Mo Wilde is a forager, resear̲ ̲ ̲ ̲ ̲ ̲ ̲ ̲ ̲ ̲ st.
She lives in West Lothian in a ̲ ̲ ̲ ̲ ̲ ̲ ̲ ̲ ̲ ̲ es,
where she encourages medicinal and foraging species ̲ ̲ ̲ ̲ ̲ ̲ ̲ ̲ ild,
teaching garden. She has been teaching foraging formally since 2005.

After many years travelling she settled in Britain. She ran Napiers, Scotland's oldest and most trusted herbal medicine company, and achieved a Master's degree in Herbal Medicine at the age of 50. Mo is a Fellow of the Linnean Society, a founding Member of the Association of Foragers, a Member of the British Mycological Society and a Member of the International Lyme and Associated Diseases Society (ILADS). She practices at Napiers Claid Clinic specialising in integrative medicine in the treatment of Lyme disease, lectures in herbal medicine and teaches foraging courses.

### Praise for *The Wilderness Cure*

'*The Wilderness Cure*, her diary of the year, is many things: an unpreachy manifesto, a recipe book, a celebration of friendship, a passionate love song to the wild, a textbook of empathy, a cabinet of ecological curiosities, a masterclass in how to tread softly, a survival guide, a journal of quiet epiphanies, a primer on the art of relationship, a meditation on the significance of mycelial networks, a map of the collective unconscious, an impeccably researched account of many of the medical perils of modernity, an inquiry into the healing power of the natural world and an evolving reflection on what it means to be a human . . . A triumph' **Times Literary Supplement**

'With the seductively readable style that comes only from the light poetism of wisdom and knowledge speaking from the heart, Monica Wilde relates the story of a year eating nothing but wild food. The result is a masterly work of information and erudition, one from which I am still buzzing with the pleasure of its reading' **John Wright, author of** *The Forager's Calendar*

'Mo Wilde's story of foraging for food and medicine is an inspiration to us all. She brings home the need so many of us have for the wild redeemer as a part of our diet and our lives' **Stephen Harrod Buhner, author of the bestselling** *Herbal Antibiotics* **and** *Earth Grief*

'Mo Wilde has retraced [our ancestors] steps . . . A delightfully humble, funny and wise guide, [Mo] leaves tentative footprints for us to follow. Perhaps if we do that, we can all make it home in time' **Miles Irving, author of** *The Forager Handbook* **and host of the** *WorldWild* **podcast**

'Mo Wilde's year is an inspiration. What an incredible woman and an even more impressive book' **Cat Thomson**

'This book is utterly fascinating, and written in a wildly refreshing manner. Though embarking on such a wholesome journey, Mo doesn't sugar-coat the difficulties however, she also celebrates the many positive sides, [offering] advice on how we could better live, without ever preaching' **Michael Perry, Garden Media Guild award winner and author of** *Hortus Curious*

# THE
# WILDERNESS
# CURE

## MO WILDE

**SIMON &
SCHUSTER**

London · New York · Sydney · Toronto · New Delhi

First published in Great Britain by Simon & Schuster UK Ltd, 2022
This edition published in Great Britain by Simon & Schuster UK Ltd, 2023

3 5 7 9 10 8 6 4 2

Simon & Schuster UK Ltd
1st Floor
222 Gray's Inn Road
London WC1X 8HB

www.simonandschuster.co.uk
www.simonandschuster.com.au
www.simonandschuster.co.in

Simon & Schuster Australia, Sydney
Simon & Schuster India, New Delhi

A CIP catalogue record for this book
is available from the British Library

Paperback ISBN: 978-1-3985-0865-1
eBook ISBN: 978-1-3985-0864-4

Typeset in Perpetua by M Rules
Printed and Bound in the UK using 100% Renewable
Electricity at CPI Group (UK) Ltd

*This book is dedicated to Gaïa,*
*soul of my beloved planet, Earth.*
*I have known you and loved you my entire life.*
*Without you, I would never have written*
*a word, let alone breathed oxygen.*
*Until death do us part, x.*

# CONTENTS

## PART FOUR: SUMMER

## PART FIVE: AUTUMN

## PART SIX: FINAL DAYS

# INTRODUCTION

*'When you follow a wild path, you are called ever deeper.'*

Claire Paterson Conrad

## BLACK FRIDAY

*27 November 2020*

Eating only wild food for a year might sound like a completely crazy idea, but we are living in unprecedented times.

Both an inquisitive forager and research herbalist, I've been interested in wild food for many years. Always intrigued by the practical, not just the theory, I've wanted to trace the history of foraging and our culinary evolution by following a truly seasonal wild diet myself. Nature both fascinates and inspires me. I'd hoped that the coronavirus lockdown would encourage us all to reflect on our destructive behaviour towards the planet but, by the consumer excess of Black Friday – now a week-long binge of discount shopping – I find myself frustrated. It feels as if nothing has changed. It is the final push I need – almost a rebellious hunger strike!

My instincts tell me that the cure for our disconnect with the earth is through complete immersion in nature. But I have no idea if this is possible, let alone if it will change us – or me. If it can, I am determined to be the guinea pig. I've spent too long at my desk this last year, wired and tired. So I have vowed to give up buying food and eat only what I can forage here in central Scotland starting today – Black Friday, 27 November

As if the coronavirus hasn't tested us enough, climate change continues to rapidly alter our ecosystem. Temperature extremes; crops without bees to pollinate them; floods one minute and water shortages the next; soil degradation; chemicals and microplastics . . . and I'm an optimist! We are also being warned of food shortages as one consequence of Brexit. Most of our food is imported and certainly, during the winter, pretty much all of our fruits and vegetables are from overseas, apart from the ubiquitous seasonal Brussels sprouts whose name seems very ironic right now.

Food, and the sharing of food, is at the heart of what it is to be human. In our old tribal cultures, a traveller was always offered free food and hospitality. In this modern-day free-for-all – as we face climate change, extremes of wealth and scarcity of resources – the current state of free, wild food and our access to it, reflect deeper themes in our survival as a species on this beloved planet. Eating wild food is both culinary and healing, social and political, and will inspire future generations in their quest for a deeper relationship with nature and Earth-centred solutions.

Foraging is not a novelty. It is not a middle-class culinary experience nor the province of billionaires. The foragers that I know from around the world represent the complete diversity of our species. Nature is mother to us all. She doesn't care if we are poor, rich, a person of colour, white, female, male, binary or any other. After all, she loves diversity. Amongst fungi there are over 36,000 genders – some of us are just coming to terms with the fact that humans may have more than two! In nature, every colour under the clichéd rainbow is represented, and life is expressed through so many 'other-than-human' species that we are still finding new species each year – although not as fast as we are waging war on them. Foraging is an epigenetic Post-it note on our genes that we all share. It defines us as simply 'human'. Whether we just pick a handful of hairy bittercress to add to a city park salad, or a bonanza banquet of autumnal wild mushrooms, it is one of the last wild acts of defiance against the concrete world. Humans versus humanoids. It's a crack in the dam, a chink of light; wild food nourishes your very soul.

I truly hope that the pandemic lockdowns have awakened a new appreciation for nature, whether we encounter her in the country-side or between the cracks of paving slabs. I've noticed, especially amongst young people, there is a hunger to connect with a simpler, more authentic way of life and being. This book is for those who hunger.

# PART ONE

# WINTER

# CHAPTER ONE

# THE DAY BEFORE

*'I went to the woods because I wished to live deliberately,*
*to front only the essential facts of life, and see if I*
*could not learn what it had to teach, and not, when*
*I came to die, discover that I had not lived.'*

Henry David Thoreau, *Walden: or Life in the Woods*

I'm quietly scrubbing beetroot over the kitchen sink. An observer might say, 'in a mournful way', and I guess there is an element of that, but I would say, 'with reverence'. Beetroot is not usually something that I pay this much attention to. When I was a child, pickled school beetroot was my nemesis and I got into real trouble when I smuggled it, uneaten, out of the dining hall tucked into my knickers. The bright red juice bled through my lightweight, turquoise, summer uniform dress causing a major panic when I was spotted, and rushed off to the school nurse. I was only seven years old at the time! Half a century later, beetroot and I have made our peace. In fact, I quite like it. Roasted until the edges are sweetly chewy or blitzed with mint and cream into a dip, I would even go so far as to say that I'm going to miss it. Suddenly, I appreciate this very large root. Even two or three small ones will make a meal.

I'll miss it because from tomorrow, I am going to eat only wild food for one whole year. And so, this beetroot will be my 'last supper'.

I am acutely aware, on this rainy November morning, of exactly how many wild plants I will need to gather to equal the calorific value of this beetroot. I am also conscious of the irony that, although wild beet was commonly found in abundance by our ancestors, at the time it didn't have a swollen root. This was a modification brought in by the ancient Romans who highly valued the beetroot as an aphrodisiac. I'm told that the frescos on the walls of the Lupanar (the official Roman brothel in Pompeii) depict abundant beetroots, nestled between copulating couples, attesting to its popularity. So it was the Romans who first hybridised this vegetable to produce the swollen, edible root that we enjoy today.

Like our Stone Age ancestors, I love wild beet leaves. Steamed with a little melted butter . . . and there's another problem. How far back am I going to go? Will I include butter? Butter is not wild, but humans have been keeping goats and sheep for at least 12,000 years. I can see that I am going to have to establish some very clear ground rules.

## THE CONDITIONS

The Collins dictionary definition of 'foraging' is 'the acquisition of food by hunting, fishing or the gathering of plant matter', to which I would also add fungi and seaweeds. I've been teaching people how to do this for about fifteen years now and the number one question people always ask me is: 'Could *you* live entirely off the land for a year?'

I've thought about this for a long time and I do think it is possible, as long as four conditions are met:

1. This isn't TV, so unlike wilderness adventurer Bear Grylls, I would *not* be dropped into a landscape I have no knowledge of. Instead, I must be familiar with the land – in all its

seasons. Like us, other species have strong preferences
as to where they live, so knowing the habitat is essential
to survival.

2.  I must have access to roam over a variety of terrains:
    seashore, hedgerow, forest and the right to harvest whatever
    food I find because, as the seasons change, the locations of
    wild foods change too. Thankfully, in Scotland we have the
    Right to Roam.

3.  Although my main focus is plants, seaweeds and fungi,
    I may need to eat wild meat and fish, so that I don't
    completely starve in the winter. Until now I've been 90 per
    cent vegetarian but I must be prepared to eat anything –few
    bananas grow in Scotland.

4.  The experiment should start after the spring equinox, to
    give me enough time to prepare for the winter. (Well, I've
    already blown this one!)

Unlike my ancestors, though, I do have three particular modern
advantages.

- **Electricity**: a dehydrator, a fridge and a freezer – these
  make it possible to store food over the winter.
- **Fuel**: an oven and a car – without the latter my ability to
  travel to areas where I might find food and carry it home
  would be my toughest challenge.
- **Shelter**: a well-insulated home with a roof over my head –
  without which I would need far more calories just to stay
  warm and not freeze to death during the winter months.

## THE RULES

1.  I will eat only wild food. This includes native or naturalised
    species that have gone wild. For example, hairy bittercress

is native, but ground elder, feral apples and fuchsias were initially cultivated but escaped from cultivation and now also grow wild.

2. The food will be local to the habitats I travel through during the year – no foraged bananas! I won't be growing vegetables either this year.

3. No money! I can't buy anything. All my food must be picked, hunted, gifted, traded or swapped for my skills. Any gifted food should be made by the person gifting it with wild harvested ingredients and not be bought or commercially produced.

4. Although our ancestors would have eaten wild birds' eggs it is illegal and unsustainable to do so now. So I am going to substitute wild eggs with eggs from my own free-range, organic hens. However, my rule is that I only eat them in the same season that wild birds are laying eggs.

5. When the goat kids are born in the spring, I may try to trade for some milk with a crofter or smallholder. This reflects our pastoral nomadic past.

6. Ideally, I'll be eating food that is seasonal. However – especially during winter – I will also eat wild food that I picked earlier in the year and either froze, dried or preserved.

## THE EXCEPTIONS

In retrospect, it's a tough challenge to begin my wild year in the winter when foragable food is scarce, with little planning and proper preparation, but I am impetuous. And, with so many daily reports on the threats to the natural world, I feel an urgency that cannot wait another year.

1. With winter already upon us, I've had to buy some hazelnuts from a British orchard to supplement my own, as I didn't know that I would take this path in September when the nuts were ready to pick. Next summer and autumn, I will collect the same weight myself, to show that this can be done in the wild. I have an allowance of twenty nuts per day until mid-April. I also had to buy 3 kilos of nut flour because I left all mine too long in the back of my van; the nuts sprouted before I could process them into flour. I vow to gather the equivalent in the next season. I'll keep a list of all the stores and calculate, over the course of the year, anything bought in advance versus everything collected and make an end-of-year tally.

2. My one and *only* non-native exception is olive oil. Much of the food that I preserve each year is pickled and preserved in oil. For instance, common hogweed shoots and various wild mushrooms are lightly boiled in a solution of home-made vinegar and brine, drained and then packed into glass jars and topped up with olive oil. As well as preserving the food, the oil negates the strong taste of vinegar. I will use the olive oil out of the jars to cook with as it would be a waste to throw it away. The Celts have been trading with Europe for at least 2,500 years or more and possibly some of the Etruscan jugs that made their way from Sumerian potters to the ancient Celts had olive oil in them!

3. Finally, I don't want to waste anything that was picked and lovingly preserved in previous years. So a bilberry jam, for example, may have been made with wild bilberries and a little sugar. Whilst I won't be buying or using sugar, if I have made jam which might not keep, then I won't let it go to waste. Everything that will keep for a year is now boxed up in the attic.

## SOME SCIENCE

Having read a lot about the difference in gut microbiomes of ancestral people like the Hadza' (a Tanzanian tribe who still follow an exclusively foraged diet) compared to your average Westerner, I thought my wild food diet would also be an interesting scientific experiment. So I'm sending a stool sample to a laboratory to analyse my gut bacteria on 'day one'. I'll repeat this at intervals as the seasons change to see if and how my gut microbiome changes.

I'm also monitoring my weight, my fat-to-muscle ratio, and my blood pressure and blood oxygen levels. I could stand to lose a few kilos, and while this journey is not about losing weight – it's about discovering what life has to teach me – this could be the most drastic diet yet!

## MY PRECONCEPTIONS

*Food*

Never has this simple word generated so much passionate debate as in this century. As essential to our survival as air and water, nowadays food seems such a complicated issue. With low-fat diets, low-carb diets, vegan, pegan and many more, food is always in the news.

On the rare occasion that I visit a modern supermarket, at first glance it seems as if there is infinite choice. There are acres upon acres of food in brightly coloured packaging, and yet really the selection is limited. Over the course of our collective history there is evidence that mankind has eaten over 7,000 plant species. Ethnobotanical research shows that many hunter-gatherer communities tuck into anything from 100 to 350 species over the course of a year. Today however, over 50 per cent of the world's daily calorie intake comes from just three species – wheat, corn and rice. At 60 per cent add in soy products from the soybean, and I'm sure the potato is not far behind because 80 per cent of calories come from *just* twelve species. Yet all of these are winter carbohydrates that once we might only have eaten in the winter months.

Obesity is leading to increased rates of heart disease, diabetes, metabolic diseases, cancer and an ecological footprint that dramatically increases our need for resources. On the other hand we also have a newly classified psychological condition – orthorexia.[2] A type of starvation caused by a fixation with eating only healthy, or 'raw' and 'pure' foods. Those affected run the risk of becoming severely undernourished. We live in a world where children and adults still die of starvation and malnutrition while millions of others are obese; tragically this includes children. Obesity and diet fads can also hide malnutrition, leading to ill health of epidemic proportions. It seems that we really have lost our way with the most basic, fundamental and instinctive human need – that of feeding and nourishing our bodies while enjoying food without angst or anxiety.

What happened? To understand how we became so divorced from our annual food cycle, perhaps it helps to trace our evolution and remind ourselves where we came from.

Humans, in our earliest incarnation, before *Homo sapiens* even evolved as a distinct hominid species, harnessed fire and learnt to cook some 1.5 to 2 million years ago. Whether eating raw meat or cooking it,[3] unlike other animal species we weren't confined to a narrow range of foods and we didn't need to spend hours a day grazing. Nor, unlike our monkey relatives, did we need such long intestines to digest all that fruit and fibre, sitting around for hours as it worked its way through our stomachs. Thus we had time to play, to invent, to explore . . . to migrate north – out of Africa. Even Neanderthals gathered around the hearth for a Sunday roast that they'd speared with a home-knapped flint blade. They became extinct 10,000 years after we joined them on the Mediterranean coast, and little is left of them other than a 2 per cent to 3 per cent contribution to European and Asian DNA. We fished, hunted and survived the northern winters when vegetation disappeared under the snow. We learnt to eat almost anything. And our numbers grew.

Judging from fossils, friendly wolves evolved into domesticated dogs between 33,000 years ago (Siberia)[4] and 11,000 years ago (Israel). They helped us to round up herds for hunting and by around 10,400 years ago[5] we were certainly herding flocks of sheep and goats, to keep our food close at hand. Around 8,000 years ago humans began to cultivate the land, leaving our Palaeolithic past for a new Neolithic era of farming.[6] This didn't happen overnight. Archaeological remains show that both hunter-gatherer and farming groups coexisted for at least 2,000 years.[7] Hunter-gatherers held out for a while, as agricultural labour takes up so much more time than foraging, but as the land was claimed and defended by farmers their range decreased. Human bodies adapted a little. For instance, many groups started to develop a tolerance for milk proteins. But overall, we haven't changed much biologically. For the first few thousand years, farming provided us with winter calories, but we *continued* to eat a wide range of foraged fruit, vegetables and herbs that provided the flavour and nutritional elements of our diet.

As we became experts at farming we stopped moving around and, growing larger by extending the period that we ate 'winter calories', we also increased the size of our families. The population expanded dramatically, land use became fixed to one place and the foragers, nomads and hunters were gradually squeezed out to the margins of society.

Around 5,500 years ago the first cities started to develop.[8] Concepts of ownership were now firmly established and we were born, not into a small tribe of relatively equal members, but as kings or slaves depending on the accident of our birth. As land continued to be claimed, the concept of nation states emerged. Medieval man was no longer free to roam nomadically but was tied to the land. Most men were slaves, beneath the lords, and women were down there with the animals. After the Enclosure Acts of the seventeenth century,[9] when common land and open field systems were abolished thus ending self-sufficiency, many of the landless poor flocked to live in cities. Yet food storage logistics meant that it was still predominantly seasonal – except for the wealthy. Despite these challenges, the cities still grew.

By the eighteenth century, overcrowding, lack of good-quality fresh food, poor sanitation and poverty encouraged disease to spread.

Only the rural folk or the rich had a wide variety of vegetables and, for the latter, meat was how you proved your worth. Venison, ox, mutton and pork graced the banqueting table. Vegetables were often an afterthought.

The Industrial Revolution speeded up the pace of change again as we moved from a plant-based organic economy to a fossil-fuel economy.[10] In the nineteenth century, sanitation saved the day[11] and dramatically improved the nation's exposure and resistance to infectious diseases. New drugs were pioneered at the turn of the century and by the 1940s, the launch of antibiotics was heralded as a new era, when mankind would soon see 'the end of all disease'. We pretty much eradicated polio, leprosy, smallpox and (for a while) tuberculosis yet now one in two of us born after 1960 will get cancer.[12] The post-war industrialisation of food since the 1950s changed the food scene dramatically and for ever.[13]

Every day, when you open a magazine or flick through TV channels, you will instantly find recipes, features and programmes on what to cook and how to cook it. Chefs are the new superstars and restaurants cater for every taste. Food is flown daily around the globe in our quest for greater choice. Modern life features a proliferation of diet plans. Some are just barmy, but others get results. Although many dieters may thrive on these extreme plans initially, in the long term balanced food cycles are vital. Health gurus abound and we now obsess about eating healthily, and yet most of us end up fat, despite the fact that there's a diet for everyone: calorie counting, LifePoints, the Atkins diet, the cabbage soup diet, fruitarianism, vegetarianism, the Paleo diet, breathairianism, Weight Watchers, veganism, detoxes galore. However, we still get fatter, sadder and sicker, or destroy the environment in our desire to get what we want to eat regardless of local, seasonal availability.

So what has gone wrong?

We managed to survive for millennia without knowing what a vitamin was – let alone a calorie. Our concerns were previously less about *what* we ate, but about *when* and *where* we could catch a fish, or hunt a deer, pick tender green salads or harvest nuts and berries, storing up enough to see us through a harsh winter. This started to change significantly when we gave up our nomadic life, reducing the number of edible species we would encounter over a year. Those food species that are available now are sold in and out of season, all year round.

Howard Draper, American anthropologist and expert on Inuit nutrition, warned us as far back as 1977:

> *Industrialised societies have (at least for the time being) removed the danger of starvation which was a constant threat to most primitive societies. Science and technology have greatly enhanced the efficiency of food production and preservation and have increased the number of nutritious foodstuffs available. Concomitantly, however, there has been a marked increase in the production of foods of low nutritional quality. Moreover, these foods have been made attractive and appetising with the result that their consumption has increased at the expense of better quality foods.*

Draper remarked that consumers were finding it difficult to make the right food choices when low-quality foods were made to taste good.

Most animals will self-select a range of foodstuffs, instinctively knowing how much or how little of each to eat to remain healthy.[15] We are animals but the availability of processed foods confuses our ability to naturally select nutrients. This has led to the advent of dietary rules outlining which food categories we need to choose from to achieve a 'balanced diet'. It requires thinking with our heads and not following our 'gut' instincts. Hence the need for traffic-light systems and nutritional data labels on our foods to educate the bewildered consumer, further complicated by complex foods, such as artificially flavoured instant noodles, reconstituted Turkey Twizzlers and sugar-laden spaghetti hoops, that don't even look like food any more. It is no wonder that 'healthy eating' has become such a minefield!

Food should not have to be complicated. Yet I wonder if even 'seasonality' is truly understood. We *think* we know, but when I ask people what it means to them, they invariably attribute seasonality just to the origin of fruits and vegetables. If asparagus is flown in from Peru and not yet growing in Norfolk – it's out of season. If the raspberries are trucked over from the hillsides of Spain and not picked in Scotland's Glen Lyon – they're out of season. However, this is a simplistic way of looking at seasonality. The truth is that entire food *groups* go in and out of season.

I imagine that it's April already and I'm foraging in a hedgerow. There is an abundance of edible new spring vegetation. Spicy cuckoo-flowers and hairy bittercress leaves; iron-rich, protein-packed nettle tops; bitter dandelion leaves and tender chickweed – the iceberg lettuce of the foraging salad. There is new, vibrant green growth all around me. My question is, 'If I wanted to eat carbohydrates right now, where would they come from?'

I suspect it would be hard to lay my hands on carbohydrates in April or, to be precise, from January to the end of July. They are mainly found in grains (wheat, barley, oats, corn) that are harvested from the end of July onwards. Nuts and other carb-rich seeds start to ripen at the end of the summer and are picked in the autumn. Roots and tubers count as carbohydrates; they are harvested in their first year of growth. Over a year old and they become woody, fibrous and too tough to eat. In the spring of their first year they are tiny, so they are also harvested in the autumn once they have reached a decent size and still remain tender. The ubiquitous potato didn't reach our shores until the late sixteenth century.

Therefore, traditionally we would eat a lot of carbs only in the autumn and winter for, in a pre-farming community, we would have run out of them by the spring season. In that context, there are implications for eating carbs out of season. Given that we can eat bread every day, 365 days a year, with cereal for breakfast and pasta for dinner – day in, day out, year after year, is it any wonder that we are getting fat or that gluten sensitivity has become such an issue?

Conversely in winter, fresh vegetables are seldom found. We could only survive the winter by eating meat and energy-giving carbohydrates from roots, tubers and grains eschewed by the

Paleo diet. Abandoning all carbs all the time is not the answer. But what is?

We are omnivores. Over millennia, humans have tried all sorts of diets in all corners of the globe and most ancestral diets appear to have suited us well.[16] For every diet that's recommended as the ultimate fix, another one quickly confounds us, with results that are just as exemplary. So what is the answer? What are the common-denominating factors between ancestral diets? In fact, are there any?

We have proven that we can eat almost everything (a few poisonous species apart) and that, when we found it, we ate a lot of it before moving on – which also allowed the habitat time to regenerate. But there is one huge proviso and it is that we had dietary *variation* caused by seasonal change. Even the Inuit people living mainly on a high-protein fish diet went foraging for berries, and the Maasai living on a high-protein diet of blood and milk also ate a range of vegetables. Here in the northern hemisphere, we ate a huge range of foods and our diet included meat, dairy, grains, fats, carbs and sugar – not just lots of plants – but a pre-Neolithic lifestyle prevented us from getting obese. As fast as we found food to eat, it would change with the turning of the seasons. Variability and variety were built into the natural order and we were rarely able to overeat from a single food group even if we tried. We also burnt a lot of calories tracking it down.

Many people assume that, as a forager, I'm going to be following a Paleo diet, but to me this is just an example of a 'winter' or 'high-altitude summer' diet. The thinking behind the Paleo diet originated from archaeological finds in South Africa – predominantly animal bones. This is supposed to prove that we all mainly ate meat. There are some problems with this evidence when applying it to all ancestral people: the South African coast is mild, lacking the severe winter with its climatic extremes experienced by Neanderthals and early European *Homo sapiens*; food eaten on trips that wasn't brought back to camps; and the fact that only peat bogs and marshes seem to preserve material records of ancient food plant use. So archaeological records have large gaps. Studies of modern indigenous tribal peoples may be flawed. They have often been driven off the most productive lands due to centuries of land ownership, colonisation and exploitation, and forced to adapt their diet to life on the fringe.

The most important thing to remember about 'diets' is that no single modern diet encompasses the variety of foods that we used to eat, nor should they be the same throughout the year. Paleo is a great summer diet, when there is a lot of game and fish. In summer there are few vegetables – the plants are all in flower while nuts, seeds and grains are yet to be harvested. Veganism would have been a very short spring diet full of fresh green vegetables although lacking in fats and calories; so better as an autumn diet of nuts, berries, grains and roots, but impossible in the winter. Veganism in Scotland is only possible by importing food that is in season elsewhere across the globe. The classic official government food pyramid, with its heavy base of bread, pasta and potatoes, belongs only to the winter months in a farming community. Most diets have something to recommend them when followed for limited periods. History shows us that the key to thriving is variety.

I feel that to truly understand 'how to eat' I need to rediscover the annual rhythms of food in each of my unique local terrains. The only way I'll know what an ancestral diet truly is (in Scotland), is to get outside and see what there is to eat, in every season. Even if next year I do end up having to source much of my food from a shop, at least I will know what to emulate.

Whatever my thoughts have been so far though, tomorrow I'm going to start to find out exactly what is available to eat and what I have to do to stay alive.

I am tucking into an evening snack of cheese and biscuits, an all-too-regular habit that has contributed to the extra kilos I am carrying. And, I confess, an all-too-frequent glass of wine (or two) as well. It will be interesting to see what I really miss. What will the world be like without coffee, chocolate and cheese? I have to admit to some trepidation but it's too late to back out now!

I love this planet. Don't brush that remark aside. I really do *adore* this Earth that is our home, as deeply and passionately as any lover, with all her myriad organisms, creatures, fungi and plants — especially the plants. So I grieve to watch how consumerism and capitalism are destroying life. Nothing epitomises consumerism like Black Friday so today's the day that I leave it all behind.

# CHAPTER TWO

# EARLY DAYS

*'A story has no beginning or end: arbitrarily one
choices that moment of experience from which
to look back or from which to look ahead.'*

Graham Greene, *The End of the Affair*

## BLACK FRIDAY

*Daisylea, 27 November*

I wake early this morning, snug as usual in a cocoon of warmth. I
turn to face the window, my view unencumbered by curtains and
framed by the waney-edged oak with which we built this house
ten years ago. The wintry half-light is streaked with pastels of
orange and red as the sun tries half-heartedly to rise in the east.
With winter now a nip in the air, the field below is dotted with
the sheep that Rab, my farmer neighbour, turned out to graze after
the last cut of hay. Both my window and this rolling expanse of
short grass are bordered by two stands of elegant beech trees, now
without leaves. The misty vista down the valley, uninterrupted
by houses or roads, stretches all the way to Cairnpapple Hill – an
ancient Neolithic landmark in this part of central Scotland. A lone

wood pigeon softly coos and everything in the world of nature is at peace.

Despite this tranquil scene, I feel tense. I'm aware of a gnawing feeling of trepidation. I've woken with mixed emotions: fear, curiosity, foreboding, excitement! I've been looking forward to today with a sense of exhilaration but I'm now wondering what on earth I am doing. A quick glance at my phone, flooded with Black Friday offers, quickly convinces me that turning my back on the crazy world of consumerism does feel really good. Perhaps, some day, people may need to resort to the path that I'm following willingly. I'm under no illusion that this is going to be an easy experiment, but I think I have the knowledge to do it. Of course, I should have prepared better. I should have spent the entire year building up stores and making ready for winter, but . . . sometimes, when you're me, you just dive in at the deep end!

Today is a weekday and, with four weeks to go until the winter solstice, it is dark in the mornings. So I don't have time to go for an early walk. I am relying on the plants that I've picked this week in the afternoons to feed me.

Breakfast is . . . 'interesting'. Usually I have a big stir-fry of organic vegetables – bought weekly in bulk from a local organic wholesaler – with nuts and any mushrooms that have been found in the last day or two. This morning I'm having a chunky salmon fished from the River Tay that I froze in the summer. I've also dug up some crispy white marsh woundwort tubers, now well scrubbed to remove the heavy West Lothian clay, and picked a few fresh common hogweed leaves.

The first issue is cooking without butter or liberal amounts of oil. So I decide to bake the salmon on a bed of fresh yarrow leaves to stop it sticking to the pot. With tiny leaves reminiscent of ferns, yarrow tastes like a pungent, slightly bitter wild rosemary. I also cover the fish with a thick blanket of this wild herb, nature's tinfoil. It cooks perfectly and the boiled marsh woundwort tubers are excellent. A nine-star dish. (Ten stars would require the addition of some butter!)

It's a workday so I'm busy. I need to write up all the letters and prescriptions for the patients I've seen in my herbal clinic this week.

'Seen' now sadly meaning Zoom or WhatsApp. I talk to each person for an hour as Lyme disease, my specialism, is so complex.

Lunch is the same as breakfast, served cold. Last weekend I made some excellent mustard by soaking a handful of wild black mustard seeds in a vinegar home-made from fermenting small, sharp, hard feral apples. It is a winning combination and lifts the taste of the fish. After lunch, I nip down to the postbox to send off the stool sample for my gut microbiome test. I am going to repeat it every two to three months as the foods I am eating vary, to see what impact this has on the bacteria.

Throughout the afternoon, I drink plenty of herbal tea made from flowers and aromatic wild herbs which I picked during the summer and dried. My dehydrator is probably the one piece of kitchen equipment that I would really struggle to do without, as Scotland is not known for its dry, sunny days! When each plant is dried I store it in a brown paper bag. Our daily herbal teas live in giant jars on the open shelf in my kitchen. When one runs low, I get down all the small jars and packets and empty handfuls of this and that into a bowl, mix them up thoroughly, and then refill it with handfuls of these fragrant herbs and petals. Every time it tastes a little different. If I'm a bit stressed plenty of roses go in, or if my immune system is low I add violet leaves for their vitamin C.

The sturdy shelves were recycled from old scaffolding boards by Géza, master builder *and* – as luck would have it – master of home-made ciders, beers and wines. He's been my best friend since he arrived in Scotland from Hungary twenty-two years ago. He physically built this wooden house that we share on a windy hilltop. Matt is also living here. A gentle, kindred foraging soul who earned his nickname 'Mushroom Matt' from twenty-five years of growing fungi. I often think he is part mushroom himself. Our three independent lives are enriched by the benefits of sharing our skills and resources – a micro-community. Matt is an Association of Foragers member too, and is joining in my crazy experiment eating only wild food. He's wondering if it will help his diabetes. His participation is really helpful as Géza – while he loves foraging for fungi – has decided to stick to his usual diet of soups, stews and stir-fried vegetables. However, he has promised to keep me supplied with wild elderflower wine and honeysuckle mead, for Géza is the ale-meister supreme.

I add lots of hawthorn flowers and leaves to the Géza Chai tea blend; they help to keep blood pressure in balance. If I have problems sleeping, I add bright yellow mullein flowers and pineappleweed – a type of soothing wild chamomile – to the Calm Mix. Today the House Blend is watermint, rose petals, rosebay willowherb, ground ivy, pineappleweed, pot marigold, red clover, mullein leaf and ground elder. I steep a liberal handful of herbs in a large three-cup cafetière. Fragrant and delicious, it infuses me with the warmth of the summer past.

I am happy here on the hill. My three grown-up children no longer live at home, forging lives of their own, so I am free to roam without care. I'm sure they think I'm quite mad!

## A SLOW START

*Daisylea, 28 November*

Saturday has arrived and I am really not in the mood for fish for breakfast again. It's raining at the moment, a steady drizzle, but the weather forecast is good and it should clear up by mid-morning, so I sneak an extra hour in bed. I really shouldn't read the news. It's full of Brexit doom. Topshop and Debenhams are going under and the Chancellor of the Exchequer, Rishi Sunak, gets a smack on the wrist for accidentally forgetting to declare several millions of his family's financial interests on the ministerial register. Luckily my stomach intervenes and I head for the kitchen.

My attempts at breakfast turn out some reasonable pancakes – considering that I'm using ground chestnut flour, water and a tiny Cuckoo Maran egg – my substitution for a wood pigeon's. Luckily wood pigeons lay all year round, although far less in December. But when I accidentally scare one off its nest while foraging in the woods, I earn an 'egg point' and can use a hen's egg. Wood pigeons are easy to spot as they fly like cargo planes in the film *The Dam Busters* – a low and bumpy start until they finally take off, just clearing the tops of the bushes before they crash. They're so ungainly they make me laugh.

Without my heavy non-stick pan, this unfamiliar batter would have been a culinary disaster, but the pancakes only char a little. Sadly I am forgoing butter and – although they're a bit stodgy and won't flip – they taste perfectly acceptable. They are crumbly without the gluten to hold them together but with the addition of some pickled cherries from my summer stores I'm happy to devour them.

Once the rain finally stops, I go out to forage for vegetables. At the base of some clumps of grass near the stream I spy common sorrel with glee and pick two handfuls for a salad. My fingertips quickly go numb from the cold as I try to separate the leaves from the surrounding damp dock stems. I also find a few late shoots of common hogweed growing where I scythed the path two months ago. Unlike their volatile relative the giant hogweed, they rarely cause burns unless attacked first – especially with a strimmer. Their white-bristled stems remind me of my grandfather's overnight stubble whereas giant hogweed sports vicious crystal spikes. My favourite spring treat is hogweed tempura. I spot a handful of small nettle tops to add to the basket too but there is not much here. A fallen beech tree glistens with white porcelain fungus and the neighbouring elder is flush with bizarre, brown jelly, wood ear mushrooms. The rain starts again though and I'm quickly driven back inside, taking refuge in the warmth of the kitchen with a nutritious, filling stew on my mind.

Slow cookers are perfect for stews and all the old one-pot dishes that were once so common. Apart from those at the top of the old feudal system, right up to Victorian times the majority of people only had a single small stove or open fire.[1] Hence, the majority of lunches and dinners were one-pot affairs. The most common dish was pottage, a term that covers a wide variety of dishes but all made in one pot, from a thin *ronnyng* soup to a porridge or a thicker *stondyng* stew depending on what went into it. Vegetables, grains or dried peas were the staple ingredients but sometimes meat or fish was added, and occasionally they were thickened with eggs.

We were probably making soupy stews even before humans invented pottery. After a successful hunt, a deer might be roasted over the fire but its stomach would be filled with meat, grain or herbs and water, and hot stones from the fire dropped inside. The heat from the stones was intense enough to bring the mixture to the boil and adding the occasional extra one kept it going until the stew was cooked. It became popular in the Victorian era to think of our ancestors as savages. However, we now know that they were just as intelligent as we are today. I am sure they would have been just as curious, experimental and fond of good food too!

It unites us as humans across the globe, that so many different cultures still have a traditional variation on the hearty one-pot meal. Here in Britain there's the Lancashire hotpot; in Ireland, the Irish stew. There's seafood chowder, osso buco, coq au vin, pot-au-feu, potjiekos, Brazilian feijoada, Jewish cholent, Polish bigos, Hungarian goulash . . . the one-pot dish is truly universal.

I spent some time living in the West Indies, and there you find pepperpot. This is passed on, allegedly in the original pot, from generation to generation. The casserole is boiled up every day to keep bacteria at bay and more ingredients are added, including cassareep, the liquid by-product from grating bitter cassava roots, which is also great as a food preservative. I imagine that the innkeepers of medieval Britain would have had a similar pot on the go all the time, with more ingredients added as needed, in a perpetual, never-ending stew.

For this meal, I am using a shoulder of venison that I found at the back of the freezer. My friend Bob is seventy-two years old but still monitors some of the deer herds for farmers and estates. When he was culling in November he gave me a young doe. In return, I am keeping him supplied with herbal elixirs.

I cube the meat, taking it off the bone, and brown it in a casserole dish with a little deer fat. I add wild mushrooms – translucent porcelain fungus just plucked from the beech and some gelatinous wood ears from the last ancient elder in Rab's field. The wood ears will suck up all the piquancy of the stock and in return enhance the flavour with their natural glutamates. The dish is seasoned with cow parsley, wild marjoram, the red haws from the hawthorn hedge, toasted hogweed seed for spice and a little home-smoked sea salt. Cooked in the oven at a low temperature for two hours, this is a most tender and fragrant dish. A few late hogweed shoots are stir-fried with a little water to accompany the meal and both heart and belly are happy. I'm relieved that I've been finding fungi and plants so late in the year. Perhaps this won't be quite as difficult as I imagined.

## FIRST FROST

*Oakbank, 29 November*

Sunday now dawns with a stunning red sunrise that on closer inspection reveals a very frosty landscape. My fleeting appreciation of its Narnian beauty is quickly eclipsed by the full realisation of the consequences. I'm kicking myself for being smug and not picking more sorrel yesterday. Frost is a brutal killer. Today it will be limp and slimy and it may not decide to revive itself for weeks.

Breakfast increases my apprehension as the success of yesterday's pancakes is not to be repeated. I've only spotted one wood pigeon on a nest – it is November – so have run out of 'egg points'. Without an egg my pancake quickly ends up as a very weird, fried nut-flour porridge. Flavoured with some dried bilberries, it nevertheless fills a soggy gap.

On Sundays, away from my desk, I have more time to look for food and this is pressing. A twenty-minute drive away is a stretch of ancient woodland called Oakbank. It is bordered by Linhouse Water on one side and Murieston Water on the other, before they meet and thread their way through the expanding commuter belt to meet the broad River Almond. It's not a place I often visit but one November, three years ago now, I met up with a friend there for a walk and picked some pink purslane sheltered by beech trees in a warm nook in the curve of the great river. I may sometimes forget where I've put my car keys or what I came into the room for but, like every good forager, I *never* forget where I once found food.

Foraging triumphs imprint on a different, ancient, primeval part of your brain. I once found some fabulous porcini mushrooms while lost in a giant plantation wood of hectare upon hectare of battery-farmed conifers. They were overcrowded and skinny, with dead lower limbs and the only green growth concentrated at the top, reaching desperately for the sun, rooted in acid, lifeless soil. But eight years later, without paths, signs or a compass I could immediately find my way back to that *exact* spot and the awaiting porcini. My feet remembered the path for me. In the depths of a forest I enter liminal space, where all my instincts come alive again. Something animal inside me knows the way as surely as birds fly from the southern to the northern hemisphere or a wolf returns to its lair after a summer on the tundra.

I park in the last remaining space off Pumpherston Road and grab two calico bags for my anticipated haul. Once over the river bridge, passing all the dog-walkers, I turn off the main path by an abandoned barn – now graffitied with 'Suck Ma Baws' in two-foot-high letters which does little for my mood. I'm down in the valley and the cold air along the riverbank is damp and bone-chilling. Frost still lingers as the winter sun is too low to peer above the embankment but I find three wood blewit mushrooms encased in a block of ice. Luckily the frost hasn't done too much damage and they'll be fine if cooked soon. I'm feeling a bit gloomy at this stark reminder that winter is before me not behind but, as always, getting outside lifts my spirits.

As predicted, pink purslane leaves are nestling in the crook of the rushing Almond, protected from the frost by an insulating duvet of rust-tinted field maple and crispy brown beech leaves. The dark green leaves are still small but plentiful enough to fill a large salad bag and I'm dead chuffed that I remembered this spot. I am going to cook them with some seaweed that I picked and dried earlier in the year. A delicious plate of greens. On the circular route back to my van I pass a feral apple tree. Bounty! Small, sour, hard, scabby, spotty little apples that would never make it to a supermarket, but I know they will be amazing baked or pressed to release a sharp, tangy verjus that substitutes for lemon juice.

# CHAPTER THREE

# FORAGING HABITAT

*'It has always been my understanding that truth
and freedom can only exist in wild places.'*

Daniel J. Rice, *This Side of a Wilderness*

## HOME TURF

*Rab's Wood, 5 December*

Stewed feral apples for breakfast with some chopped hazelnuts. All that
is missing is the crumble!

Plans for both lunch and dinner are left to fate in the slow cooker.
Two roe deer shanks, a handful of hawthorn berries for flavour, some
jelly ear mushrooms, a bundle of common sorrel and the hogweed
stalks separated from some leaves I ate yesterday. I also add some
sheathed woodtuft mushrooms. I am 100 per cent confident they are
woodtufts, but due to their similarity to the 'funeral bell' mushroom
I always double-check. After all, the clue is in the name! Grabbing my
basket, I head up to Rab's Wood to see what else I can find. I am hoping
for more mushrooms and anything green.

Rab's Wood is just a thirty-minute walk from home. I live right
in the middle of Scotland's 'Central Belt'. If you trace the three big

motorways that link Edinburgh, Glasgow and Stirling and then find the exact centre, that's where you'll find me. It's like living in the Bermuda Triangle. The fields and woods around me are vanishing fast, as the commuter towns encroach. The windswept hills are now dotted with towering turbines; a new fishery attracts cars and their trail of discarded cans and burger boxes; and land profiteers have carved up the last, quiet forest into woodland 'allotments' for city folk who'll pay their inflated prices – despite my failed attempt to buy it for the local community and keep it intact.

This stretch of land on the Heights is like an old lady now. You can see in her cheekbones how beautiful she once was. There are still traces. Overgrown hedges, missing bushes like gapped teeth, that you can find on the 1818 Ordnance Survey map. Hints of the old monks' road that crossed from Ogilface Castle over the windswept moors, so the clergy of 1253 could safely avoid the raised blanket bogs of Blawhorn Moss. This area comes alive in the summer with fluffy white bobbing heads of cotton grass and heath spotted orchids. At least the moss bog – unchanged in 8,000 years – is now a national nature reserve and protected from the invasion. There are wild cranberries there too.

I know this place like the back of my hand. Any forager would. Before you even start to think about *which* plants or mushrooms you might find to eat you have to think about *where* you'll find them.

## LOCATION, LOCATION, LOCATION

It's all about knowing your local terrain; deeply knowing it. Like us, plants can be very particular about where they like to grow – or not, some just don't care. It's the same with mushrooms. An orange birch bolete will be found under a birch tree. So, if you're after birch boletes it pays to look in a birch wood. The longer you forage the more you get to know their personal preferences. Down at the coast, for example, the best pepper dulse is always found nestling behind rocks on the moist, cooler, east-facing or north side. It doesn't like to be hot or out of the water for too long. Although it is often found in other places – out of sheer exuberance – it never tastes quite as good as on the ocean's edge. The importance of location goes beyond the taste of the food. When I decided where to build my house, I specifically chose a spot from where it would be easy to forage the foods that I *prefer* to gather. Now it is a matter of survival.

Where humans originally chose to live and roam was critically influenced by our food choices. Understanding how location is connected to our ideal food terrain makes it easier to understand not only the evolution of modern food but also how to rewild our diet. It can be hard to trace the most popular early sites as the best were transformed from camps into villages, towns into cities. Niche groups have, over time, learnt to live at the extremes of the world on very specialised diets. However, most humans require a balanced diet and there is a core group of nutrients that we need in order to remain healthy. *Homo sapiens* evolved in Africa over 315,000 years ago and migrated to Europe some 134,000 years ago. I'm interested in trying to figure out *where* they chose to hunt, forage and camp as it helps me to understand where to look for food myself in pursuit of my 'off-the-grid' diet. Although our ancestors lived around the Mediterranean for a long time – climate-wise an Eden compared to Scotland – they did eventually make it to Britain.

As ancient nomads we didn't wander about aimlessly in a random fashion any more than we do today. Like them, my every trip is now filled with intent. Our path through the year would have been a series of circles away from our campsites.[1] Like the petals on a daisy, taking us back time and again to well-known terrain – where we knew we'd find food – according to the season. Each hunter-gatherer community would have based their seasonal camps in areas of naturally abundant nutrients, from which to base their nomadic activities.

In Britain, it's possible to work out where these camps were located from the archaeological finds of stone tools and other lithics (non-degradable artefacts). I've spent a lot of time pondering the question of where we chose to settle by using the Megalithic Portal app from megalith.co.uk and Andy Burnham's lovely book *The Old Stones*.[2] It is no surprise to me that the top ancient sites closely relate to my own experience of where to find the widest variety of foraged foods.

Most of the major sites found in Britain, and on the west coast of France, that were habitations rather than ceremonial sites, are on a floodplain, near a river and within 2 to 23 kilometres of the intertidal limit. In other words, our ancestors chose places where they could easily reach the most diverse variety of foods within a day's march. In Scotland, Clava Cairns, an important Bronze Age site, is situated on a small river just two and a half hours' walk from the Ness estuary, a four-hour walk from the Nairn estuary and eight hours from the Findhorn estuary. Nearby is Daviot, one of the oldest stone circle sites, also a two-and-a-half-hour walk from the Ness estuary, a four-hour walk from Loch Ness and surrounded by a large ancient forest for hunting.

Cramond, the village where the River Almond empties into the Forth estuary, dates back to 8,500 BCE as evidenced by mounds of hazelnut shells. It was superseded by a Roman fort, transitioned to a medieval village, and was finally engulfed as a suburb of the City of Edinburgh. I imagine that most of the evidence of our Neolithic past is now buried under tons of concrete and asphalt as humans have gravitated to the same perfect locations since time immemorial. Today, nearly 6 per cent of the British Isles is covered by man-made surfaces, up from just over 4 per cent only thirty years ago.[3]

Sites that are not on rivers within reach of estuaries appear to have been colonised much later. Some were located away from camps and villages for specific reasons. The latter seem to be mainly ceremonial sites such as caves with paintings – for example, the Lascaux cave in France – religious or burial grounds such as stone cairns, circles and standing stones, or hunting sites. The oldest known site in Scotland, dating from 12,000 BCE, is Elsrickle where stone tools from an ancient hunting campsite have been found.[4] Interestingly, the current name comes from *elsrick* – in Gaelic *eileirig* – which means a place where deer were taken to be slaughtered. The topography of Elsrickle supports the theory that animals were driven from high ground down the steep bank, where the panicked animals were likely to fall, only to be killed by hunters waiting at the foot of the slope.

I am convinced that our nomadic hominid forebears came along the coast, before starting to colonise the inland countryside, and that our first bases were on these sites near the coasts, around which we made hunting and gathering forays following 'daisy-shape' trails. In winter we would relocate to a camp further inland, closer to the forests, from which we also made smaller looped hunting and foraging excursions.

This all makes total sense when you think about the seasonality of food too. In the winter, ancient peoples found shelter and prey in the forests. As the snow cleared and the ruminants moved out seeking grass, they – like me – experienced the hunger gap, before the land plants realised it was spring. So there was no choice by the end of the winter than to return to the seashore, feasting on oysters, other shellfish and seaweeds. As the land plants appeared, and birds nested, we could move away from the coast again but by midsummer all the plants were in flower. The need to follow a Paleo diet during the summer, hunting the deer in their alpine pastures, was critical. Later on, in summertime we also used the milk from the earliest domesticated sheep and goats. In the autumn, we foraged for a huge abundance of berries, and collected grains, nuts and seeds for the winter. Like squirrels I am sure we made secret caches of them, perhaps in the forests to which we returned in the winter. So location was inextricably linked with the seasonal availability of our food until farming ended our nomadic existence.

In one of my favourite places on the east coast of Scotland, I can harvest 100 plant species in a day within 4 square kilometres. Extend that to 25 square kilometres and I could live there all year round – assuming I could remove all human habitation boundaries and forage freely. Victims of their own popularity, many of our ancient sites are now buried deep under the streets of modern towns and cities. The land that once gave food freely to our ancestors and many non-human species is now privately owned.

I try to think like the plant or the fungus I want to find. Nettles and thistles love rich soil that has been disturbed, so I look for them where ditches have been dredged, leaving banks of soil along the edges; or on dung heaps; or fields once ploughed that this year lay fallow. Wild garlic likes humus-rich, damp, semi-shaded woodland banks while crow garlic likes sandy soils in open sunlight, with coastal grasses for its neighbours. Chanterelle is particularly fond of birch trees surrounded by lush, deep mosses that hold humidity. Hen-of-the-woods prefers oak by far, when given a choice, while chicken-of-the-woods likes to rotate trees. The first ones of the year come out on old willow, cherry comes next, and lastly the oak. Pignuts like the sunny side of well-drained banks with some light-dappled shade. I find that they are easiest to dig up from the soft banks of fine tilth that centuries of ploughing have pushed up against fences and hedges. I always find pineappleweed by the farm gate. It loves dry soil compacted by tractors and cattle stomping in and out.

Sometimes the clue is in the name. The larch bolete is faithful to the larch tree, and sea wormwood, sea kale and sea radish never venture far from the coast. Another clue is the nature of the habitat itself. On a round-Britain trip it surprised me to see that, for hundreds of miles, the central reservations of the motorways bloomed snowy white in the summer. This is Danish scurvy grass which left the poor, salty soils of the coast to travel inland – loving the salt and grit put down each winter that accumulates by the side of the road.

It's a privilege to get to know each species; observing them closely, recording their idiosyncrasies and preferred habitats.

Over the fence and into Rab's Wood I find what I am looking for. I'd noticed the fallen beech tree in the summer – it must have come down in the spring storm last year – and luckily no one has chopped it up. Lying like a dark, shiny whale across the diagonal riggs that span the woodland, it has produced exactly what I had hoped and expected it would. Along the split edge, layer after layer of oyster mushrooms are fanned out in contrasting cream just waiting for me. I return home as both my energy and the winter sun fade, with a full basket, to be greeted by the aroma of an excellent pheasant stew cooked by Matt.


## FREEZER AMNESTY

*Daisylea, 6 December*

It's raining again this morning and it's coming down too hard to get outside without a soaking. After yet another breakfast of stewed feral apples with hazelnuts, I've decided to hold a freezer amnesty. This delights Géza who doesn't share my hoarding traits.

Oh, joy! Forgotten, at the back of the freezer, I find a tub marked '*Wild Gremolata 2019*'. I am over the moon. I've been eating meat every day which has been a challenge for me as, up until Black Friday, I was mainly a vegetarian. I'm beginning to find that just the smell of it puts me off – especially pheasant. Without a wide variety of spices it isn't always easy to disguise gamey flavours or bitterness. I think I've been avoiding eating a lot of the meat because of this. I feel suddenly dizzy – my blood sugar must be low. My calorie intake is much lower than it should be and all I have had to eat – again – is four small nut-flour pancakes with a little grated feral apple for brunch and a few cups of herb tea.

Finding the gremolata has instantly given me a lift. Traditionally, it is the most delightful mixture of fresh green herbs and wild garlic, very finely chopped and traditionally immersed in olive oil with lemon zest or orange juice. But, for this forager, the juice of sea buckthorn berries makes the perfect citrussy alternative. The juice, on its own, is like fluorescent orange battery acid; it always needs to be mixed with a sauce or a syrup. Incredibly healthy, it has an antioxidant profile to rival açaí berry – without having to be flown in from the Amazon. *Zingy* and *zesty* are two words that sum it up perfectly. Now, not only is there something green on my plate but it instantly adds familiar flavour to the pheasant stew that I am struggling to get down.

This afternoon, Bob drops off two hares from a farm he's been culling on. In return I give him some more of my wild elderberry elixir. I am grateful for the hares as there are so few wild vegetables at this time of year but I have very, very mixed feelings. They are so beautiful and I love watching them racing across the fields up on the hills near the Heights farm. No one, that I have seen, troubles them up there where it is mainly cattle, but they are often shot when they encroach onto arable farms. Hare coursing, a brutal way of hunting hares with dogs, is illegal in Scotland but there are still three or four arrests every year. It's much more of a problem in southern England, especially on the flat lands of Lincolnshire and East Anglia, where large groups of men with huge spotlights, mounted onto four-wheel-drive vehicles, set greyhounds on hares, livestream the chase and take bets on the fastest dogs.

Shooting for sport is a very different matter to managed culling for habitat conservation. In a perfect world, we would have lynx again as the keystone predator to keep deer, hare and rabbit numbers under control, making culling unnecessary. However, I have quickly realised that, like it or not, eating meat during the winter is my only reliable source of protein as there are no wild peas, beans or grains right now. So I thank the hares and promise to return their kindness by planting hawthorn into the gaps in the hedges up on the Heights. This will give their kin more protection and provide some winter food. Then, with Matt's help, we carefully skin them, so that nothing is wasted.

When Bob brought me the deer in November, we skinned it without knives. Both of us have, coincidentally, collected old stone tools in the past. It's not uncommon when fields are ploughed to find flint tools that have worked their way to the surface. Matt has a 5,000-year-old flint hand axe and some razor-sharp flint blades. I have a stone knife of about 3,000 years old. Using these ancient tools turns the act of butchery into an act of reverence. There is no slashing or carving. Instead, there is a slow, rhythmic, gentle quality as the sharp side of my stone flake eases the skin away. This is how ancient humans did it and, suspended in liminal time while working away, I have plenty of space to think. My thoughts descend like floating prayers over us. Spending this slow time with her brings home that she isn't just a slab of meat but a once-living creature that deserves our gratitude and respect.

It's hard to explain but this creates a different, poignant relationship; a marvelling at how skin and sinew, tendon and muscle combine. A wondering about where spirit lives on. A link back to our mutual human–animal past when our relationship was more conscious. I become aware of my own death in the natural cycle of life.

## TINNITUS

*Daisylea, 8 December*

I woke just after 4.00 this morning. I try to get back to sleep as I am still tired, breathing deeply to trigger an autogenic state of relaxation. However, my attempts at stilling myself are thwarted by my nemesis – tinnitus. Three years ago I had to have a tooth pulled and within a week, I became aware that the faint background whistling noise – which I'd attributed to noisy light bulbs – was getting louder. My biggest sorrow is that this internal and infernal noise accompanies me into the forest. Two years ago, climbing up an arroyo in the Gila Wilderness with another herbalist, my friend Julie McIntyre, we stopped by a pinyon pine. It had oozed thick resin into great globules on the surface of the trunk that had set into hard, glittering crystals. Once I'd finished prising off a few lumps to take home to make ointments, I sat down beside Julie on the hillside in the wintry February New Mexico sunshine.

Suddenly, for one single magical minute, the tinnitus was miraculously gone. The joy of hearing uninterrupted silence again was indescribable.

Of course, I use the word *silence* loosely, as nature is never completely without sound. But when humans are quiet you can hear the air breathing, the plants growing and moving, the insects going about their chores. You feel immersed and connected as one with nature. Tinnitus is like a customs checkpoint on the border, always reminding you that you are actually not one vast landscape but separate countries. Coming home I decided to get rid of it. I mixed up some herbs but, as I remind myself this morning, it would help if I then actually took them! Recently I have been trying acupuncture to treat it, so wolf down some wild apples stewed with dried bilberries before rushing out to my appointment.

Acupuncture is an interesting form of medicine that humans have been practising for thousands of years. Archaeological research suggests bone or stone needles were used in China as long as 8,000 years ago but, astonishingly, primitive acupuncture was also practised in Europe.[5] I have always been fascinated by Ötzi the Iceman. He was found, extremely well preserved by the ice, in 1991 when a glacier started melting in the Tisenjoch Pass of the Ötztal Alps bordering Austria and Italy. Around his neck he had, strung on a worn leather thong, pieces of two bracket fungi that I still harvest today – tinder hoof and birch polypore.

It also emerged that he had DNA traces of Lyme disease, the stealthy bacteria *Borrelia burgdorferi*, nibbling away at the collagen and cartilage in his hip joint, no doubt aggravating the osteoarthritis found in his right hip. I feel for him.

Ötzi also had a number of curious tattoos – little blue crosses and sets of stacked trigram lines – ascending his legs and back. Unlike facial tattoos, or those on more visible parts of the body designed to catch attention and convey a message, these were more like the tattoos that result from stabbing yourself with an ink pen on the back of your hand, in the fifth form at school *circa* 1975!

Researchers suspect that these were 'medical tattoos'.[6] They measured all Ötzi's tattoo stripes and crosses and overlaid them on the meridian charts used today by Chinese acupuncturists. Amazingly, they match the acupuncture points used to treat pain in the low back and hip, with one set also for stomach pain. Someone, somewhere, had given Ötzi acupuncture, probably with a flake of flint or a sharpened bone, and then carefully tattooed the points in permanent ink so that Ötzi could self-administer pain relief to his body in the future. And all this a little over 5,300 years ago!

For myself, acupuncture lessens the noise in my ears but when I am quiet, it is still annoyingly there.

Today the wind is from the south. In the woods, at the edge of my hearing, I can detect the distant hum of traffic from the motorway; a constant drone of cars and rumbling lorries. This background of traffic noise is ubiquitous now in almost every part of Britain. It penetrates the depths of the countryside, echoing up hills, pulsing across plains, omnipresent. And in the wildest of places – where traffic noise has not yet penetrated – the whine of wind turbines often vibrates through the air and the soil itself. It occurs to me that humans are nature's tinnitus.

One remarkable thing that happened during the first corona-virus lockdown was that – like my single glorious minute on the New Mexico hillside – for a brief period of time Gaïa's tinnitus was silenced. In scenes reminiscent of post-nuclear Chernobyl's 30-year recovery,[7] deer took to sunbathing on the hot asphalt of the nearby A802 dual carriageway while – without the over-zealous council clearing the 'weeds' – pigeons got fat on dandelion seed from the central reservation, produced after the stunning yellow blooms had faded. Everywhere was uncannily, eerily but wondrously quiet. I miss the silence so much.

## CRYSTAL WORLD

*Fallen Tree Wood, 13 December*

The air is crisp and fresh and every lungful seems alive. As the sun never really left its bed at all today the frost is still hard on the ground and the leaves crackle underfoot. I mentally note some dandelion leaves, earmarking them for a salad, but the ground is solid and digging for calorie-dense roots is out of the question until it thaws a little. I slip into Fallen Tree Wood, where it's warmer. As I jump the stream, the water is still flowing despite the ice curling at the edges. In a bed of slowly decaying needles between the threadbare conifers there are still a few winter chanterelles, elegantly dressed in grey above their spindly yellow legs. A grey squirrel suddenly darts out, takes one look at me, and races up the nearest Sitka spruce. He knows this is hungry weather! I pick the winter chanterelles now. They store well in the fridge but left out they are liable to be hit by a harder frost that will render them soggy and sad.

Winter has its challenges and finding food is getting tougher. If it wasn't for Bob giving me that roe deer I would certainly be starving. The transition from vegetarianism is strange but continues to deepen my appreciation for animals. I wonder if the bacteria, fungi and moulds which will one day eat me will feel so grateful.

This morning my belly is full of fruit flan. I used ground-up dock seed and crushed walnut kernels mixed with pasteurised bramble juice to make a biscuit base. I then rehydrated and stewed chokeberries, bilberries and bird cherries with a little carragheen seaweed to make it set. It took time to make but it was wonderful to revive the flavours of summer again.

Along the quarried cutting through the rock that towers on each side of me, some low-lying angelica are still proudly flaunting seed heads. The frost has added hundreds of tiny glittering crystals to each seed and pedicle. You could not buy a Christmas ornament as beautiful as this with its biodegradable 'sequins'. I stand entranced until the cold bids me 'move along'. Enchanted by its magic, I feel like a child again.

# CHAPTER FOUR

# DIGGING ROOTS

*'I prithee, let me bring thee where crabs grow; and*
*I with my long nails will dig thee pignuts.'*

Shakespeare, *The Tempest*

## WILD GARLIC

*Almondell, 18 December*

Today the sun is shining. In Scotland at this time of year there are few daylight hours. The sun is barely up by 8.45 a.m. Hiding behind a blanket of clouds, it feels that as soon as it's risen it's time for an early night at 3.45 p.m. On an overcast day we are sunk into perpetual gloom. There are great Scots words to describe the weather: dowie, draggled, dreep, dreich, drear, dribble, drookit, dour. Taking advantage of the short window of light, I go down to Almondell Country Park to see what I can find along the River Almond.

I admit to an ulterior motive. One thing I am missing a lot right now is the onion family. Brown onions, red onions, spring onions and garlic. These used to make their way into nearly every meal that I cooked – until Black Friday. In the spring, Almondell sports a huge, long bank of wall-to-wall wild garlic. So far, this winter has been very mild and, over the past few years, one noticeable effect of climate change is that many plants start to sprout long before the spring.

I am not disappointed.

At first glance, the hillside looks little more than a monotone mass of dried leaves, twigs and other debris but here and there, as my eyes adjust, I start to notice tiny tips of green amongst the leaves. On my knees with my nose full of the earthy scent of the humus, gently brushing away the thick pile of leaf insulation, these tips are revealed as emerald shoots – some of them 7 to 10 centimetres long. I slip a knife gently down the side of each spear and wiggle it, signalling to the bulb to let go of its tight grip on the shoot. It then slides out of the ground easily, leaving the bulb and root intact to grow another. It is illegal to dig up a plant without the landowner's permission and anyway, would be unsustainable without a community harvesting plan. I gather the equivalent in shoots to two brown onions. This is Gaïa's kindness – even in the middle of winter.

I carry on down the track that chases the river to the next spot I have in mind. Here, fallen logs stack up at the base of a forlorn ancient beech tree that still stands, without branches or limbs. The jumbled piles of wood create a warm microclimate and here an abundance of pink purslane carpets the ground. Well . . . did! They're in the bag now and I'm picking opposite-leaved golden saxifrage; its cheeky yellow-streaked tips will make a tasty and pretty salad.

This morning I was stunned by the news headlines that UNICEF is providing breakfast boxes to British children who usually have free school meals, for two weeks over the Christmas holiday – so that they have at least *one* good meal a day. It is still on my mind – a stark contrast of their tragic food poverty with the generosity of nature's larder today.

Walking back up the hill to the car park, I pass two giant beech trees that have been felled. I feel anger and a pain in my heart for these older trees, cut down so thoughtlessly today in the name of 'health and safety'. It is not only the trees that are no more. The fungi that champion the underground health of the forest are deprived of prime real estate. The protected lion's mane mushroom, for example, only grows on old decaying trees. We have also lost the wisdom and memories that trees, plugged into the woodland via the mycelial network, impart to all the others to which they are connected.

The fallen leviathans have sprouted a huge flush of turkey tail mushrooms, breath-taking in their abundance. Grey zonal rings, which look just like a turkey's tail with a white edge, show they are ready to produce spores and perfect for picking. Each one produces millions of spores and, as they also reproduce asexually, collecting a few causes no harm. I take out my knife and cut a piece, putting it into my mouth to chew on while I work. I'm planning to make some immune-boosting decoctions for the coming winter months. It makes perfect mushroom-flavoured chewing gum.

Back home I reheat the pulled roast hare casserole. The flavours of the wild mushrooms and damson prunes have melded together in a delightfully savoury, umami union. I roast some tuberous comfrey roots – a first. They taste almost like Jerusalem artichoke and, as I will find out later, have a similar effect on the colon. This is accompanied by a salad of all the fresh greens picked today: winter purslane, golden saxifrage, wild garlic shoots and watercress – such an important source of winter vitamin C. I feel nourished by this supper and grateful.

## PIGNUTS

*Daisylea, 19 December*

I'm on the hunt for calories. There are three copses that provide shelter for the birds and wildlife in Daisylea field, one of which crests a warm, south-facing slope. In the summer, nestled in the dappled shade between the beech leaves, the small white flowers of the pignut shimmer, enjoying the warmth. Now, on this chilly winter day, the flowers are gone without a trace but I remember *exactly* where they were. Farmer Rab kindly gave me permission a few years ago to dig them up. I'm sure he thinks I'm mad, but harmless! Today, as well as a small wicker basket, I also have a hand fork and a Korean *homi*. The homi, a type of hand plough used for removing grass from rice paddies, turns out to be the perfect implement for capturing these elusive delicacies.

The pignut is a chubby member of the carrot family (Apiaceae). It tastes great, a cross between a chestnut and a parsnip. The only problem is that they are tiny. They are usually the size of a hazelnut although foraging legend has it that sometimes they can grow to the size of a golf ball. I'm currently losing 1 to 2 kilos a week on my wild diet – not that I'm complaining as the weight is there to lose, but I am aware that there's a distinct lack of carbohydrates in my diet. The hazelnuts that I am rationing over the winter won't last very long at this rate. I try not to think about it as it fills me with trepidation. I've divided the berries I have into five bags, each labelled with the name of a month from now until April. I find it reassuring to look at them sometimes, knowing that for each wintry month there will be some food.

Wild tubers, the underground starch storage larders of plants, have several key attributes that make them particularly attractive hunter-gatherer foods. Most significantly, they can be harvested across a greater proportion of the year than many fruits and seeds. Several research studies show that one's calorie-to-effort 'return on investment' for digging tubers, roots and corms should average around 1,000 to 3,000 calories per hour. Return rates are higher for resources such as honey or meat but, in hunter-gatherer tribes, roots are frequently included in daily dishes because of the greater predictability in finding them.

I am sure that this is true in the tropics where most of the studies on hunter-gatherers are researched but I am rapidly learning that this doesn't apply in Scotland. Here the winters freeze the ground solid and the heavy clay is not conducive to big, fat, easy-to-harvest roots. The book I'm reading, *The Lifeways of Hunter-Gatherers*,[1] points out that roots often provide reliable returns because the areas where they grow are well known, and can therefore be scouted in advance to check out their condition before investing energy in harvesting parties. Time spent searching is then negligible and digging produces a more reliable outcome than hunting or fishing. The predictability of wild roots as fall-back foods helps survival when there is low availability of protein and fat resources.

Strangely, wild roots are not eaten much in the UK. This may be partly due to the illegality of uprooting a plant without the landowner's permission. But, unlike our Polish cousins, for example, we do seem to miss out on this natural source of goodness. Although modern Paleo diets eschew carbs based on 'archaeological evidence', contemporary studies of living hunter-gatherers show that 'underground storage organs' are critical to most diets.

In Venezuela, the Yaruro people – known as the Pumé – gather so many wild tubers, corms, bulbs and roots that they make up approximately 25 per cent of their diet, comparable to that of other savannah foragers. In gathering wild roots, they manage a return of 2,449 calories per hour. South African studies also show that 50 per cent of foraging outings to collect underground storage organs provide enough calories to meet the 2,000-calorie daily requirements of a hunter-gatherer in under two hours. They also grow near the soil surface and can be gathered with minimal effort. With such a readily available food resource in the southern Cape landscape, roots and tubers probably played a critical role in providing food for early humans. It would amaze and delight me if this was something I could achieve in Scotland. All my daily calorie needs in just one hour!

It is slow work as I dig up the pignuts and I start to think about other plants that will yield a better return. The difference between foraging as a hobby and foraging to live is as much about quantity as quality – unlike the popular saying.

Marsh woundwort tubers are lovely and crunchy; they taste like bean sprouts and grow abundantly in the boggy meadows around here. Their disadvantage is that the tubers are usually tucked under a mat of rushes making them virtually impossible to dig up without a struggle and, as the leafy foliage has died back, they are going to be hard to locate. On the plus side I translocated some about three years ago – when I was rewilding an area I thought they would like to grow in – so I can certainly find enough for a few meals.

Reedmace is easy. There is a big swamp of it at the back of the gasworks. The prospect of getting into a cold, muddy swale to dig them out at this time of the year is a bit daunting but I know they will be a good return on investment.

Dandelion roots are a favourite of mine, best roasted with a little parmesan, salt and black pepper. Sadly, parmesan and black pepper are obviously off the menu. The challenge with dandelion is that its favourite place to grow is right by the edges of roads. They like the salt that's put down in the winter to stop ice building up. Here, where it's gravelly, the roots are knotted and twisted and probably so polluted that I wouldn't want them anyway. I do know a field that's run wild up on Torphichen Hill. I must find out who owns it and ask for permission to dig.

Thistles are fairly easy as they are everywhere in Scotland, and I love the roots as they taste just like globe artichokes. Will winter thistles that have flowered be stringy and tough? The stems are often too fibrous. Or will they be as delicious as artichokes? Other high-calorie options occur to me as I dig. Tuberous comfrey (lower in alkaloids than its cousins), wild carrot, common hogweed, sweet cicely, lesser celandine . . . a potential foraging 'shopping' list!

I'm on my hands and knees now and think I've perfected the technique. Using the homi, it's easy to slice under the sward – below the level of the grass roots – and carefully peel back the turf. The delicate stems of the pignuts pierce through this matted tangle and, as they dwindle into a fine white thread, snake their way deeper into the soil. It's not like digging for carrots where you know the root is right under the leaves. I get the sense that pignuts learnt a long time ago that this tactic just leads to discovery. So instead, as soon as they've breached the soil, they twist and turn, under a root, around a stone, and try to end up as far away as possible from the point where they emerged into the light. Luckily, here the soil is crumbly and I can brush it away fairly easily, following the fragile thread carefully as, only too easily, it snaps and all is lost. Eventually the prize is revealed. Some are even slightly larger than a hazelnut, some quite a bit smaller. I try to resist scratching the brown outer wrapping off with my thumbnail to reveal the glistening white 'nut' inside and crunching them up raw. After an hour of digging I have about thirty. That's just one side dish, eaten twice.

Géza laughs at me when I get home. So much labour goes into collecting such a small amount and, being an engineer, he thinks the inefficiency of pignut collection is crazy. 'That's why agriculture was invented,' he reminds me – again. I spend the next hour washing, scrubbing and peeling them – loving them into being!

I am saving these for Christmas.

For supper tonight I cook up some pheasant breasts that have been marinating all day in some olive oil that I strained off a jar of pickled hogweed flower buds from last spring, some home-made elderberry vinegar and some red elderberry paste that I use in a similar way to tomato purée. I miss the ease of tomatoes as I used to use them a lot, although they weren't actually eaten in Britain until around 1597. I bake the pheasant with wild garlic bulbs and olive oysterlings – a slightly bitter, late-winter mushroom. Though they are hugely popular in Japan as *mukitake*, hardly anyone here seems to eat them so they are easy to find even in December. I add tuberous comfrey leaves, home-smoked sea salt, grated feral apple for a little sweetness, and some water.

While it is cooking I rehydrate some sea spaghetti, collected on the last low tide of the season. It took several days to get it all dried, despite having two dehydrators so I can do twenty trays at a time. I think it was the delay in drying that's made it smell somewhat fishy, which is slightly off-putting, although thankfully it doesn't taste of fish food. Oddly, Matt doesn't notice the smell at all.

Despite all this effort, I don't really enjoy the pheasant casserole and only eat a tiny portion. By contrast, Matt tucks in heartily. I am rapidly going off meat completely and my gut transit time has screeched to a near halt. I am really missing the dietary structure of my old life. Longing for big, colourful, morning veggie stir-fries that would keep me going the whole day with just a light lunch. In the evenings, a few crackers with some cheese. Well, probably a lot of cheese!

To console myself I have a glass of honeysuckle mead. Soon after Géza and I built this house I started making some 'country wines'; elderberry, bramble, gorse flower, crabapple and meads from wild-flowers and honey. After they had matured for a year Géza tried them. 'They're rubbish,' he announced, wincing at their acidity, and set about making some himself, injecting some organisation and hygiene into my haphazard process. However, the following year, these were also found lacking so over the last five or six years they have all sat, collecting dust, under the bookshelves. This aged hon-eysuckle mead is now one of the finest. Dry and not too sweet and cloying like so many meads, with a hint of honeysuckle on a warm summer's breeze. Just the tonic I was after, so I have a second glass. Like all things that are precious, they just needed time!

# CHAPTER FIVE

# BROKEN LAND

*'To love a place is not enough. We must find ways to heal it.'*

Robin Wall Kimmerer, *Braiding Sweetgrass*

## THE DUMP

*20 December*

There is a tug in the air as you approach Yule. It's hard to describe but everyone is feeling it. Tomorrow is 21 December, the winter solstice. Earth, heading toward the end of the year, will be at the point of its furthest tilt away from the sun. It feels as if everything is slowing down. Groaning like the engines of the *Titanic*, hard to starboard and full steam ahead to avoid an iceberg, the earth seems to grind to a halt before tilting her face back to the sun. From that solstice moment onward we will be given an extra two precious minutes of light every day. We all feel this pause before the great shift. Everyone in the house is apathetic, as if all cosmic energy has been sucked out of our bones, with a serious, somewhat gloomy, face. The sort of heavy face that says, 'We should all be hibernating.'

To cap it all, the government has just cancelled Christmas. So there is also the psychic pressure of the entire nation feeling pissed off at yet another U-turn. The government has known about the new coronavirus variant since September. In fact, variance is what coronaviruses do. We all suspect that focusing on the latest one is a way for politicians to avoid looking as if they've got egg on their faces for not being sensible and telling us sooner. It would have been nice to tell the public before people had bought Christmas turkeys to feed three households, only to find out that they'd be eating them on their own. Except in my case, there'll be no turkey. I have a haunch of roe deer to roast. All I want from Santa is vegetables.

I procrastinate in the morning, over a cup of 'coffee' made of roast acorn and dandelion root, giving in to the mood of the dying year. In today's news I learn that 'early humans may have survived the harsh winters by hibernating'. The article[1] goes on to explain, 'Evidence from bones found at one of the world's most important fossil sites suggests that our hominid predecessors may have dealt with extreme cold hundreds of thousands of years ago by sleeping through the winter.'[2]

I am not at all surprised by this and finally rouse myself to go out at 2 o'clock. It's late in the day. There are only one and a half hours of daylight left now, so I can't go too far, but getting outside to forage always lifts my spirits. Each lungful of cold air revives me and returns me to myself. It's as if the trappings of the twenty-first century that create the working *digital self* are quickly eroded as my *wild self* reclaims me. I decide to go to the Dump to see if there are any green plants at all.

The Dump is a miserable place. It was a quarry in a past life so is indented in a hollow protected from the wind that bites over the wet heath moss. I used to love it, as in its shelter I found a huge range of edible plants but, about seven or eight years ago, the owner decided to start using it to dump farm waste. Now the terrain has been remodelled with huge piles of manure and soiled straw bedding, interlaced with black plastic, that sit in stinking fetid ponds unable to drain through the scraped rock. The manure mounds are host to all kinds of weeds including large bull thistles. I imagine their tasty white roots reaching easily into the rotting heaps but never pick them. I'm wary of the agricultural chemicals that probably also inhabit the sludge.

I scale one of the manure mountains, carefully testing that the ground beneath my feet will not suddenly give way, to reach a row of broad-leaved docks lining the top like sentinels. Their green leaves – with holes bored by sparkly green dock beetles – have long gone but the crisp red-brown seed is what I'm after. I'll add them to my acorn flour to make it last longer. The wind has dried them and they are easy to pick. As I run each plume through my hand, the nutlets detach easily and I soon have a full bag of them.

I look behind the hedge along the inner slope of the bank that separates the Dump from the road. The leaves of the dog violets are barely 4 millimetres across. I will have to leave them three or four weeks to grow larger. I was hoping they would have put in a growth spurt during this unseasonably warm December as I'm aware I need a bigger supply of vitamin C than the few carefully dried berries that I have tucked away. Wild violet leaves have five times the vitamin C per 100 grams than an orange and they make a great herbal tea.

From the bank I cross up to the wet heath that encircles the Dump. I spy sorrel leaves hiding in the edges of large clumps of grass that surround a hawthorn tree. It's a beautiful tree with red berries thickly thronging its upper branches. There are none below because 'someone' picked them months ago. They are now nestling in jars on my kitchen shelves labelled '*Hawsin Sauce*'. A take on hoisin, this is a delicious ketchup-like berry sauce that I adore. It has its roots in a medieval recipe and helps to bring flavour to a monotonous winter diet.

The wet heath is a thick carpet of bilberry bushes even though every tiny wild blueberry has long gone – the prize of the competition between myself, the rabbits and the deer in the late summer just past. Many of the berries ended up in my dehydrator and I'm reaping the benefit now. On the back of the windswept slope, the thick spiny clumps of gorse bushes have an edible treat. They are already coming into flower, bringing some bright yellow cheer to the drab vegetation that surrounds me. I pick a few flowers to go in a salad with the sorrel, some lesser celandine leaves that have also come up this week, and some watercress tops. I make a mental note to pick the rest of the watercress soon, as there is frost forecast which will decimate this food source.

It's 4.00; the starless sky is rapidly darkening as I wander back along the road. I haven't finished yet and I can still see the telltale spikes of reedmace beckoning in the quickening gloom. I pull up four of them, careful not to slide into the stagnant ditch. They resist and then suddenly give, coming out of the mud with a loud, satisfying, sucking noise. I snap the rhizome off, careful to heel the thick clump of roots back into the ditch to carry on their colonisation of this little waterway. I'm not going to harvest any more next to the road, where oil and traffic dirt drain into the ditch, but I want to perform a test.

Back home with ice-block fingers defrosted, I peel off the scaly exterior skin of the four rhizomes to reveal the pithy white fibres of their snow-white interior. I pull them apart and pound them with some hot water, using the end of my rolling pin in a small glass bowl. Then slipping in a clean hand, I massage the fibres. At first, they are slippery and feel almost as soapy as if I were hand-washing laundry. After a while I feel a change in texture as the fibres become dryer to the touch. I separate them from the now milky water. All I have to do is wait for the water to settle and the starch to sink to the bottom. I'll siphon off the clear water, dry out the starch and use it like arrowroot flour or cornflour. This little experiment will give me an idea of yield, so I can calculate how many rhizomes I need to pull from the large swale at the back of the gasworks, in order to get a single kilo of reed-mace flour.

No one ever said a foraging life would be easy!

# CHAPTER SIX

# THE SEASONS TURN

*'To one in sympathy with nature, each season,*
*in turn, seems the loveliest.'*

Mark Twain

## YULE

*Daisylea, 21 December*

As I open my bleary eyes, the sun is just starting to peer through the black silhouettes of bare beech branches, standing proud against a grey and orange-streaked sky. I fully understand why ancient cultures worshipped the sun. How faithfully it rises every day, always reliable, no matter what happened yesterday. It grounds me and reminds me that we are very small beings, in a huge cosmos, existing in a brief sliver of time.

I'm excited when I remember it is finally Yule. Today marks the turn of the seasonal wheel and a step change in the dance between the sun and the earth. Each day a little lighter than the last and every extra minute counts when you live in Scotland!

From the Neolithic era when farming was introduced, the winter solstice was traditionally the time when the last of the animals were slaughtered. Over the winter, with less and less food to find, they would lose condition and require feeding from the stores of grains gathered in the autumn. Unless it was a bumper year, the grain was also needed for people to survive. This period was marked by a great feast, the pagan feast of Yule (Juul) that was later replaced by Christmas. By the Middle Ages, a feast of wild game such as three-bird pie, venison or a boar's head might be served and, if you were a farmer or wealthy townsman, you would dine upon a fattened goose, ham or roast beef.

Hunkered down in a shelter over the cold winter, eking out grains, nuts and preserved foods, I can easily imagine the joy when my Stone Age tribe caught the occasional deer in a forest and the celebration that would have accompanied such a triumph.

Today is slightly overcast so I had better get a move on. It will be too dark to see by 4.00 p.m. I'm out scouting to see what will be ready to pick in the next few days to add to our Christmas dinner.

To be honest, I am really hoping for gifts of food!

## VEGETABLES!

*Yellowcraigs, 23 December*

Down to the coast today. The plants here in the warmer coastal climate are thick with glossy leaves and tender young growth. Matt and I harvest as much as we can fit into our baskets. The alexanders are already coming into flower, with fat buds about to crack open. Their leaves make the most delicious alternative to spinach and the buds are excellent for lacto-fermenting and pickling. I cannot describe how much joy I feel luxuriating in such promiscuous greenery after a month of abstinence.

We pick sea buckthorn berries. This tart, battery-acidic, vibrant orange fruit will keep me in vitamin C for the rest of the winter. Here in East Lothian, sea buckthorn is a rampant coastal weed, so a little judicious pruning helps to keep the path clear. There is no danger of the birds missing out on their winter food as there are tangerine bushes stretching as far as the eye can see, and you can still find berries, clustered thickly together at the ends of the twigs, in January and February. They are murder to pick as each one is so full of juice, under the fragile skin. They pop under the lightest pressure and cover you with a sticky juice. It is much easier, when they are so abundant, to cut the end tips off and take them home. Some people put the twigs in the freezer and then pick off the frozen berries but I never have enough freezer space. Once I am home I 'milk' them at my leisure – running the twigs through my hands, collecting the juice in a bucket. Today's haul will give me 10 litres from the two large bin bags we gathered. We hide them behind some bushes to collect on the way back.

It's a fresh and sunny day, with a westerly breeze so it's not too cold. I'm as happy as a clam. The Forth estuary is where the river, that winds its way down from Stirling, broadens and feeds into the North Sea. Here, once great oyster beds covered 50 square miles. Now, aided by a major marine restoration project, they are starting to move back in again – a hopeful sign that perhaps human pollution of the waterways is improving. The beach and dunes are beautiful and there are a few people out with children and dogs. Playful shrieks and yelps are echoed by the swooping gulls as I pick my way along the sandy path that divides the vegetation from the beach, around the rocky point to where the succulents live.

Above the line of marram grass, much of the green foliage still growing, under the mile-long sea buckthorn barrier is poison hemlock. This is deadly but easily identified by its lacy cut, green feathery foliage and telltale purple spots on the stem.

Where the bushes have died back and let the light in, pink purslane leaves are starting to sprout. They wait for the competitive grasses and buttercups to die back, before starting their growth cycle in November. They make delicious salads and I've been eating an awful lot of them recently. There is no spring beauty, another type of purslane, yet. This comes into leaf much later, in the early spring.

Descending the sandy path, I rescue a few dandelion roots exposed where the sand has fallen away from the trail. Down on the shoreline there are more green treats in the form of scurvy grass. Its round, plump, almost heart-shaped leaves are glossy and polished. A mouthful of this wakes me up instantly! Hot, pungent, bitter. I've brought some cold roast venison with me to snack on. The fresh leaves sandwiched between the slices are like an instant wild wasabi paste.

I gather Scots lovage seeds. Half of what I pick I scatter along the shoreline to help regenerate and spread the plants' range, the other half I take home to use as a spice. After all, Scots lovage is in the same family as fennel, cumin, coriander and many other household seasonings. Walking back along the beach I find tree mallow – perfect for making *molokhia*, a thick Middle Eastern soup. Later in the year I plan to come back for a few more. They are ideal for wrapping food – like vine leaves – into edible parcels. By the time we retrieve the bin bags of sea buckthorn berries there is quite a harvest and we head for home. I am tired, but there are still several hours of processing the berries ahead.

## CHRISTMAS EVE

*Daisylea, 24 December*

A short morning walk has yielded treasure! Some late watercress that survived November's frost, reliable pink purslane leaves, peppery hairy bittercress and pretty yellow gorse flowers that are just coming into bloom. Their sensitivity to sunshine is so great that, once spring has arrived, you can reliably navigate by tasting your way around a gorse bush. The flowers on the sunny south side of the bush taste strongly of coconut while the flavour of those on the shadier north side is of green peas. They still taste of the latter now. There is not enough warm sunshine yet to generate the essential oils responsible for the transformation.

On the way back I notice that the mahonia in the garden is in flower. It also has yellow flowers – insects can see yellow better in the early months of the year but prefer reds, pinks and purples in the summer. These taste of sherbet lemon drops. I don't take them

all because the berries will be useful later in the year and you can't
have both!

The green leaves and flowers all go into a bowl together to make
a lovely winter salad. Dressed with a little crabapple vinegar I eat
them with a baked smoked salmon seasoned with wild garlic salt.
It isn't quite as smoky as I'd have liked. I cold-smoked the fish after
defrosting it but now think it would have been better hot-smoked.
It's a bit on the dry side, so I strain a little precious oil off a half-open
jar of pickled chanterelles, beat it up with an egg yolk – treating my
pet ferrets to the white – and make a little mayonnaise. I also make
some horseradish sauce to go with it. My horseradish sauce is not for
the faint-hearted as, made from freshly grated roots stirred into the
mayo, it blows all the cobwebs out of my head.

Just grating a single root makes my eyes water more than an entire
sack of onions. The tears rolling down my face are not of sadness.
Quite the opposite. I feel a contentment and peace within my soul.
This new way of living with Gaïa isn't going too badly . . . so far!

## CHRISTMAS DAY

*Kinross, 25 December*

This Christmas is very different. I am going to my mother Ursula's
house, a forty-five-minute drive away, as she can't travel to me.
Now eighty-two years old, she is valiantly joining me for her first
Christmas dinner of wild food. I treat myself to an egg for breakfast, remembering with nostalgia the fragrant orange I used to find
nestled at the end of my father's long, itchy, woollen 'Santa' sock, on
Christmas morning. I would appreciate it as much today as I did in
the 1960s, when an orange was a rare treat! I haven't seen that many
pigeons nesting in the snow so using 'egg points' is a bit of a stretch
but my four hens, who had stopped laying, have produced two eggs
between them this morning. I whisk one up with some preserved
wild garlic pesto and pour it over some gently frying, just defrosted,
cubes of ceps to make an omelette. I wolf it down alongside a cup of

acorn and chaga 'coffee'. I added precious chaga today for a winter boost but, surprisingly, I am not missing caffeine hits nearly as much as I thought I would. Eventually I load up my van and wend my way along the edge of the majestic, cloud-shrouded Ochil hills to the market town of Kinross.

I've brought with me some garnet-red hawthorn gin, now mellowed with age to the depth of a rich madeira. Careful not to include the murky sludge that has settled on the bottom over the last four years, I give my mother a 'sherry'. I've saved a roe deer haunch from November to roast. First it is rubbed over with deer fat that I carefully melted down when I skinned it. Every last drop is precious. Then I sprinkle over sea salt, crumbled smoked dabberlocks seaweed, and powdered scarletina bolete – a startling relative of the porcini. Scarletinas do look very scary, so are often avoided by mushroom hunters. The cap is a rich nutty brown moleskin on top, but underneath the pores warn you off with a vibrant orange hue. The stem's deep red colour is created by hundreds of tiny bright carmine dots. To terrify you even further, as you cut the mushroom open its fluorescent yellow flesh immediately, on contact with oxygen, turns a vivid Prussian blue. Mercifully when you cook it, it changes back to lemon yellow. I wish they were still fresh and in season now, to make a welcome and stunning flash of colour at such a dreary time of year. Unfortunately, most of my meals are now unappetising shades of brown and dark green.

With the venison haunch in the oven, there is time to make some 'cakes', as Christmas isn't Christmas for my mum without a pudding. I whip up an experimental batter using the second egg with chestnut flour, ground dock seeds, and some dried cranberries I have pre-soaked in sea buckthorn juice. Their colour stands out like glistening rubies. I add in some precious honey, eked out with some rosehip syrup for sweetness and some toasted, ground hogweed seeds to replace cinnamon spice. These bake quickly in their reusable silicone cupcake cases and once they are out of the oven and cooling, I pierce the tops and dribble in some of the hawthorn 'sherry' to moisten them while Mum tucks into a second glass.

By the time the venison is cooked there is also an array of vege-tables. I'm eating roast alexanders root with its earthy yet perfumed flavour, some wild fennel root and abundant roasted tuberous com-frey tubers. I've put a parsnip and some domestic carrots in for Mum. I had planned to have wild carrots but once dug up they were barely 2 millimetres thick, fighting their way through the thinnest layer of topsoil into the hard subsoil below and, damn, I forgot to bring my precious pignuts!

For greens there are steamed alexanders, baby wild leeks and tuberous comfrey leaf. Two handfuls of fresh sheep's sorrel, found growing round the back of Mum's house, become a fresh, perky microgreens salad. I've defrosted some porcini mushrooms (picked in September) that round the meal out nicely, especially with a sumptuous thick gravy poured all over them. The gravy is simply the roasting pan juices thickened with smoked oyster mushroom powder and acorn starch. There are some pickled chicken-of-the-woods mushrooms to have on top. All of this is accompanied by my best vintage red '*Bramble de Lothian, 2017*'. I can't say that there was much left over afterwards, and we didn't manage to fit all the cakes in, but we had a good try! All in all it was a pretty good Christmas banquet, although I could have murdered a Yorkshire pudding.

The hawthorn sherry gives way to sloe gin and a suitably Christmassy nap. It's been a sterling effort and a lovely, peaceful day but I am missing my grown-up children – who were not as surprised as I thought they might be when they heard of my latest project! I think this is the first Christmas that I haven't seen at least one of the three. My sadness is tempered knowing that many families have lost loved ones this first Covid Christmas. My heart goes out to them.

# CHAPTER SEVEN

# GAME

> 'Soon, coyotes, ravens and eagles will become food for
> soil micro- and macro- fauna, which will become plant,
> which will become herbivore, omnivore and carnivore yet
> again, which will become soil, in endless transformation.'

Fred Provenza, *Nourishment*

## SNOW

*Daisylea, 27 December*

Today it is snowing. Through the frost-laced window it's impossible
to see the light green flush of early spring herbs any longer – the
ground elder, wild leek, purslane, dandelion and hairy bittercress.
All I can see is a white fleecy blanket of icy snow. Outside, all sounds
are muted and breath hangs suspended in the air in frozen drifts.
Snug in my warm home, with a cupboard chock full of ferments and
a freezer of mushrooms, I wonder what it was like before fridges and
food storage long ago. What would I eat today?

Breakfast is rather inevitably more stew from Christmas leftovers.
During the morning I have a go at baking. I have plenty of dock seed
retrieved from Yellowcraigs, ground into a rough flour in the blender.

Mixed with chestnut flour and hot water it makes a decent dough. Rolled out and baked for fifteen minutes on one side, then turned for another five minutes, I manage to produce some pretty reasonable crackers! This, along with venison liver pâté, topped with a wicked winter salsa, makes a very civilised treat. Matt and Géza join me in making short work of them. The salsa is all the hot, mustardy, garlicky, bitter herbs: scurvy grass, hairy bittercress, three-cornered leek, wild garlic bulb, alexanders leaf, minced together and mixed into a paste with crabapple vinegar.

It's a month today since I started. Weirdly, it feels like both the shortest and the longest month I've had for a while. I veer between slightly anxious when outdoor pickings are scarce but also joyous when I find unexpected gifts. I think the delight of self-sufficiency is outweighing the worry and I really don't miss going to the supermarket at all.

## HOGMANAY

*Daisylea, 1 January 2021*

My wooden house up here on the hill is still surrounded by a thick layer of snow, innocently sprinkled over a treacherous ice rink. Six days in this remains a novelty and dramatically beautiful. Today, 1 January is a new start. Surely 2021 has to be better than 2020?

I wake up with a bit of a hangover as Géza and I stayed up to see the New Year in. One of the problems with home-made wine is that one is never quite sure how strong it is. Bramble wine, for example, is light, lacking the body of wine made from grapes and can seem a little thin, more watery. But it can also pack a huge punch and it's a long stretch between sundown and midnight at this time of the year in Scotland!

I start the morning rather late with a last cup of roasted cleavers seed 'coffee'. In Scotland, for some obscure reason lost in time, our name for cleavers is sticky willy. It's also known as goosegrass.

Before I started this crazy undertaking, I knew that cleavers seeds could be roasted and ground into a coffee substitute but I had never bothered to try it. It amuses me that on my foraging courses over the last few years, I would tell people that this could be done but joked and dismissed cleavers coffee as a post-Brexit survival tactic. I take it all back. This is an absolutely delicious drink, and it actually contains a little caffeine.[1] Its genus Galium is in the family Rubiaceae, which is also the family of the great *Coffea arabica*. I thought I would really miss coffee on my wild food diet as every single morning started with a cup, followed mid-morning by a second, but I have been completely happy drinking herbal teas made from the various flowers and leaves that I picked and dried last summer. Sadly, I am paying for ignoring cleavers because by the time I realised I might need it, there was barely enough to last three days. I will need to search the fences for more. However, this shortage has just made each cup taste the sweeter and every sip is laced with appreciation. As James Duke, who wrote *The Handbook of Edible Weeds*, comments, 'Foragers are spiritually rich, if financially poor.'[2]

Brunch is an 'egg points' treat. The crossbills nest in January and the pigeons are still at it – possibly not in all this snow – but the eggs my hens have been laying are accumulating. I have been saving them up and giving them to Bob in return for the game that is currently keeping me alive, but they are the gift that keeps on giving. Around 11.00 I make an omelette with alexanders and scurvy grass pesto beaten into the eggs, with a little smoked salt. I then fold it over some pickled hogweed and pickled chicken-of-the-woods. It is exquisite and a stunning, vivacious, bright green! After a month of food that is getting monotonously brown it is a delight simply to look at. And it tastes just as good.

In the afternoon, I venture out into the cold crisp air and walk up the road to my neighbours. Allan had sent me a text earlier, offering me some geese and ducks that have been given to him, and I have learnt never to say no. The birds are waiting outside on top of the wheelie bin and I leave a little bottle of hawthorn flower brandy in return. They're heavy and the ice is slippery – very treacherous – and I'm very careful not to end up on my back again! I still get a twinge from a fall two years ago, when a pesky rabbit burrow beneath a footpath collapsed under me.

Back home, I look at the birds. There are four pink-footed geese, two wigeon ducks and two teal ducks – all matched in drake–duck pairs. The teal in particular are so beautiful. I've never seen them close up before. Their wings are trimmed with shimmering jewel-like green and blue feather patches. I look them up on the RSPB website. The page on teal tells me that the UK is 'home to a significant percentage of the NW European wintering population'. I realise that only 2,100 nesting pairs are left in Britain and that they are on the Amber List for protection. However, during the winter, they are joined by tens of thousands of northerly teal flying south to warmer climes and it is perfectly legal to shoot them between 1 September and 31 January inland, extended to 20 February for ducks on the foreshore.

I feel heartbroken. I shall have to eat them now as not to would be to dishonour them. I wonder why my feelings about eating the deer are so different and I realise it's because of the *intention* behind the killing. The birds were randomly shot in sport despite their declining numbers. The deer were individually culled to manage the habitat because their numbers were too great. I realise that to me it makes a big difference.

## FROZEN

*Drumtassie Wood, 7 January*

I am still surrounded by snow and ice. How long will this last?

Feeling very cold and hungry, I retreat into the woods. Here there is shelter from the wind, a little more warmth among the trees, but little to eat. In the snow underfoot, I can clearly see the tracks of all the animals. The deer have come to eat the grasses of the woodland glades. The skeletal tree canopy and the sweeping boughs of evergreen needles have protected the land beneath from all but the heaviest snowfall. The rabbits have been nibbling on young saplings, ring-barking them and killing them off. Here, signs of a scuffle: a fox has caught one.

In this wintry landscape, with the ground frozen too solid to dig for roots, no laying birds other than the odd isolated pigeon, and no greens, there is so little to forage. With my meagre hoard of back-up nuts and grains rapidly running out, I cannot survive without meat. My first-day microbiome test results suggest my protein intake was insufficient on my vegetarian diet before I went wild. Despite my love of animals and my preference for a plant-based diet, in a pre-Neolithic world it's a fact that without the food in my freezer, I could not survive in this climate on foraged food alone – until the spring comes again.

I wasn't expecting my relationship with meat to change so much, so quickly. But the very real issues I've thought about so much surrounding commercial meat production – climate change; dairy farming; the standards of meat; health issues; land inequality – are not relevant to my current situation. Perhaps that's made me see things differently? Death is all around us in nature. It's unavoidable, and it's even more apparent when you're trying to forage for every meal, witnessing this fact daily. I know I now have fewer years in front of me than behind. Life and death form a continuous, renewing cycle and, from the moment of my own death, fungi will start eating me. Perhaps some bacteria already are. Surely what counts is the quality of the living moment – and every human and animal deserves a decent life.


## HALLUCINATING

*Elrigside Wood, 8 January*

It's mid-morning and fuelled by a cup of acorn and chaga 'coffee', to boost my immune system as I fight off a cold, I am trying to catch up with work to free the weekend for foraging. It's pointless as I can't concentrate. Today I'm feeling weak, blurry-eyed, dizzy and wobbly with very loud tinnitus. My mouth is parched with the sensation of a lump in my throat. I'm getting waves of nausea and feeling very faint with a horrible sensation that I'm going to suddenly break into a hot or cold sweat and vomit. Am I having palpitations or am I just panicking? It isn't a hangover and I'm not on drugs, so what is going on? My appetite – which has been decreasing over the last week – has gone completely and the thought of yet more 'brown food' makes me want to retch.

Matt soaks some wild berries in a little water to rehydrate them and bakes them with some nuts in the oven for me. I drizzle a little of the precious bottle of birch sap syrup over them and eat them slowly. Then gradually, in slow motion like the time-lapse footage of a flower unfurling from bud to blossom, I come around. I am sure this is either low blood sugar or a protein overdose. My bowels are so slow that I have to resort to a half-teaspoon of magnesium citrate in a little water – the only supplement I've had this year as I'm not taking any extra vitamins or minerals.

I need more green vegetables. My body is craving them, craving their fibre.

Lunch is a little more substantial. The last of some roast wild boar tenderloin that I was given, cooked with grated feral apple. I am amazed at how well the apples are lasting in the fridge, even as the flesh is losing its crisp sweetness and they turn shrivelled and pithy. There is a little sea beet still at the back of the fridge that joins them. Strengthened by the food, I head out to Elrigside Wood.

Ducking under the beech boughs, I notice a strange feeling in the woods, as if I am being watched. Not in a sinister way, as if a human was hiding there, but nevertheless, nature seems to be 'on alert' at my presence. I have noticed that the smell of my body has changed on this meat-heavy diet. It's become much stronger and more intense. I wonder if animals can tell the difference in our intent by how we smell? They can detect urinary 2-phenylethylamine in other carnivores.[3] Do they avoid us if we smell like meat-eaters?

# SQUIRRELS

*Daisylea, 8 January*

As if fate intends to really test me, today my neighbour has caught
three grey squirrels that were raiding horse oats, in a trap, and hung
them on my front door handle. Once out of their furry jackets, the
squirrels are covered in fat. There has hardly been any on the deer
and geese that I've had. Perhaps by midwinter, they have used up most
of the store they put on in the autumn, but to date there has been a
serious lack of fat in my diet. There is more on the bellies, rump and
under the limbs of the three greys than there has been in a whole deer
or a brace of wild geese. I carefully cut it away and melt it gently in a
frying pan. Once cool, I will pour it into a jar to use in baking. This
is a very precious resource.

I marinate the rest of the squirrels in a mixture of sea buckthorn
juice, wild raspberry vinegar and a little oil saved from the pickled
hogweed shoots and leave them to mature in the fridge. I roast them
whole inside a lidded clay pot in the oven until they are tender. Then
I use a fork to pull the meat off the bones. Chopping finely, I mix
it with chestnut flour, some chopped three-cornered leek, water to
moisten the mix and a little wild garlic salt, then roll it into balls.
Each ball is then dipped into a batter of acorn flour and water (with
a scoop of carragheen gel to make it stickier) and fried in a little
squirrel fat. A dipping sauce, made by reducing some venison stock
and sweetening it with the last of the wild plum sauce, is the perfect
accompaniment. As is the winter salad of sea beet, three-cornered
leek, winter purslane dressed with an elderberry vinegar and birch
sap syrup vinaigrette.

I have to admit, as barbaric as it might sound, that it is delicious
and I haven't tasted a finer dish yet in a Michelin-starred restaurant.
It certainly gets the Géza seal of approval. But I am longing for plants
to eat and they are all still under the snow.

After dinner, I start an umeboshi-style ferment using wild damson
plums. I've defrosted a big bag of them to free up badly needed

freezer space. I spoon them into a large ceramic fermenting crock with rock salt and weigh them down with stones. They will take a few weeks to mature. I check on the sloes: they are happily fermenting in a little brine with a piece of kombucha scoby and are well on the way to becoming 'kalamata olive' sloes.

A lot of effort! I shall be *so* glad when spring comes and the plants return.

# CHAPTER EIGHT

# COMMUNITY

*'For small creatures such as we, the vastness
is bearable only through love.'*

Carl Sagan, *Contact*

## GLACIAL

*Daisylea, 10 January*

The ground is frozen and as hard as rock.

## MORE SNOW

*Daisylea, 13 January*

More snow! There is nowhere to forage here. We're in the third national COVID-19 lockdown and I'm panicking that this latest restriction is really going to affect my ability to find food. We're forbidden from leaving home except for essential purposes. I feel a desperate need to get to the out-of-bounds coast to stock up on vegetables. If I get stopped, even if my excuse of 'foraging' is believed, I don't think I'll get away with being two counties from home. I am so thoroughly fed up just eating meat with pickles and a tiny half-handful daily ration of nuts and dried berries. My bowels are fed up too but I won't go into lurid detail. It will be interesting to see what the impact of this is when I do my next gut microbiome test.

## FOOD PARCELS

*Daisylea, 20 January*

As news of my crazy wild year project and the snow siege has slowly leaked out, parcels have suddenly started to arrive out of the blue with gifts of wild food. I am amazed and overwhelmed with gratitude for my foraging tribe. Whilst I can survive on what I have stored up, these treats have made my spirit soar.

Wild garlic pesto, mackerel and seaweed pâté, and a bottle of wild vermouth. Freshly picked three-cornered leeks, alexanders, sea beet and delicious tender navelwort. Fat hen seed, acorn meal, violet leaves, sea purslane, wild cabbage, black radish and a Babington's leek. Burdock roots, myrtle berries and smoked blewit mushrooms. Cleavers seeds, Scots lovage seed, dried flowering currant flowers, a bottle of reduced rosehip juice and to cap it all, a 250-millilitre bottle of birch sap syrup. Smoked pigeon and pheasant breasts, deer fat, a bunch of fresh wild garlic, smoked ceps, smoked wild garlic salt, pickled mushrooms, pickled pears with hogweed, smoked powdered hen-of-the-woods and chanterelle and some fermented smoked wild garlic. What bounty! I didn't ask any of my friends for help. I know how precious these gifts are and am humbled. I have never experienced this abundance of kindness before.

Food is both the least and the greatest of gifts. In every culture that I have lived in, food is central to important traditions of hospitality. I grew up to believe that feeding a stranger, finding a bed for a traveller passing through, sharing water and the resources that you have with others was the way the world worked best. And it was reciprocal.

In nature, there are no cultural boundaries, national borders or gated communities. Gaïa gives to all who have need. I am touched by the generosity of my friends and their care for my struggling stomach in this unusually snowy winter.

## ELF CUPS

*Muiravonside, 29 January*

A light coating of snow. Again! There has now been snow on the ground for the last thirty-two out of thirty-four days. There hasn't been a winter like this for at least ten years.

I go out anyway to find that 'off the hill' there has been some rain and the rest of the country is pleasantly mild and snow-free; only we are still besieged. Down at Muiravonside, I head straight for the slope with well-rotted birch branches where I know there will be scarlet elf cup mushrooms. They're not there. I'm about a week too early as I spot only one, barely 4 millimetres wide, peeking out like a tiny red eye from the vibrant green ferny moss.

Coming home empty-handed, I make venison mince and dried berry bolognese, served up with rehydrated, boiled sea spaghetti plus a tiny green salad punching above its weight with sour and tangy flavours that delight my taste buds. In the afternoon I try my hand at crackers made from nettle seed, fat hen seed, chestnut flour and mushroom powder worked to a firm paste with hot water, then rolled out into rounds. Straight out of the oven, they make a delicious, crisp biscuit. Later on in the evening, with some elderflower wine and hazelnut hummus, it's almost like the old cheese platter days. Minus the cheese!

Sixty-five days into this wild food diet, I'm 12 kilos lighter than when I started and my jeans are no longer straining at the seams. Whilst I didn't decide to live on wild food to lose weight, I'm delighted nevertheless.

Soon it will be Earrach, the Celtic spring. It's just started snowing again.

# PART TWO

# EARRACH

# CHAPTER NINE

# CELEBRATING IMBOLC

> 'The goal of life is to make your heartbeat match the beat
> of the universe, to match your nature with Nature.'

> Joseph Campbell, *A Joseph Campbell*
> *Companion: Reflections on the Art of Living*

## THE SEASON TURNS

*Daisylea, 30 January*

Snow is still on the ground and the birds have yet to return, but when I go outside I can see that life is moving. There are hints of green in sheltered corners and, when you look closely, some plants *are* growing – coiled up like springs under pressure, waiting for the day that they can explode into the sunshine. I find clumps of tender, delicious pink purslane, cosy in nests of fallen leaves under the skeletal grey beech trees. Here the snow cannot reach them and their light blanket of slowly composting leaf humus shelters them from the frost. My winter supplies are getting low, so I'm delighted to notice the return of the light. It marks the start of Earrach, the Celtic spring, with early signs of new life.

Traditionally, here in Britain there are four seasons – spring, summer, autumn and winter – but I've noticed that it's not as simple as that. The seasons overlap each other and, where I live in Scotland, it feels as if we have five. Spring is longer than the others and, from a food availability perspective, divides into an early 'spring of scarcity' of seafood and early greens, and a later 'spring of green' when the trees come into leaf and the birds are laying. The Celtic word for spring was Earrach and started on Imbolc as January turns into February. Spring as we know it now was associated with the period after Easter in late April and May.

Earrach is 'the hungry gap', the Lenten period when winter supplies are running low but domesticated fruits and vegetables have yet to sprout. However, many wild plants do grow throughout this period. They enjoy the lack of competition from the grasses, buttercups and nettles and quickly flourish to have their day in the sun. I am relying on them until I can get to the coast!

# IMBOLC

*Daisylea, 31 January*

I wake from a restless sleep. I can feel the call of the sea. The waves whisper urgently to me in my dreams at night and I have a craving for succulent seaweeds. Whilst the land plants still slumber, the seaweeds have awakened, sending out new and tender tendrils into the salty source of all life on earth. On the coast I can forage for the sea vegetables and shellfish that thrive in the cool waters. They promise to supplement my diet in this period of scarcity on the land but not yet, as we're still in lockdown.

However, it's a good food day today! I need it badly in this hungry time. Breakfast is baked feral apple and hazelnuts, with a little toasted hogweed seed powder to conjure a cinnamon-esque twist. I remembered to soak some hazelnuts overnight and now pulverise them in water to make a nut milk. Once it's been strained and cultured with kefir for a few days, I am going to make some 'cheese'! I yearn for cheese. Giving up all dairy products has been so hard. I'm in two minds about making it as I cannot afford to waste the few nuts I have left on luxuries. I resolve this dilemma by straining off the hazelnut meal from the nut milk, then dehydrating it to reuse as a 'flour'. Nothing wasted!

All day long my slow cooker quietly stews me a haunch of venison with wild garlic bulbs, rehydrated black chokeberries (from garden shrubs) and wild prunes, blackening russula mushrooms (from frozen) and molokhia greens (leaves from coastal tree mallow, dried and rehydrated). I have seasoned it with birch bolete powder, red elderberry paste, black elderberry jelly, hawthorn 'hawsin' sauce, smoked oyster mushroom and smoked sea salt. With a full and happy belly, I am lighting candles to celebrate Imbolc – a reminder that winter is now past the halfway point and that life will return.

As the twilight deepens, pricks of light – which intensify inversely to the blackening sky – begin to illuminate this polar landscape. I've placed thirty small glass bowls in the snow with large tealights inside them. Imbolc is a kind of Celtic Diwali. This year, as the thermometer plummets, I'm watching from inside the house. Although we don't have central heating or a log stove in our wooden house, the recycled glass fibre insulation is so thick inside the walls that it's always cosy. We generate and trap heat from cooking and washing with just one energy-efficient portable heater on low at each end of the house. Even the insulated concrete floor absorbs the low winter sun that creeps in, radiating it back during the night into our passive house.'

With the lights off, sitting in darkness in front of the large glass doors, I meditate on the light. The night is bright, lit now by the full Wolf Moon three days past its zenith, and the flames dispel the shadows. It is stunningly beautiful and tranquil.

The flickering warmth of the candles warms my soul and, in Celtic prayer, I give thanks for all that is to be born this spring. The lambs and kids, fawns and kits, my friend Christina's baby due in March. I've nicknamed the baby 'Fish' as that's what the first grainy ultrasound picture revealed – curled up inside her like a coiled fern. Fish has grown steadily, rounding out Christina's surfer-lean body with maternal curves, kicking her ribs and waking her at night.

The evening is calm and I send love up in the flames, with prayer for all new beginnings. Even alone, it is important to me to mark the days that punctuate the seasons and our lives.

Living wildly, directly off this land that I'm coming to love even more passionately every day, awakes a deep yearning to connect more closely with my tribal roots, my ancestral heritage. But where is Britain's indigenous past? Our continuous lineage has been broken – shattered into pieces – but we were aboriginal peoples once. We were tribal, we too spoke to the plants and the spirits. We *were* connected to nature, rooted in our landscape, with steaming rituals, shamanic journeying, healing with plants and mushrooms.

I think we became disconnected from our ancestry when the Romans invaded this island. They came, saw and conquered when our ways were not written down, our festivals not filmed, our rites not recorded. Left only with fragments of poems, we lost our old ways, our tribal knowledge, our traditions bit by bit. Our alienation with nature began, or was accelerated, by this Roman invasion.[2] The invading army slaughtered the last druids – our Celtic priests, healers, magicians and shaman – at their sacred home on Mona (now Anglesey). Under Suetonius Paulinus, the Roman legions faced the defiant druids and wild women across the Menai Straits with trepidation until commanded to cross. Then, according to Tacitus, 'They bore down upon them, smote all who opposed them to the earth and wrapped them in the flames they had themselves kindled.' Welsh historian Phil Carradice presciently states that 'with the demise of the druids the people of Britain had lost their spiritual driving force'.[3]

I would have been a wild woman then, as I am now. I would have fought with every breath and spell in my body.

# THE CELTIC SWEAT HOUSE

*2 February*

I can't shake this fascination with our past; with how this land was used by the people who lived off its bounty as I am living now. I'm in deep, reading archaeological papers about the growing evidence of sweat lodges in Britain, while absent-mindedly chewing my breakfast of cold, leftover roast venison from the back of the fridge and a wild Eggs Florentine on steamed sea beet leaves flavoured with wild garlic pesto. On top sits a poached duck's egg sprinkled with green wild garlic salt. Tracing back the details of our heritage is like trying to capture the fleeting, vanishing footprints of our Bronze Age ancestors in the mud flats.[4] Flashes of clarity in a tantalising moment, then gone without a trace.

Through the technical detail of the papers that I'm reading, a ghost becomes clearer – more tangible. Remnants of burnt mounds in Britain date from the Bronze Age; there are over 100 in England alone. Many are clearly not cooking sites, like the 4,000-year-old sauna house in Orkney.[5] Located outside settlements, the burnt mounds are nearly always next to water, with several sometimes occurring along the same stream. Stones marked with concentric ring patterns surround the mounds on Yorkshire's Barningham Moor. Studying the layout of the site up here on the high moor of How Talon Ridge, Alex Loktionov, a Fellow of the McDonald Institute for Archaeological Research, has an interesting theory about the location of some of the burnt mound saunas.[6]

Water from the spring, rising below the hilltop altar and the funerary cairn, carried messages from our ancestors downhill to the sauna, while the prevailing south-westerly wind captured prayers and messages from the sauna's steam and carried them back up to our ancestors. He believes that while a 'ritual hydraulic cycle ... hypothesis can in no way determine exact functions of burnt mounds, it does at least unlock a new spiritual dimension which goes some way towards explaining why the phenomenon is connected with the Bronze Age.'

I am fascinated by this window into our ancient past. Around troughs dug to contain water heated by hot stones, a small group of friends could sit on benches beneath lightweight covers made from bent sticks and animal skins, and commune together in the steam. The very sophisticated, beautifully preserved sauna found in Orkney, at Westray, is a large building with a complex network of cells off a central structure. Here, a sizeable tank of water produced boiling water and steam. The archaeological team thinks that its scale, elaborate architecture and sophistication confirm that our ancestors used it for more than just cooking. Perhaps for rituals, negotiations, comfort for the sick or dying, or even just relaxation and winter warmth.

Ancient stone sweat houses still stand in Ireland[7] – in magical clearings alongside sparkling brooks half-hidden by rambling foliage. Often forgotten, the search is part of the thrill. One, St Hugh's in Leitrim, is so tiny that you crawl in the door, as if entering an igloo. Inside is a small chamber where up to six people might have sat together. In ancient times, rural folk lit a fire inside it to heat the stone walls. Once hot, they swept the fire out, put down grass matting to protect their feet and crawled in to sweat. Early written accounts record folk saying they did this to ease arthritis or rheumatic pain. However, country people do not divulge their secrets so easily to city researchers, and there is always the hint that more happened in these spaces, especially when so many were in areas known for the prolific growth of psilocybin mushrooms. The Gaelic word *púca* (pooka) means both mushroom or pixie and is still sometimes used to describe these fungi with their pixie hats.[8]

With all of this spinning inside my head, I go for a walk up on the heath, sustained by some duck soup that has been simmering in the slow cooker with wild garlic shoots and some tuberous comfrey, its leaf tips already peeking out of the soil. Today started with snow but the subsequent rain is melting it fast. The land is living up to its habitat name of 'wet heath' – that so accurately describes this stretch of acidic, nutrient-poor, waterlogged heathland. It is windswept and beautiful, in a wild way, savage as the wind gets up. There are small tunnel entrances into the spiky gorse thicket where the deer shelter and rabbits burrow around the gnarled roots, interspersed with mouse holes. There is nothing to forage up here at this time of year. I slip down the hill again, into the back of the dump, and gather more juicy pink purslane leaves for a winter salad.

On an old log, I find the familiar liquorice-black rhizomorphs of edible honey fungus spread out along its length. It has ripped the cambium away from the heartwood, precipitating the tree's demise. The threads of the rhizomorphs in my hand trace back through the centuries of our violent past. Our current divorce from nature triggered by the displacement of invasion.

I ache deeply for losing the human to Gaïa connection that our ancestors once had.

# CHAPTER TEN

# THE HUNGRY GAP

*'It has been said that next to hunger and thirst,*
*our most basic human need is for storytelling.'*

Khalil Gibran

## INDOORS

*Daisylea, 5 February*

It is so dark in the mornings still. Eventually I emerge from hibernation. Poking around in the back of the freezer I find a lost herring, probably caught by my friend Norrie, that somewhat resembles a home-made kipper. I have it for breakfast. The smokiness goes well with the sharp sea buckthorn-citrussy wild gremolata I'm still eating, that in turn disguises the slight soapiness of a fat hen seed 'couscous'-type salad.

It rains most of the day with a biting east wind that keeps me indoors. When I was growing up in Kenya, we only ever seemed to have two seasons. The rainy season and the dry season. At the end of the dry one, we would all breathlessly await the start of the rains. Yet day after day, the sky remained cloudless and blue, while the merciless sun carved cracks into the earth. Then one day something strange would happen. Thunder would start to rumble, far away on the horizon, and then lightning flashes. Before the first drop of rain hit the earth, hundreds of tiny seedlings would suddenly sprout out of nowhere. How the plants knew that the rain was coming mystified me as a child. Researchers at Imperial College London have recently deduced that plants can detect the electricity that accompanies a storm and, anticipating the rain that follows lightning, their metabolism moves into gear. They are truly amazing.

Lunch is minced duck or possibly goose. I'm not sure which as I forgot to label it before putting it in the freezer! Served with sauteed alexanders stems and wild garlic. The bitterness of the vegetables and the gamey chewiness of the meat – it must be goose – means that I only eat a little. I must admit to feeling a bit flat. Winter seems interminably long this year and it's sometimes hard to stay cheerful. February isn't called the 'suicide month' for nothing. I daydream of a beach in Mexico and phone Christina for a chat. Fish is kicking hard, she tells me. We laugh at the nickname. She wants the baby's gender to be a surprise.

Supper is better: Matt has made a tasty mushroom soup with venison bone stock, birch bolete powder, winter chanterelles, blackening russula mushrooms, wild garlic salt and a dash of elderberry vinegar. As it's Friday, we crack open a bottle of home-made dandelion wine to share. Vintage 2016. Unlike our mead and cider, it probably contains some sugar as it was made five years ago, but it's been that sort of week.

## STORMY WEATHER

*Daisylea, 6 February*

It is snowing again, and it's bloody cold up here on the hill. According to the news, we have a rendezvous with Storm Darcy – which sounds like a ballsy stripper but is actually a real tempest. The blizzard is coming in fast and over the next few days we are forecast 30 centimetres of snow and a temperature of minus 5 degrees C.

Breakfast is late today. I get up to find Matt cooking a wild herb pesto omelette with leftover duck mince that also doubles up as lunch. There is absolutely no going out today, so I spend most of the day reading.

Another surprise parcel has arrived, just when I need cheering up most as foraging is still impossible. I am amazed that the postman got through the storm. There are burdock roots, dusky purple myrtle berries, smoked blewits and some violets. Supper is more experimental than it has been recently. A pheasant breast has been marinating overnight, ready for the pan. I sauté it with chicken-of-the-woods mushrooms and wild garlic shoots, and serve it with a sort of fat hen seed polenta still with a hint of soapy bitterness – despite several rinses and the heavy disguise of wild garlic pesto.

I julienne the burdock roots, along with some alexanders roots, into matchsticks and soak them in some mushroom 'soy' sauce, damson umezu, birch sap syrup and gorse vodka. Then they are fried until tender. (Well, as tender as burdock roots ever get.) The ritual of preparing food is comforting. Even scrubbing and peeling roots is meditative and, with winter still raging around me, creating a chef-class meal gives me so much pleasure. I rarely follow recipes but use them to inspire me. So tonight, despite the storm pounding out a tattoo on our tin roof, I lay the table with tiny porcelain dishes of wild umezu dressing to dip the Japanese-style gobo burdock in. Serenity reigns!

With a full belly and a woollen blanket wrapped around me, I'm tucked into an armchair reading up on the Ice Age when most of the British Isles was either cold tundra or covered in ice sheets. In Scotland there is no trace of us prior to the Ice Age. Scottish human archaeological history dates from 12,000 BCE.[1] What these people ate was mainly deduced from animal bones found in archaeological sites. Much less is known about fruits and vegetables eaten in Palaeolithic diets because plant remains are perishable. Those that survive tend to be seeds and grains, burnt on the bottoms of cooking pots or stuck in tooth calculus. Plants in even earlier hominin diets are seldom found except in scanty amounts at a handful of sites. This has led to people assuming there was only animal protein and fat in the prehistoric diet.

To me this seems a very reductionist approach. It pretty much ignores what was available to eat, which doesn't make any sense to me as a forager. I bet I could find between 200 and 300 species to eat across the year. Why would ancient humans be any different?

This summer I'll be studying ancient meadows on a field trip in Poland. My friend there, wild food fanatic Professor Łukasz Łuczaj, records the ethnobotanic use of wild plants in different communities around the world. Łukasz has found that although some families may eat as few as 19 species,[2] as many as 185 might be eaten across a community.[3] However, he tells me, the average edible wild species *available* per community is usually around the 120 mark. This matches Stone Age sites in Finland, where 97 to 103 species of edible plants were discovered.[4] The existence of plant remains in peat bogs where vegetation is better preserved proves my point. A 780,000-year-old site, Gesher Benot Ya'aqov in Israel, records fifty-five species, including nuts, fruits, seeds, vegetables and tubers, eaten all year round.[5] Comparisons of differences between charred and waterlogged samples at European Neolithic sites also revealed that a wider range of wild food plants is found in waterlogged sites due to the better preservation of plant material.[6] This is common sense as people would generally have eaten what was around them. I think that knowledge of local plant food history and studies of the last few forager tribes alongside the archaeological evidence is the only really sound approach.

Off to bed sleepy, I dream of cheese ripening in a jumbled mix of Stone Age caves and the cheese caves of Cheddar. What wouldn't I give for a slice of cheese!

## FAT

*Daisylea, 8 February*

Monday is bin day. This is usually a chilly 500-metre trundle, taking the wheelie bin down to the main road, but I'm let off the hook today – we are not generating any waste! My only naughty treats are books. They're posted in cardboard envelopes that I recycle, with a neighbour's horse manure, into a nutritious layered 'lasagne' bed in which mushrooms grow.

Early February is freezing cold, a total washout from a foraging perspective. We're snowbound again and it's just as well that the UPS van driver got through yesterday to collect the next set of microbiome tests.

It will be interesting when the results start to come back so I can compare sets and see if there are any changes. I feel as if my gut has completely transformed. Meat, albeit healthy, lean, wild meat, is in at least one and sometimes two of the day's meals. There are greens of course, but just not in enough quantity to provide significant fibre. The most abundant wild vegetables at the moment are alexanders and wild leeks. Each has a pungency – one fragrant, the other garlicky – that doesn't lend itself to eating an extensive amount in a single sitting. My portion sizes are also smaller than they have ever been. I'm just not hungry.

I wonder if my very poor appetite is an instinctive attempt to balance the amount of meat to the amount of vegetables. What is happening with my hunger hormone, ghrelin, and why isn't it kicking in? Have I gone into some sort of hibernation mode? With a mug of hot 'summer lawn' tea, I'm back with my nose in a physiology book trying to work this out.

Ghrelin is a hormone released by our guts when we haven't eaten for a while. Both exercise and fasting increase ghrelin blood levels. Basically, it makes us feel hungry. A lot of hormones in our bodies work in pairs, as if on a see-saw. Leptin, another hormone, inhibits ghrelin. Working in tandem, leptin suppresses appetite and then ghrelin increases it. A high-protein diet suppresses ghrelin, making us feel less hungry than a diet high in fat which doesn't, encouraging us to eat more when there's fat on the plate. Leptin blood levels are increased if we have a higher percentage of body fat and need to eat less until, ironically, we become obese. Obesity makes us leptin-resistant – losing our appetite's brakes, tempting us to eat more than we need to feel full.[7]

Trying to get my head around all this, I realise that, from an evolutionary perspective, it makes sense that the ghrelin–leptin dance isn't always predictable. Ghrelin is satiated and kept happier for longer on a high-protein diet. As hunter-gatherers, we could easily obtain protein. We used to dry meat into long strips of chewy biltong, or dry it, then grind it with nuts and berries to make pemmican. So when we did kill a mammoth or a bison we didn't need to eat it all at once!

However, fat is much harder to store in a world without fridges or tupperware. Our only reliable form of storage was as fat on our own bodies. Ghrelin is exceptionally good at making this happen, and it also helps us to hang on to our body's reserves in case the next mammoth gets away. This is why the ghrelin–leptin balance goes awry when we're presented with fat and the appetite's brakes come off. It is nature's way of telling us to gorge, as the fat will go off and won't be around tomorrow. It certainly explains why fats are so hard to resist in the modern diet.

It's interesting to see the changes in my body, beyond the obvious 12-kilo weight loss. Perhaps with so few fats or carbohydrates in my meals, my hunger hormones are working together better. My ghrelin seems to be satisfied by all this protein, keeping my appetite small until the leptin levels in my body fat decrease – assuming I continue to burn off body fat. Was the reason that I couldn't 'hear' the hormones before because I was leptin-resistant?

Yesterday's burdock gobo was very exotic but the portion size was about a heaped tablespoon. Today, I ate a veggie breakfast: sea beet leaves sauteed with sliced ceps (from frozen) with wild garlic leaves and sea salt. I've skipped lunch and am now having venison mince with leftovers for supper with a glass of elderflower mead.

There's certainly little fat and not a lot of carbohydrates in my diet but surely hunter-gatherers weren't constipated half the time? I find a journal paper on ancestral diets and learn that the transit time of food through the human gut of a modern hunter-gather is protracted, averaging sixty-two hours with low-fibre diets and forty hours with high-fibre diets.

Today Matt and I finished leaching a large batch of acorns; it's taken about three weeks, changing the water every few days to leach out the bitter, brown tannin, until it ran clear. Some I had picked from the oaks at Dalkeith with Andy and Christina's help last autumn, along with some acorns Miles gave me. They will end up dried and ground into 'flour' while the fine acorn paste that settles on the bottom of the tubs makes a useful starch. Géza is very fond of the simple acorn crackers I make, although he's only tasting, to avoid depleting our supplies.

In the outside world, it has been lightly snowing all day with some hail. Spring feels very far away.

## FOREBODING

*Daisylea, 9 February*

I looked in the hazelnut basket this morning and realised my worst fears: I'm running out. I feel a tremor of fear at the dwindling supplies which were supposed to last until at least the end of April. After my parents divorced, I spent my teens in Malawi, with my father (who took a job in the government there), my brothers and sister. I learnt to cook fast for my ever-hungry siblings and experimentally, as the Mozambique war impacted the railways and there were often long food shortages. Empty larder shelves always fill me with the deepest dread and foreboding so seeing the bottom of the nut basket makes me extremely gloomy.

There has been very heavy snow overnight. It is piled up in dramatic drifts, looking spectacular. Going out on the deck is dangerous as a wind-slammed door creates tumultuous avalanches that thunder down off the roof. There is not a plant in sight . . .

Breakfast is sea beet and ceps (again) with venison fillet and pickles. I carefully save every drop of oil from the pickles to use later for cooking.

I skip lunch. I'm not that hungry.

Supper is a stew of hare legs – I try not to think about them – with alexanders stem, hedgehog mushrooms, blackening russulas, fermented wild garlic, a wicked winter salsa (variation on gremolata) and sea buckthorn juice. I make a salad of violet leaves, hairy bittercress, wild garlic and alexanders leaf with an elderflower vinaigrette, and eat mainly the salad.

## WAVERING

*Daisylea, 11 February*

I am gagging on food. My body just doesn't want to eat anything. I have no pleasure in it. Today I have a light-headed dizziness all day. Low blood sugar. Lack of calories. It's crazy as there is food in the house. What has got into me? I'm not even craving anything illicit and even if I was there is nothing in the house.

## HUNGRY AGAIN

*Daisylea, 12 February*

Breakfast is a gooseburger made of chewy mince, chestnut flour and ground chicken-of-the-woods to thicken it and some rehydrated cranberries for flavour. A little sauce of cooked feral apple and cranberries in an amazingly concentrated rosehip reduction helps. I can only manage one but Matt easily eats my second.

Lunch is a thin mushroom soup.

Supper is a few acorn and chestnut biscuits made with wild honey, cranberries again and water. I smear on a smidgeon of precious walnut butter that I made in the blender, and a teaspoon of 2019 gooseberry jam. It's not exactly substantial but the sugar feels great!

By 8.00 p.m. I am starving hungry. I look in the fridge but everything needs preparation. There is nothing on the shelves that I can instantly eat and snacking on the last of the nuts would be a sacrilegious waste. A glass of elderflower mead helps but I know that's empty calories. I feel very low. I haven't been outside much this week as work has been busy and there are few plants growing to lure me from my desk. I should make more effort as foraging always makes me feel better.

## VALENTINE'S DAY

*Daisylea, 14 February*

It is 7.05 on a Sunday morning. The sun is still below the pale silver horizon and the Earth is silent, waiting for him to beckon life out of this dark, cold, lifeless place. I've been awake since 4.48 and up since 5.50. I've tidied the kitchen, emptied the dishwasher, made some herbal tea and performed a few other displacement activities. There are tears streaming down my face. The rain woke me up, drumming on the tin roof. It means the snow will melt. I feel that I am melting with it. I look at my email inbox. Matt has forwarded me a diagram showing the depth of the roots of meadow grassland plants. Who knew that the roots of red clover and greater burnet went down so deep?

I try to remind myself that it is mid-February and I always feel blue at this time of year. It doesn't help that it's Valentine's Day. I start to think about all my stupid mistakes and loves lost in the past. In Matt's diagram, the root structures are thick and well formed, the healthy plant above ground is reflected in perfect symmetry. In the real world it is not like that. Damaged roots make damaged plants; twisted, stunted, diseased, weak, they never reach their destined potential.

Occasionally one – usually a tree – overcomes all odds. Often growing on a rock, its roots probe tiny cracks in the surface and snake out like elephants' trunks in all directions as they sinuously search for water. There is a hawthorn I know like this, deep in the

Avon Gorge, and a beech tree at Rumbling Bridge. These survivors are few and far between, so I know them by name. Most fail and fall at the first frost or summer drought.

Humans are like this. Those of us wounded as seedlings with poor roots make damaged adults. With time we learn, but not before leaving a trail of destruction in our wake. We become stable, yet, when caught off guard, can still be strangely vulnerable. The oak that stood for centuries suddenly one morning falls to the ground.

I sometimes think of myself as a giant waterlily, the *Victoria amazonica*. Its leaves are huge – from 1 to 2 metres across when fully grown – with upturned edges and the strength to stay afloat under objects of up to 45 kilos in weight. In pictures you often see a child sitting in the middle of a huge leaf, as proof of their stability and endurance. This giant leaf is anchored by a thick stem that flows into a delta of thick roots reaching down, down, down into the sludge, mud and mire in the bottom of the lake.

*Victoria amazonica* sprouts only one incredibly beautiful flower at a time and it lasts a mere two days. The first sultry, tropical night that it opens she is female. Clothed in white she emits the sweet scent of pineapple as, inside her, a heady thermochemical heat starts to build up. Nearby, innocent beetles who have been going about their business pollinating other plants, come to her with gifts of pollen. But careless of them she closes, trapping them inside her petals. Overnight she becomes he. A male with anthers that produce pollen and, by the evening, when he opens his now purple-red flowers, the scent and the magic have gone. The beetles desert the flower. It closes and sinks.

I know that this plant could not survive in any other habitat, just as I cannot change my roots embedded in the mire of my past. I grew, putting out big leaves, and so many creatures came – resting there for a while. I have even, occasionally, produced some flowers! But, although it seems that over time the weather has become more predictable, the pond that I live in is subject, sometimes, to a violent wind that rips down the valley like a hurricane. It flips up and batters my trembling leaves, which hold on with all the strength of the thick stem I have grown to anchor my fragility. But roots are fibrous and flimsy. They carry the vibrations of the storm which tries to tug and wrench them from the mud, awakening the swamp monster that always lurks in the grimy deep. Up it roars as I quake, until the storm passes.

I often say I would not change my past because who would I be today if it were different? But I think I say this just to comfort myself. Perhaps I could have been a daylily instead. Or even a rose (preferably one without thorns). A tall, elegant mullein festooned with so many yellow flowers that all you have to do to receive one is gently touch her stem. Or maybe a cheeky primrose or nodding cowslip? The truth is that my roots cannot be transplanted into any other soil, no matter the price I have to pay. The murky pond is what sustains me and nourishes me whether I like it or not.

A blackbird calls and a robin answers. Day has dawned and although the sun is sulking behind a solid grey sky, it is light – brightly reflected by the snow still on the ground. The rain did not last.


## THAW

*Muiravonside, 16 February*

It's 7.07 in the morning and the sky is the strangest shade of bright slate-blue. The sort of sky you only usually see from an aeroplane, high above the clouds. It is slashed across from side to side, the edges curling back into wisps of dark grey cloud to reveal a caldera of molten red-streaked lava beneath. The wound inside is striped: intense pink, citrus-sharp orange, and ocean turquoise. And then, suddenly, it heals shut and, in an instant, only the slightest hint of warmth is traced in the quiet blue and grey sky. Soon even that hint is gone and the sky chills to a lighter pallor. The black outlines of the beeches and the lone Scots pine are silhouetted against this cyclorama, dramatic in their winter nudity. The trees are trembling, gently chided by the scolding wind that is bringing warm air from the south. There is not a drop of snow left – just the eager green of grasses awaiting the explosion of spring.

Up in the Muiravonside birch wood, the fallen boughs of years past are silently rotting in the wet thaw. The only sound is when they crack underfoot, protesting my weight. A furry green moss covers the oldest branches and here – nestled down amongst the soft fronds – are scarlet elf cups. Cheerful, bright fungi, they range from young vermilion to elderly carmine red, beaming happily for all who spy them, replete on decaying cellulose. Within the hour they are nestling on my plate in an equally bright-green riot of lightly fried, three-cornered leek – whose flavour is now too intense for hungry rabbits to bother it. My fresh fungi breakfast is delicious, and the vibrancy of these new colours – shimmering jewels on a chipped plate – feeds my eyes and my soul. Colour! It is a love song to my psyche and re-energised spirit.

Bob has come over with a deer. 'This winter's been hard for them,' he tells me. 'So much snow – there's no food for them. They're all starving, thin and losing condition.'

Certainly there's no fat on the one that he gives me. Bob has been so kind to me, like a wolf bringing a kill back for a cub, as if it were completely normal to find a neighbour on a strict wild food diet. I hang the deer in the shed. It needs to be skinned and I use my stone tools. I take time to pause and reflect during this slow, gentle process as my fingers work the same grooves in the worn stone blade as the hands of my ancestors.

# CHAPTER ELEVEN

# ON SEAWEED

*'Limitless and immortal, the waters are the
beginning and end of all things on earth.'*

Heinrich Zimmer, *Myths and Symbols
in Indian Art and Civilization*

## SEA HARVEST

*Tyninghame estuary, 28 February*

Seaweed grows in the primordial soup from which all life began.
When you analyse the phytochemical make-up of seaweeds you find
that they have an incredibly wide spectrum of vitamins, minerals,
antioxidants, polyphenols, protein, amino acids and trace elements.
Nature's ultimate multivitamin! The seaweed I dried last year has
been a vital part of my winter diet and I need to replenish my stores.
They are running low and there are still months to go before the
land plants arrive in any abundance. This last month my diet has
become so predictable – meat, pickles, defrosted fungi, bittercress,
purslane and the daily eked-out allowance of nuts. I am *aching* for
fresh greens. Browsing through the tide-tables I have spotted what I
need: a 0.3-metre low tide in daylight!

Wrapped up well against the biting Scottish wind, I am exhilarated by the elements and enthused by the new foods I'm about to add to my monotonous diet. I love heading out to my 'supermarket' on the edge of the world. Joining me at dawn, Andy and Christina are in good spirits too. Christina, now eight months pregnant with Fish, waddling carefully so she doesn't slip. This is definitely *not* the terrain for an early delivery! I'm also cautious on the wet rocks, as slipping could be fatal – one of the laws of foraging. There are many, such as avoid going out to the edge of the sub-tidal zone alone, letting someone know when you expect to be back, and taking a fully charged phone and a whistle.

When I'm working the tide, I like to be at the edge an hour before it turns to ensure I have time to gather all the species that I want. Like the land plants, seaweeds are fussy and each has a specific area where it likes to grow. The wracks are always the first to be found. Channel wrack inhabits the upper shore nearest the splash zone – where dead seaweed is tossed up on the beach – and doesn't mind spending a few days out of water. It is quickly joined by bladderwrack, then estuary and horned wrack. As they all interbreed it can be difficult to differentiate between the species. Their young fronds, steamed until tender, taste like French beans. On the other hand, pepper dulse – one of my favourites – prefers the damp side of cool east-facing rocks and is best harvested from the lower shore. The closer I am to the edge the more peppery it tastes. The long tender blades of young kelp remain firmly attached to the rocks a metre down from the sub-tidal zone and can only be reached on a very low tide.

With the larder at home looking bare, I am after all varieties of seaweed today. Instinctively keeping an eye on the others spread out along the foreshore, I work quickly, using topiary shears rather than scissors. They look like a miniature version of the hand shears used for shearing the wool off sheep – before we went electric. Unlike scissors, which are awkward to use with frozen fumbling fingers, a quick squeeze and the job is done. I only take a little from each weed, cutting off just a part of the fronds, leaving plenty to grow and reproduce. Conservation and sustainability for the forager is about a lifetime of survival, not just a single year. Cut them above the stem (stipe) and they can carry on growing.

I place them in an old wire shopping basket so the heavy seawater can drain away, picking what I think I will need for the next few months. Experience has taught me not to pick too much as it all has to be washed, sorted and set to dry as soon as I get home. If I leave it overnight, I'll wake up to some very soggy, slimy seaweed in a bucketful of purple iodine-rich seawater.

Fresh seaweed doesn't have a 'fishy' taste. Each has its own flavour and its own tradition, and I use them for all sorts of things – most helpfully, perhaps, as nature's tinfoil. I wrap my Sunday joint with long strips of oarweed kelp and cook it in a covered terracotta pot. The seaweed retains all of the moisture and flavour from the meat as well as enhancing it with the wonderful umami flavour of kelp – and it's infused with iodine and B vitamins essential for good health.

Thinking of food makes me hungry and we stop for a while, behind a big rock that shelters us partially from the now biting wind. Out of its noise, we can hear ourselves talk for the first time. Christina and Andy want to know what Matt and I have been eating this week with our dwindling supplies. They are full of encouragement and it's my friends' belief in me that has sometimes kept me going. Their picnic is a spicy, cold chickpea salad. I shell two hard-boiled eggs I've brought from their biodegradable wrappers and eat them with mouthfuls of fresh pepper dulse – it's not known as the truffle of the sea for nothing. What could taste better? This is food for gods.

My basket is overflowing, and I know my arms are going to ache lugging it all back but the thought of the feast ahead keeps me cheerful. At the bottom of the basket I have folded strips of young oarweed and sweet sugar kelp. It keeps them tidy and also reinforces the bottom of the basket. Sugar kelp crisps are my weakness. Above them I have a heap of young sea spaghetti. This is the most excellent vegetable boiled until *al dente* and served with my favourite, a sun-dried rosehip sauce. We say goodbye in the car park, each going home with our slippery bounty.

Supper is late as most of the afternoon has been taken up with sorting, rinsing and prepping the seaweed. I boil some fresh sea spaghetti for just three minutes, and pair it with a minced venison ragù for Matt and me. Cooked with elderberry paste and wild garlic bulbs, it looks just like a bolognese sauce. There's a little pepper dulse salad on the side.

The house is festooned with seaweed hanging up to dry on both the laundry racks. Géza is a bit grumpy as he doesn't like the smell. Hungary is a landlocked country after all, I tease him! He is snacking on takeaway fried chicken which I wouldn't touch. We've learnt to live with our differences. The dryer is going – on low – releasing the 'pepper gas' smell of pepper dulse. I have learnt from first-hand experience to respect it. Last year, after my big annual February pick, I was standing in our walk-in wet room, rinsing all the seaweed in cold water, freezing and tired. The last thing I had to do was to rinse a bucket of pepper dulse, checking for shells, grit and little shrimps. 'A little warm water won't hurt,' I thought. How wrong I was! As soon as the warmth hit the pepper dulse it released a cloud of pepper gas. I ran from the room, my eyes smarting and teary. It was like a CND rally in the 1980s.

## LAVERBREAD

*Daisylea, 1 March*

I have spent an hour at the sink already this morning, hands plunged into freezing cold water, dreaming of hot water. Being fossil-fuel free works for heating the house, but only the electric shower provides hot water. I'm rinsing and re-rinsing the laver seaweed to make laverbread – not actual bread, but a thick, dark, oil-slick paste. Traditionally it was spread on bread or toast, or mixed with oats and formed into balls or cakes that were then fried in bacon fat for breakfast. I use laverbread a lot. It has a very savoury, umami taste and is as essential to my cooking as concentrated tomato paste or garlic purée is to other cooks. Its intense flavour is unlike anything else.

Making good laverbread requires some understanding of older cooking methods. The only way, in my opinion, to make good laverbread is *very* slowly. I learnt this at first hand: one dinner and a few glasses of wine later when I went to bed completely forgetting the laver I'd left in a cast-iron pot atop a woodburning stove. To my surprise, in the morning it was perfectly cooked. Of course, at the turn of the century, most people had a wood-fired, cast-iron range cooker rather than the high-powered hobs and ovens of today. This experience totally changed the way I read old recipes. Now I think carefully about what stoves and fuel were available at the time each was written.

Humans are a species transformed by fire. If the 'cooking hypothesis' of influential primatologist Richard Wrangham is true,[1] then our ancestors were inviting their friends around for a barbecue some 1.8 million years ago. Being able to harness fire to cook our food was, he argues, the nutritional impetus behind our development from small-brained *Homo habilis* to small-toothed, larger-brained *Homo erectus*.

Our human brain has not changed over the last 300,000 years. I'm beginning to find it hard to believe that our hunter-gatherer ancestors would have been content with a boring diet. Especially as they probably had more time on their hands than twenty-first-century humans.

## GOOSE

*Daisylea, 12 March*

The warming sun calls me to get up and out. I slip my feet into boots as the dew glistens heavily on the long grass. There is a strange cackling, low down in the hedge. My neighbour's goose has wandered over and found a quiet spot in my field. She hisses madly from the rough nest she has made before deciding to rejoin her flock. Behind her she has left an enormous egg. This is definitely foraging! At 190 grams it is triple the weight of the 64-gram egg our brown hen has laid. The yolk is also three times bigger.

I breakfast on scrambled goose egg Matt-style. It is absolutely delicious – despite the lack of butter, milk or cream. Matt gently coddles it into being with chopped wild garlic and a pinch of smoked salt and I am grateful for a well-seasoned pan that doesn't stick. After months of brown food offerings this is like nectar!

## CAR PARK FORAGING

*Straiton, 14 March*

I'm dropping in to Ikea. Just joking! Its vast car park is surrounded by a long boundary hedge of flowering currant. Its deep pink flowers taste as if rosemary, lavender, thyme and rose have all got into bed together. Flowering currant is a wonderful herb, especially for infusions. In previous years, I would have put them into a gin and tonic but today I am going to dry them for cooking with.

The store is closed for lockdown and the car park is eerily quiet, like a post-apocalyptic sci-fi scene. I haven't missed shopping at all and one wonderful side effect of foraging is that I'm saving a fortune in food costs. In the absence of humans, nature is busy filling the gap. Through a crack in the tarmac, a tiny spindly birch tree sapling reaches for the sun and, along the edges of the walkways, stinging nettles emerge into unpolluted air.

Birch trees are always the first to make a new woodland, and nettle is an avid coloniser of barren lots. They're called pioneer species and their job is remediation. Nettle sends out strong, tough, lateral yellow roots, sideways through the soil, that will exploit any weakness in concrete. When humans leave, nature will reclaim the place for her own, slowly breaking up the ground and cleaning up after us.

The 'tough guys' are the first plants to arrive on broken land: nettles, thistles, docks and willowherbs, as well as the opportunists:

mustards and cresses. As if they somehow know that desecration of the land marks the poverty of people, all these plants also provide a rich food bank of nutritional values and medicinal powers. Nettle tops, thistle roots and stems, willowherb shoots, bittercress rosettes: these are foods for the hungry and there for the taking. Free for all.

# CHAPTER TWELVE

# SAP RISING

*'A society grows great when old men plant trees
in whose shade they know they shall never sit.'*

Anon.

## SAP RISING

*Craigengall, 20 March*

Today is the spring equinox. It marks the halfway point between the winter and summer solstices when the length of the daytime hours is equal to the darkness of night. It is a joyful day – the worst of winter is over, the joy of summer is ahead. As if in celebration, the birch sap is rising. Walking out this morning before breakfast, I broke a small twig belonging to the large, crooked birch by the reed-filled pond. I snapped it up and bent it in half. Within a few minutes, it started to drip. I laughed. That slow drip, drip, drip heralds the two weeks when the sap is running and the *tapping* window is open. I love it – such a promise of spring.

Birch sap is a pleasant, refreshing drink, without much more flavour than water, although there is a subtle, earthy hint that distinguishes it. It is full of nutrients: amino acids, sugars and salts. The sap is to birch trees as plasma is to us humans. We humans are all much closer to plants than we think. For example, if you compare the chlorophyll that colours a plant green and the blood that flows red in our veins, there is only one molecule of difference. In chlorophyll there is magnesium and in our blood there is iron. We breathe in oxygen and exhale carbon dioxide. Plants breathe in carbon dioxide and exhale oxygen. It's a mirror dance of interdependence.

Breakfast needs to be sustaining today for working outdoors in the cold. Matt is going to help me collect sap and we feast on hedgehog mushrooms cooked in pepper dulse oil, fresh wild garlic and salt with burdock 'oven crisps'. The crisps are made from slicing burdock root, then soaking it overnight in a marinade of sea buckthorn juice, mushroom ketchup and pickle oil. After roasting them on a tray in the oven, they are umami, filling and delicious.


It takes me a while to find the tree taps in the 'safe place' I stored them a year ago. Géza lends me his cordless drill, a bit and some rawlplugs. Twenty years ago, it was rare to tap birch trees before April but I now do it earlier than I used to – I think due to climate change. For the last five years, I have always tapped in March. Łukasz, who has studied sap collection in Europe, tells me that there are records of its use in Russia from AD 921 and a long tradition in northern European countries.[1] In the Arctic lands of eternal winter every calorie was valued. One of the earliest British recipes for birch sap wine was recorded in 1675. In Scotland collection of the sap was popular until the 1940s. It was thought to prevent baldness and Queen Victoria drank it during her visits to Balmoral Castle to remedy her thinning hair.

I choose a birch with a decent-sized girth. I apologise to this graceful tree and explain my intentions, then drill a small hole and push the tap snugly in. Below the spout, I place a 5-litre bucket. The sap will drip out slowly overnight giving around 2 litres per tree. I like to think that there is an understanding, but of course there is no such arrangement, no matter how much I try to anthropomorphise the birch next to me. Yet I know they have awareness even though it's on a different level. This century we've learnt that bacteria can 'talk' and count; this is called *quorum sensing*. And birds like the Clark's nutcracker can harvest well over 100,000 seeds each, plant them in separate locations (three to five seeds at a time) and, over the following couple of years, remember where they buried them all. I can't always find my car keys! Their memory involves incredible navigation by triangulation – the sort of maths that would defeat most humans. So if the abilities of bacteria and birds are being reassessed, why not plants and trees?

Scientists are looking into it. Suzanne Simard, Professor of Forest Ecology, has revolutionised the understanding of tree relationships and inter-species communication in the forest.[2] She taught us how 'mother trees' can recognise the offspring from their own seed, through the mycelial networks of fungi that connect the roots of trees to form 'colonies'.[3] Molecular biologist Anthony Trewavas believes that plants can save and reuse information from their 'experience' to guide their growth,[4] a concept taken up by plant-research scientist Monica Gagliano.[5] Gagliano demonstrated, through her fascinating mimosa experiments, that plants do indeed learn and retain learning through memory.[6] Birch trees emit methyl salicylate which smells of wintergreen when they are injured. This is sensed by other birch trees who then begin to manufacture higher levels of protective chemicals in their sap. Many plants use volatile oils to communicate with pollinators and insect predators. So if plants can 'talk', then what language are they speaking?

I believe that biochemistry is their 'language'. All living organisms use biochemical processes to navigate the complexity of life by controlling information flow via biochemical signalling. It explains how many living organisms communicate with themselves and with others. I like the word 'biosemiosis',[7] a suitable twenty-first-century synonym for this biosphere Esperanto. I'm sure all of us, in our relatively recent past, once had a far greater ability to understand the signs and codes of other life forms. The longer I spend outside amongst the trees, the more I feel that growing close to nature in spirit brings a convergence of thought that is more than just synchronicity.

I thank the birch for its sap. Trees work on a long timescale and I hope that in the 80 to 140 years that this birch will live, it will regard this moment as a tiny blip in the same way that I eventually discard the memory of a vicious cleg bite from a particularly nasty horse fly. I take care to sterilise the drill bit so not to infect the hole which I'll plug tomorrow when I collect a brimming pail of sap. Tomorrow I'll boil some of it down to concentrate the flavours and natural sugars into a sweet, smoky, mysterious birch sap syrup – a labour of love as it takes hours. This makes a delicious sweet treat seldom found on a forager's menu; we never make a lot for it takes 100 litres of sap to make just 1 litre of syrup.

As I walk home, I'm still thinking about the scientists who devote their lives to studying plant intelligence. I have begun to suspect that it's not always that we are learning more about the natural world around us, but rather that we've forgotten so much.

## JOURNAL PUBLICATION

*Daisylea, 21 March*

Today is a celebration. A wonderful spring equinox gift. My first peer-reviewed academic paper – on foraging – has been published in the journal *Sustainability*.[8] I've been working on this for over a year with Łukasz and Leanne, an Aberdeen-based forager. I didn't go to university until I was fifty so the whole process has been new to me. Better late (in life) than never! We're going to discuss a new one in July during my Polish field trip.

# TEMPURA

*Daisylea, 23 March*

I wake up to a now familiar edge of hunger. It's not overpowering but it's a new aspect of life. Yet despite feeling it, I also know that I won't eat a lot today. My appetite has changed and I wonder again how much it has to do with the ghrelin-and-leptin dance.

Skipping breakfast, I make more of an effort for lunch as I'm cooking for Matt as well as me. I use ground-up dried chicken-of-the-woods mushroom mixed with laverbread paste to make laverballs. I've also found some early common hogweed shoots and the temptation to cheat is impossible to resist. The deep-fat fryer that I only use in the spring for hogweed tempura still has sunflower oil in it from last year, and it doesn't smell too bad. So I fire it up and deep-fry the laverballs and, using chestnut flour for the tempura, make some hogweed tempura. I eat these with some cold roast venison and a pink purslane salad. Géza wanders through and tries a laverball. Despite his professed dislike of seaweed he finds them 'pretty good'.

I couldn't begin to describe what hogweed tempura tastes like. To convey the flavour of wild foods there have to be some common terms of reference. So many things will be described as: 'tastes a little like parsley' or 'can be used as a substitute for asparagus'. If someone has only tasted one or two dozen vegetables in their life, how can they begin to imagine the flavours of one or two *hundred* species? This is the way of fried hogweed. It doesn't taste like anything other than hogweed.

# VISITORS

*Briggis Hill, 25 March*

Our annual visitors, the house martins, arrive with the dawn sunlight today. These beautiful birds build their cup-shaped mud nest each year, up in the eaves above my bedroom window. Their swooping arcs of flight lift my spirits with them – spring is definitely around the corner!

Despite work piling up after my clinic yesterday, Matt easily persuades me to slip out for a walk down Briggis Hill to where the wild few-flowered leeks live. There is little to see but I double-check all my foraging spots anyway. I show him where I have found plants in the past, explaining my internal food map of the area. Nothing is up yet. It reminds me of window shopping: those trips where once I might have gone to the shops, knowing that I probably wouldn't buy anything but might succumb to an impulse purchase.

Back in the garden, all the plants still slumber. 'Green time' doesn't follow the clock or the calendar; it unfolds to a programme of light. I wonder how a plant would tell the history of Earth? If a plant was the subject, how would it describe the world in a story? The mycelium that connects their communities; the biochemical chatter of volatiles; the electrical signalling; the microbes in their rhizo-biomes; the ambulatory web of human helpers and human predators; the degradation of the earth.

In human history, today will be remembered for the container ship stuck in the Suez Canal. It is blocking the canal, causing a mighty 9.5-billion-dollar traffic jam. I'll bet that to the palm trees lining the canal, it's just another day. But I am appalled to discover it's cheaper to ship Scottish fish to China to be filleted,[9] and then ship it back again – a 10,000-mile round trip – than it is to do it locally.[10] It's a very mad world.

# CHAPTER THIRTEEN

# THE SWEETEST THING

*'We don't inherit the earth from our ancestors,*
*we borrow it from our children.'*

Native American proverb

## GREAT EXPECTATIONS

*Treverlen, 27 March*

Christina phones me. It's just after 6.00 in the morning. I know as soon as her number comes up what she's going to say.

'I think I'm in labour.'

I ask a few questions and say I'll be over soon. Christina and Andy have a home birth planned, and the midwives have agreed to this despite it being the couple's first baby. Coronavirus, rampant in the hospitals, has persuaded many new mums to stay away. They live close to the main hospital (if they need it), having recently moved to a village outside the city. It still has a strong and vibrant community with a sunny orchard and sheltered walled vegetable garden that feeds the residents, both body and spirit. As both sets of their parents live in the south of England, I have offered to be Fish's adopted grandma and have been accepted for the role! I know how much new mums need practical help just after a baby is born, having had my own three bairns with little assistance. So I have offered to cook, clean, wash laundry, walk the dog, and provide moral support (and lots of cups of tea) for a few days after Fish is born. I want to give the new parents a chance just to chill out with the baby and each other, as I would love to have done.

Before setting off, I have a quick breakfast of cleavers coffee and two strawberry rock cakes I made last night from a mix of dried wild strawberries, chopped walnuts, chestnut flour, acorn flour, some honey and egg. I pushed a bird cherry, preserved two years ago in not-so-wild brandy, into the middle of each to give them an appealing moistness.

I find Christina looking like a rotund anaconda that's just eaten a beach ball. Her contractions have started but they are still not painful or close together. I remember that the first stage of labour is divided into early labour and active labour. Early labour can take many hours, even days, so we go for a walk through the community orchard with their Romanian rescue dog, climbing up the hill and resting under an ancient beech to catch our breath. I've brought wild supplies with me but I'm delighted to find a heap of young hogweed shoots with their white, bristly 'grandpa stubble' hairs, tangy garlic mustard leaves, tender dandelion and chickweed. I also find some crabapples, snuggled up in dry fallen leaves, still in excellent condition despite the winter.

In the evening, the three of us stroll along the edge of the river, pausing for each contraction. The moon, shining silver over the water, is as round as Christina's belly. Orbiting close to the earth, tomorrow is a full, perigee moon, calling that baby to come out.

Back at the house, the contractions are getting stronger and Christina is starting active labour, so we know we have four to eight hours to go. By 10.00, the couple are in the inflatable birthing pool. The lights are low, and the familiar sitting room is cosy, warm and peaceful, but with a comically large paddling pool in front of the fireplace. I take a photo of them peering over the top, smiling and happy. All is going well and I'm busy making cups of tea, refilling water bottles, handing out snacks, adding more warm water, and applying acupressure to help ease the labour pains.

## WORM MOON

*Treverlen, 28 March*

It's now about 1.00 in the morning and I prompt Christina, 'Would you like me to call the midwife?' I sense that she's nearing the end of the first stage. She agrees and I call the hospital. It's engaged. I leave it a few minutes and try again. Still engaged. I try continuously for half an hour. The line is permanently busy. I telephone St John's hospital in Livingston and explain that I can't get through to the main hospital and we need a midwife. They cheerfully offer to patch me through, much to my relief. But the line rings . . . and rings . . . and rings. No one answers.

Christina is tired and beginning to worry. I can tell she will soon enter the second stage of labour and be ready to push. Moving from the first to the second stage can be intense and emotional, hormones cranking up a gear as a mother's body gets ready to push the baby out. 'It's the transition,' I tell her. 'It always makes you feel off your stride. It won't be long now!' I sound cheerful and confident but I'm getting uneasy about how long the labour is taking and frustrated that we don't have a back-up number for the midwife. Christina is brilliant and totally focused on her body. All her preparation and yoga breathing paying off, she is serene and stoic despite the obvious pain, with Andy supporting her.

Around 5.00 Christina asks Andy to call Nicola, the doula who helped her prepare for the birth. She's not panicking but she is feeling anxious. There is still no luck getting a midwife via the permanently engaged hospital phone line and I've tried several numbers repeatedly. At 5.45 Nicola arrives. She and I sit tight like crows on a wire, offering occasional confident words of reassurance (we hope), and handing Christina the gas and air that the midwives delivered last week.

Christina is still in the pool, on all fours now, pushing and in a lot of pain. Andy is encouraging her. There is nothing we can do except to tell her she's doing fine, but she keeps feeling as if, after each push, Fish is sliding back inside her. Nicola asks if she can have a look. She tells Christina the baby is nearly here but shoots me a *look* across the room. I move round just in time to see a foot emerging into the water with a leg, closely followed by the second leg.

*Oh, shit!* I mouth. Fish is in the breech position.

Nicola signals towards the kitchen and we go out for a confab.

'Call 999 and get an ambulance,' Nicola advises and returns to the sitting room.

'Is everything all right?' I hear Christina ask, alarmed by our sudden disappearance. I make the call. By some miracle, after explaining the situation, the man at the other end of the phone seems to know exactly what to do.

'Let the baby unfold into the pool,' he advises. 'Then get mum standing with her knees bent. Support the baby with your hands, but whatever you do, don't pull the baby. See if mum can push it out that way.'

I go back in and balance my phone, on loudspeaker, on the edge of the pool. Both of the baby's arms are now out as well and its body is looking very pale and lifeless, suspended under the water. It's motionless and I can't see its head or neck. I can feel my heart pounding.

'You need to stand up, Christina.' I repeat the instructions, surprised at how calm my voice sounds. 'Bend your legs, the baby's about to be born.' I catch sight of Andy's ghost-white face. I can see the stunned shock on it. Things are moving too fast to explain all the instructions to him, so I lean in, my phone sliding off the edge of the pool to who-knows-where, and cup my hands under the baby as Christina stands, supported by Nicola.

'Push, Christina love, push!' Her pelvis is tilted at a different angle now that she's up and, on the second push, the baby drops into my trembling hands.

It's not breathing.

There are few occasions in life when time stands completely still. This is one of them. The seconds it took for that baby to draw its first breath are still suspended in never-ending eternity, where time no longer exists, even now.

I turn the baby over my forearm and briskly rub its back. 'Breathe little man, breathe!' I command. My thoughts are in turmoil. I cannot possibly tell my beloved friend that her baby is dead.

Suddenly, I hear the tiniest snuffle.

And then a sneeze.

Now a cry.

My heart is leaping and bounding like a gazelle and the joy . . . the joy is indescribable. Christina is trying to get out of the pool but the baby and I are still attached by the umbilical cord so we're crouched awkwardly behind her bum.

'Are you sure it's a boy?' she asks. I turn the little man over.

'No, she's a girl!' I reply.

'I thought so,' says Christina. I can hear her smiling – and she delivers the placenta.

At that moment, the doorbell rings and in come the ambulance crew *en masse*. There are about five of them in loud boots and rustling coronavirus-proof aprons and masks. It's like an alien invasion from another planet. The peaceful mood of the room instantly changes.

A nurse rushes to cut the cord but I'm quick to tell her that Andy wants to do it. He does, with trembling hands, and finally we're released from Christina. She sits down on a stool, a deep-red bathrobe now pulled around her shoulders, and I pass over her baby. Completely oblivious to the now chaotic scene around her, like a Madonna in towelling, she looks at Maya and Maya looks back deep into her eyes. She puts the infant to her breast.

The moon, just past the perigee now, reaches its fullest.

*

Later I sign up to the Red Tent Doula Course. Partly to be much better prepared in the future – this is the second emergency baby I've delivered that was not one of my own – and also because it is such an honour to be present at the birth of a soul, and to contribute to the joy of a new family.

But I am ashamed to say that I fell from grace.

After the ambulance crew had departed, I cooked a big Spanish omelette for Andy and Christina. None of us had eaten since the night before and we were now starving. I was too tired to forage and cook for myself. After feeding them, I went to bed on an empty stomach for a restorative nap. I woke up at 4.00 in the afternoon, shortly before the doorbell rang. On the doorstep was the midwife, and their neighbour Fi. She handed me a plate with the most beautiful lemon drizzle cake, lit up by the afternoon sun with a near-saintly halo. Slicing it up, Christina handed me a piece to celebrate Maya's safe passage. And I ate it.

This was the first non-wild food that I had had since last November. I thought the sugar might explode in my mouth but it was the sharp flavour of the lemon that was so deliciously shocking. Yet the baby was by far the sweetest thing. After all that we'd been through in the last thirty-six hours, I hope that I can be forgiven.

# BACK HOME

*Daisylea, 31 March*

It's the last day of the month so time for a pre-breakfast weigh-in. I'm astonished to find that I've lost 18 kilos in four months. Matt has lost 8 kilos. He was quite skinny to start with, so didn't really need to lose any. More compelling news is that his blood sugar has come right down. When he was first diagnosed with diabetes three years ago, I recommended a low-carb diet and gave him some blood sugar balancing herbs to take. Over two years, diet and herbs had reduced his blood sugar levels by 50 per cent on the day we started this 'wild food challenge'. This morning, for the first time, it is back in the normal range. Our gut microbiome results are also back. I now have two sets to compare and we scratch our heads trying to make sense of them. Some bacteria have disappeared completely and others have appeared from nowhere. One of the movers and shakers is a 'next-generation beneficial microbe' called *Akkermansia muciniphila*, which improves metabolic function. It has gone from 1.11 per cent of my microbiome to 8.11 per cent – an increase of 630 per cent. I'm going to wait until I have the whole year's results before getting an expert opinion on it.

I have acorn pancakes for breakfast with some defrosted chanterelles I picked in the autumn but my thoughts are miles away with Christina and Maya. They are so precious. I think about the role Maya's generation will have to play in saving the planet.

I have immense belief in the young. They can and will make this world to a better place. Thankfully, the future is shaped by the unwillingness of young people to accept the status quo. Their passion and compassion, their energy and their drive will evolve the new philosophies and beliefs we need to survive. I am so honoured to play a role in Maya's life and perhaps one day with my own grandchildren. The knowledge and skills I learnt from my adopted grandmother Mima, and the wisdom of wild women before me, must be passed on.

# PART THREE

# SPRING

# CHAPTER FOURTEEN

# APRIL SHOWERS

'. . . the lowest boughs and the brushwood sheaf
Round the elm-tree bole are in tiny leaf
While the chaffinch sings on the orchard bough . . .'

Robert Browning, 'Home-Thoughts, from Abroad'

## APRIL FOOL'S DAY

*Tyninghame, 1 April*

I breakfast on pickled feral apples that are going a bit sour, with a few pieces of rehydrated plum. Then it's off down to the coast. Today I'm taking all the chefs and staff from the Gannet in Glasgow down to the seaside for a day of foraging instruction. I usually charge for teaching but it's 'on the house' as I cannot imagine how these restaurants have survived such a brutal year. Peter, the owner, says that although it was tough it was actually a blessing too, as he got to enjoy his newborn baby's first year. It reminds me of my day out with Christina and Andy, gathering seaweed before Maya was born. It seems so long ago now!

We find a baby seal on the beach but leave it well alone. I know only too well that they are usually reunited with their mothers when the tide comes in – if no one interferes. A volunteer warden appears and confirms this.

After foraging all morning for seaweed, we light a fire at the edge of the shore and cook up some lunch. Chefs always come with excellent ingredients. I eat the scallops, pierced with birch twigs and seared to perfection over the fire, with little ferny fronds of dark, spicy pepper dulse seaweed. Sadly, I have to pass on the wagyu beef – it definitely wasn't wild. I thread shiny brown oarweed and curly-edged sugar kelp on to long pointed sticks and hang them over the coals. They soon puff up into the most delicious seaweed crisps. Although there is still a nip in the air, the sky is blue and it's warm out of the blustery breeze. The food and the company are good and everyone is enjoying being outside in the fresh air with coronavirus hardly a thought on the wind.

Back home, I dig up some white, swollen marsh woundwort tubers. Whether eaten raw, steamed or pickled, they are crisp and crunchy, juicy and succulent, in flavour somewhat reminiscent of bean sprouts or water chestnuts. Down by the stream I notice tiny florets of watermint appearing after the winter. There are also young, sweet cicely fronds, while ground ivy and golden saxifrage sprawl over the bank. Behind the still-dormant wild raspberry canes, I find the first vivid green shoots of ground elder – so hated by gardeners and so loved in my kitchen. All of these make their way into my evening salad.

## SMALL TREASURES

*Daisylea, 2 April*

A walk just after dawn this morning gives me a chance to stock up on fresh greens. Wild garlic leaves, still without their edible white flowers; tiny opposite-leaved golden saxifrage with its miniature lime-green leaves and lemon-yellow centres; garlic mustard; shiny, new ground elder shoots that taste of parsley and celery leaf. It is so nice to have daily salads again!

# GOLD ON THE HILL

*Daisylea, 3 April*

Baby yellow primroses, in full bloom, cover the hillside that slopes away from the house. I pick them with a guilt-free conscience as it was me who seeded this hillside eight years ago. They are generous with their blooms and so plentiful that I can pick a small basketful every two days. Géza is making 25 litres of primrose wine and every time I return with a load, he adds them to the fermenting bucket. In a few years, we will have delicious, light, primrose 'pinot grigio' to drink. I keep some back for a large, green salad to accompany a simple meal of cold roast venison. Being out on the hill picking flowers, under the subtle warmth of the returning sun, lifts my spirits and makes my heart glad. I love this time of the year just after the equinox. It's so full of promise.

# MONKEY FINGERS

*Treverlen, 7 April*

I'm spending the day with Christina and Maya. These first few post-partum weeks after a baby is born are a sacred time for a new mum. It is a time of healing, learning, adjusting and falling in love. It is so beautiful to witness the unfolding of this new relationship. I know from experience that this is when having a quiet friend around to pick up the household chores and offer reassurance is most needed.

Taking Christina's dog for a walk, I investigate the unmown edges of the nearby orchard, looking for lunch. I find three-cornered leek, hedge garlic, hogweed shoots and hawthorn blossom. The micro-climate of this village has an east coast warmth and the plants are definitely more advanced than they are back home on the hill. I've noticed that in Britain, the spring generally advances from south to north at one week per 100 miles. Yet this doesn't take into account the changes from coast to coast, from sea level to my roof level of

200 metres, or the pockets of microclimates. Over the years, I have got to know where the first plants will emerge and to follow their succession.

Christina, now breastfeeding, is as hungry as a horse! The fresh herbs go nicely with some quail's eggs I've been given. I whip up the yolks of two with a little oil drained off some pickled chanterelles to make a garlicky mayonnaise, then lightly hard-boil the rest. I cook a stir-fry for Christina. I just have a large plate of common hogweed shoots simply fried, without oil or fat, in a steel pan until slightly charred along with the tiny eggs. It is excellent.

I take Maya to let Christina get a few things done during the afternoon. It is heaven to lie on a rug on the warm, sunny lawn, listening to the birds, cradling a new baby with monkey fingers curled tight around my own as we look into each other's eyes. I discover that, even though she's only just over a week old, Maya loves music so I sing her the songs that I sang to my own children.

## APRIL SNOW SHOWERS

*Daisylea, 10 April*

It is snowing again, thick and fast. It's fried nettles for breakfast with scrambled eggs, followed by wild garlic and nettle soup for lunch with an experimental flatbread. There is not much variety from day to day at the moment. As a treat, I use some of the precious chestnut flour with some wild honey to make biscuits. These are so good it takes all of my willpower not to eat them all at once.

I feel too lazy to make supper and go to bed on a glass of elderflower kombucha. The snow is coming down thick and fast but the flavours of spring make it much more bearable.

## SIGNS OF LIFE

*River Avon, 16 April*

I breakfast on baked, fermented apple, that is rapidly turning from cider-flavour to vinegar, with dried raspberries. The crock of apples has the beginnings of a grey mould around the edges so these will have to be finished up fast. However, the fear of running out of supplies and going hungry has eased as new green life bursts out of the ground.

A long Friday afternoon walk along the River Avon with Matt gets me out of my head. The snow has temporarily stopped and amazingly, on venturing out, I notice that there is some sloe blossom on the blackthorn bushes. The sky is dramatic – dark clouds interspersed with shafts of light that break up the gloom. The white flowers against the black, leafless twigs are just as stunning.

Tiny clumps of delicate, green apple-flavoured wood sorrel nestle in the root crooks of old beeches, with dainty white flowers nodding in the wind. Bunches of juicy pink purslane pierce through the leaf mould, opening their pink notched petals and competing with young nettles for a place in the sunshine. I notice that there are leaf buds on the rowan trees and nibble on them, enjoying their marzipan flavour. I pick a few silky young lime tree leaves which I love in a salad but most of the edible tree leaves are still tucked up in their buds, a month away from unfurling into a chartreuse canopy. Some of the fir trees are oozing a little resin that has crystallised into sticky icicles. I scrape them off with a twig onto a sycamore leaf so my hands aren't tacky for the rest of the day. It makes a fragrant incense in an oil burner.

On the humus-rich banks of the rushing river – cascading snow-melt down the valley – some of the lesser celandine is sporting shiny yellow flowers. Traditionally, the leaves – such a valuable spring salad ingredient – are not eaten after it has flowered. They are, after all, one of the members of the buttercup family Ranunculaceae which are known for their acrid taste and ability to cause mouth blisters. Before flowering they are mild but as they age the acridity develops so each pick needs to be carefully tested before you feed them to others! I've noticed that as they age, they often get a little purple streak down the centre of the leaf. Purple spots and streaks are not a good sign in any plant! They are kind to warn us. All we have to do is to look closely and pay attention.

In the shelter of the woods I find some sweet woodruff growing, just 10 centimetres high. By the end of the month it will produce tiny white flowers and, if I dry it first, will give off the sweetest fragrance. It also imparts the flavour of vanilla or tonka bean to desserts. Just the thought of sweet woodruff cheesecake makes my mouth water. So many flavours to look forward to.

## SMELLS

*Almondell Country Park, 18 April*

After a cup of fermented, smoked willowherb tea that rivals the best Assam, and a rehydrated bilberry and acorn pancake, I'm off to Almondell Country Park. Today is Monday so I know the woods will be quiet as most visit at the weekend. Pausing in the still air I can smell the people who were here yesterday. Their odours linger in the woods, long after their owners have left. Synthetic scents of perfume, body mists, shampoo, deodorants and aftershaves fill the air, often with the tang of damp dog. Some are vaguely pleasant but still quite unnatural and a bit weird to me. I guess I've just been hanging out with the plants for too long.

I go to Almondell because it has a sheltered south-facing slope where the wild garlic comes up early. Here is another strong smell! It is peaceful in the morning sun and I harvest plenty of wild garlic leaves to eat, ferment and pickle. I stop for a while and just watch the river flowing. The swirls and eddies of the water are meditative and mesmerising, and water has a language all of its own. Here and there, the rocks trap tiny whirlpools where bubbles build up into a scummy froth. This is run-off from phosphates used in industrial agriculture and non-organic dishwashing liquid, shampoo, hand soap and bodywash.

I fill the afternoon with more pickling, cooking up hogweed seed, sea wormwood, Scots lovage seed and a little elecampane root to spice the vinegar. I also refill all the herb tea jars, a favourite task. I love blending them for how they look as much as for their flavours.

Supper is good today. Matt has cooked a venison and hazelnut stew with puréed nettles and a favourite of mine – dandelion roots roasted with a drizzling of birch sap syrup. Afterwards, Łukasz calls me from Poland. We talk about the field trip and the research we're planning in July. I'm jealous to hear that the fruit trees are already in flower there. He's envying my wild food meals and looking forward to joining in during the week that I'm over there.

## EXPERIMENTS

*Daisylea, 23 April*

The primroses are out in abundance. Some eight or nine years ago I spread seed over this bank and now each spring it is a joyous mass of yellow blossom. It's been a good week. On Tuesday I dug pignuts and, armed now with two homis, my Japanese hoes, Matt and I managed to dig out about three dozen from 'pignut hill'. I also miscalculated the days last month, so I realised we had more chestnut flour that I'd rationed for and promptly made a batch of buns. As we also had an excess of hazelnuts, I experimented by extracting hazelnut milk and have – what looks and smells like – a vegan 'cheese' on the go plus some hazelnut butter. To cap it all, yesterday, Matt got experimental with some egg whites that had been separated from their yolks to make a mayonnaise. By mixing them with some wild honey from Myrtle Hill he made, of all things, meringues!

Happiness.

Lunch is a snack of acorn crackers with delicious hazelnut butter and porcini soup. For supper, I make a chicken-of-the-woods and wild garlic curry which we have with fried hogweed.

Life really isn't that bad!

# ROOKERY

*Briggis Hill, 24 April*

The hazelnut cheese is ready for eating today. I can't wait. I go off to visit a local stable. The owner is worried that one of the horses, who escaped unaccompanied into a ride, has been eating something poisonous and needs someone who knows plants to find the culprit. The usual suspect is ragwort but I only find one or two tiny plants. There is nothing suspicious until I come across the young brown spikes of horsetail that look like aliens from another planet. I am amazed the horses have gone near these weird plants, as animals can usually smell the phytocompounds that aren't good for them. I'm guessing they've not learnt to avoid danger as they're usually kept in fields with only grass and supplemented feed. It is not just we humans who have lost touch with nature, it is also the companion animals who share our fate.

Fuelled by a snack of hazelnut cheese – delicious as expected – with pickled wild garlic stems on acorn crackers, I take the long walk home. It's a beautiful spring day and I hear the first cuckoo. Lambs have been born left, right and centre over the last six weeks. Some are stumbling on spindly legs still trailing an umbilical cord while their mothers graze nearby, unconcerned. Others race each other across the fields on chubby, sturdy legs. There is new vegetation everywhere. Ferns uncurl below the stone wall, their tight fiddleheads released from their winter hibernation under last year's dead leaves. Solomon's seal pokes its head through the first leaves of Pyrenean valerian behind the wall. Crosswort is already in full flower on the banks sloping up from the road, releasing a smell of honey into the warm air. It truly feels like spring now.

As I climb Briggis Hill, my eyes follow a stream of black silhouettes riding the updraughts over the long row of beech trees that runs down the hill by the new houses. When I draw closer, the air is filled with cawing and crying. It's a rookery! I sit on a rock and patiently count the nests. There are about thirty-seven. This is great news. Back home I can look up the rooks in my egg table and calculate the number of 'egg points' I get. I'm currently hoping it's 8 per nest – that's 296 eggs the size of a bantam's. I'm not taking their eggs, but using those from hens instead, and if I *was* taking them I wouldn't have a 100 per cent success rate, nor would I take them all. But it's still a lot and it makes me happy!

For supper I experiment making *nokedli* – Hungarian pasta dumplings rather like German *spaëtzle* – from a mix of acorn and chestnut flour. Géza taught me how to do this. Wild mushroom nokedli is one of his favourite dishes but, without gluten to bind them together, they start to lose their shape in the water and I have to rescue them quickly before it becomes a gloopy soup. Mixed with some chopped, wilted wild garlic and an oil infused with pepper dulse they make a passable dish.

## PIT ROAST

*Daisylea, 25 April*

I want to experiment with a pit roast now that the ground is so much drier, cooking underground like our ancestors once did. This method was used all over the world. I have so much respect for the ingenuity and creativity of ancient people. My pit is just 0.5 metre long and wide and about 40 centimetres deep. I line it with old bricks and set a fire in the middle, leaving it for an hour. Once it has burnt down I shovel out the coals and ashes. The bricks radiate heat exactly as I'd hoped. I use flour, not to eat, but as a clay mixed with enough water to bind it and roll it out into a sheet. I sprinkle wild carrot seed, Scots lovage seed and some juniper berries all over, then lay a seasoned venison haunch on top, pulling up the edges so the meat is sealed into a case. I had planned to use clay but ran out of time to dig it up, wash it and sift it. Next time!

I make a bed of dried grass on the bricks, nest the venison *en croute* inside and cover it completely with a protective layer of grass. Matt then shovels the earth back in and lays the turfs on top of the vents where steam is starting to rise from the ground in demonic fashion. We leave it for two hours to cook.

The fire bowl lit, Géza cracks open a flagon of his superb elder-flower mead as our whetted appetites wait patiently. I roast some dandelion roots in a steel frying pan until they are browned and drizzle them with birch sap syrup just before they char. Matt has got some einkorn, a nutty ancient wild grain, to sow an experimental plot of wild and ancient grasses next month. I pilfer a handful to make some flatbreads, grinding the einkorn berries in their entirety and making a dough with salt water. Pulled into rough circles by hand, they toast quickly in the hot pan. While we wait we pick spring leaves and edible flowers. About twenty different species end up in a deliciously fresh and fragrant salad.

We gently excavate the joint. The outside is pitch black where the dried grass has burnt away, and knocking the top of the dough case reveals its solidity. Matt flips it over as the bottom is softer, where the juices have accumulated. It is easy to cut away the slightly soggy base to leave the meat in a hard 'bowl', surrounded by mouthwatering gravy. Géza carves it easily into incredibly tender pieces. The entire meal, while simple, is exquisitely delicious. It's interesting that feasts usually conjure up the idea of stuffing yourself to excess, but I find that wild food completely satiates me and I rarely desire seconds.

My body finally feels in tune with food again. After the harsh winter, with this delicious roast, huge pile of salad greens and some dandelion roots, I feel both nurtured and nourished.

## REEDMACE

*Limerigg, 27 April*

I'm glad I borrowed waders because, despite the sunshine, the temperature is still low with freezing intermittent showers. I am up to the elbow in a slurry of mud, deep in ice-cold water, loosening the clay-like silt from reedmace roots. Once I can make out their shape by touch, groping blindly underwater, I release them, cutting through them with a sickle. Some roots are rotting and stagnant, but there are enough that are firm and crisp, with buds of new growth starting to appear, to make more than a few meals. I'm ably helped by Matt and friends Dan and Ellie. Matt particularly hates cold water so I am doubly grateful!

Once we've got the roots home and spread out on the lawn, Géza's power washer gets the dirt off in no time, much to his amusement. It's amazing how much time a little technology can save. Reedmace is such a versatile plant. Young crunchy roots can be roasted like potatoes. The older ones yield so much starch that I can wash it off and filter it for later use like cornstarch. The inner core of new shoots can be sliced into crisp roundels that taste of water chestnut and cucumber – or boiled like a giant asparagus. The immature flower spikes can be roasted or boiled and eaten like corn on the cob and pollen gathered for baking. You could also thatch a house, weave a basket and joke around, using the dried seed heads as fake cigars. They filter and oxygenate water and are really useful for bioremediation – the cleansing of polluted water that plants are so good at doing. Every plant has a gift but some are super-donors!

# CHAPTER FIFTEEN

# BELTANE

*'Forget not that the earth delights to feel your bare feet
and the winds long to play with your hair.'*

Khalil Gibran, *The Prophet*

## BELTANE

*Daisylea, 1 May*

I'm awake this morning before 6.00. Sunlight is already streaming through the window as I slowly become conscious, listening to a choral cacophony of birds. I make a cup of tea – smoked willowherb and roasted birch twig – and slip back to bed. My hair still smells smoky from last night's Beltane fire – the ancient Gaelic May Day fire and fertility festival often celebrated with a bonfire. It is 'officially spring' to me now, halfway between the spring equinox and the summer solstice in the Celtic calendar.

Reflecting on the last six months, I am quietly proud that I've got this far. I don't find that self-discipline comes easily, so I feel a huge sense of achievement that I've been able to stick to 'the plan'. The biggest challenge has been the days that I'm working – especially if I haven't prepared ahead – but it's been hugely helped by not having anything tempting in the house. Thankfully, the hardest months are now behind me.

## NEURODIVERSITY

*A802 dual-carriageway, 2 May*

I'm always amazed by dandelions. One minute the roadsides are dull grey and brown, then overnight they transform into broad, yellow ribbons snaking through the countryside. Their secret is to prepare well beforehand by developing their young leaves and immature buds just above the root, nestled at ground level, packed into tender, dense crowns like the heart of a lettuce. Just a little warmth and sunshine is enough for them to spring into full flower, as if by magic. Before blooming the crowns are crisp, succulent and extremely tasty – although I won't pick from the side of the road as there is too much pollution from the cars. There is a field above Torphichen that, judging from the variety of wildflowers and 'weeds', hasn't seen a chemical spray for decades, if at all. That is where I am going now to harvest dandelions for supper. Crowns for a spring salad detox and creamy, earthy roots to roast with birch sap syrup.

They make my soul sing, even though they are not quite as magnificent as they were last year, due to spring's cold start. Each plant can live for five to ten years, if it's not uprooted for dinner! I don't feel too guilty though as each one can bear twelve flowers, across one of the longest growing seasons of all the wildflowers. It will yield 2,000 seeds a year to colonise the 5-mile radius around them.

There are at least 235 microspecies of dandelion in Britain alone. Some have scanty, small heads, others double crowns; some have wavy-edged leaves – the lobes hardly showing – while others have deep, laser-toothed fretwork. It takes a special mental focus to see these tiny differences which makes me grateful for the neurodiversity that exists among humans. I'm sure that people who are systems-driven, as well as generalists, were critical to the survival of humanity. We forget the advantage of neurodiversity as we race at twenty-first-century speed through the concrete, steel and wiring of modern life. Yet, without a range of diverse observers, how would we know all the plants and fungi of this earth? The insects? The stars of the sky? Let alone all the species of gut bacteria in the human microbiome.

Lunch is tiny sea arrowgrass and few-flowered leek tarts. I make acorn and chestnut pastry shells – these glutenless 'flours' bound together with deer fat and water. Géza, who hates soggy pastry, likes their crisp texture. With them we have the first of the tender new rosebay willowherb shoots, simmered in a little bit of water. They remind me of a cross between asparagus and okra. Paired with fried hogweed shoots, they are welcome new vegetables that have recently sprouted. It is a delicious and *very* satisfying meal.

Supper is roasted dandelion roots, with a little birch sap syrup drizzled over them. They are chewy, caramelised and a perfect blend of sweet and bitter. I've drained off some home-made umeboshi damson plums from their syrupy umezu. Chopped with wild garlic stems, they make a salty, sweet, fruity, garlicky relish that goes perfectly with the roots.

Chewing on them and thinking about where they grow, it occurs to me that wherever humans have churned up the earth or cemented it over, there is an order to the species that return to colonise it. Many of the pioneer weeds have deep roots. They help to break up the concrete, using their muscular taproots as a lever to widen the cracks and to mine the minerals deep in the earth, bringing them back to feed the derelict subsoil where topsoil is history. So many of these plants that like waste ground – dock, dandelion, burdock, thistle – are liver herbs used to detoxify our liver. They are also detoxing the earth. They are quickly followed by nettle; a herb that builds blood. Perhaps to them we are just an extension of Gaïa that is addressed in exactly the same way. First, detox and nourish; remove stagnation and blockage; repair, realign and rebalance; restore the flow of energy. Perhaps the remediation of environmental health and the remediation of human health are not so different.

# TROPICAL

*Riggmoss Heath, 4 May*

I run up to the heath. There is a lightness in my body and heart that I haven't felt for years that makes me want to fish out my trainers. It has been a rare sunny day today despite it being May – usually one of our best months here in Scotland. The weather has been so strange and unsettled this year. The warm air is sensuous and heady, heavy with the sweet scent of coconut given off by the yellow gorse flowers to court the bees. My memory recalls the Hawaiian Tropic tanning oil I slathered on my skin as a teenager, before we knew about the perils of skin cancer. Using the tips of my fingers, to avoid the sharp spikes, I delicately pluck handfuls of the fragrant petals into a paper bag. They'll be going in my salad for supper tonight.

I have too many gorse flowers for just a salad and want to preserve some of this spring feeling in a delicate syrup. Although I'm not eating sugar this year, I know Géza has some tucked away for making his brews. In a large jam jar I layer sugar then flowers, sugar then flowers, sugar and so on. The sugar will absorb the coconut flavour whereas boiling the flowers in a syrup would evaporate off all the flavoursome essential oils. It looks so pretty.

Three days later, when I open the jar of gorse sugar a strong wave of sweet, tropical, coconut tang smacks me in the face. I almost gasp with pleasure. A finger dipped in proves it also tastes delicious. I'll let it fully infuse for a few more weeks, then I'll add hot water, gently heat up the mix and strain off the syrup. It will keep in a sterilised bottle for a year. When I'm back on 'regular food' I might make some ice cream with it but it will have to wait on a top shelf until then!

Strangely, I have noticed that I am not missing sugar or desserts much at all. It is fat that I really long for.

# SNOWING

*Daisylea, 6 May*

I'm awake. It's 5.30 a.m. and it's snowing! The weather forecast says it will get heavier until 8.00. It's no wonder the rowan tree I visited yesterday, up on the exposed Riggmoss Heath, has delayed unfurling its grey-green leaf buds. I really feel for the birds, who have already nested, trying to keep their eggs and chicks warm in this weather. Still snug in my bed, I wait impatiently for this new 'winter' to pass. This tardy snow brought in by the icy north wind is trying to drive back the spring that nevertheless hovers, trying to gain ground.

It's a week after May Day. Surely soon the plants will no longer be able to contain themselves? Indeed I can't, for every fibre of me is longing for greenery and the warmth of the sun.

# CHAPTER SIXTEEN

# THE WONDER OF TREES

*'It is not so much for its beauty that the forest makes a
claim upon men's hearts, as for that subtle something,
that quality of air, that emanation from old trees, that
so wonderfully changes and renews a weary spirit.'*

Robert Louis Stevenson, *Essays of Travel*

## FOOD OF LIFE

*Daisylea, 8 May*

For supper I had the most amazing, enormous 'tree salad' with Matt's
pickled trooping funnel mushrooms and a little cold roast venison.
We are about to enter the magical fortnight in May when many tree
leaves are tender enough to eat. They taste fresh and fabulous. My
favourite is the light lemony flavour of the beech but tonight our salad
showcased the nutty hawthorn leaf.

Food from trees is sunlight itself; I am eating sunlight!

Chlorophyll is the food that feeds all life on earth. Mushrooms do
not contain chlorophyll so they depend on eating the plant material
substrate that they colonise as their food. Some eat animals – cater-
pillars, earwigs, cadavers. However, even those animals which eat

animals will at some stage have eaten an animal that eats plants. So all food is a chain that goes back to our need for chlorophyll to make food out of sunlight.

I once read in the *New Scientist* that the human body contains around twenty different elements, mostly made inside ancient stars:[1] 'About 12 per cent of your body's atoms are carbon. The hydrogen atoms in your body were formed in the Big Bang. All the others were made inside a star long ago and were flung into space by a supernova explosion.'

We are all creatures of stardust and sunlight!

I like that thought.

I remember folk singer Joni Mitchell's prescient refrain in Woodstock:[2] 'We are stardust. We are golden. And we have got to get ourselves back to the garden.'


## LEAVES

*Briggis Hill, 9 May*

Walking past the hedge at Craigengall the new, highlighter-pen-green spruce tips are bursting from their dry, papery, nut-brown cases. The hawthorn and sycamore are in leaf again whilst the beeches are still tentatively experimenting: half are in, but half are still out.

These first weeks of May, in the late Scottish spring, are when the trees which have slumbered for the last six months spring back into life. The warming sunlight of these hope-filled days is filtered through a haze of bright, acid green. The first delicate leaves of the season are tender and tart, or soft and sweet. They are a real treat at this stage, nibbled straight from the tree giraffe-like, added to salads, fermented or captured in alcohol for next year.

Like old friends rarely seen, the joy of this short reunion is exquisite. Here's beech – lemony, slightly tart; elm and wych elm – soft, sweet, slightly mucilaginous; European lime – cool, crunchy, also mucilaginous; nutty hawthorn; sharp, antiseptic birch; and chewy, citrussy spruce and fir tips. I am in heaven eating them all again, for in just a couple of weeks they will become too fibrous and enriched with dry tannins to enjoy. A fleeting moment of joy.

The first trees in leaf (birch, crabapple) are the ones with a *diffuse*-porous wood anatomy. Their trunks contain many small vessels to transport water and minerals up (xylem) and down (phloem) the tree. Because they are narrow and numerous, the tree can cope better with the contractions and expansions brought on by freezing and thawing. Next to don their green raiment are the sycamores and beeches, who also have diffuse-porous anatomy, but are larger. They are followed – sometimes by as much as two weeks later – by trees with *ring*-porous wood anatomy; the oaks, ashes and elms, whose larger diameter vessels are fewer, so precious and more vulnerable to winter damage.

In the British Isles, as I mentioned earlier, spring arrives later by one week for every 100 miles travelled north – with a little variation due to microclimates that affect the greening of the trees. In Alladale, just north of Inverness and 200 miles north of me, spring doesn't arrive until the first week of June. I am so glad it is here now and I don't have to wait any longer.


## PASSING OVER

*Drumtassie, 10 May*

The wood I'm walking through today is relatively young but, running down the middle, is a hidden centuries-old field boundary. What was once the field corner is marked by an elderly beech who still majestically reigns over the woodland.

Why do we all walk past the young pine saplings and ignore the youthful birch, despite their scented needles, fresh vibrant-green raiment, their paper-white and silver trunks? Our eyes do not care for them. We seek the ancient mother tree. Unlike our own human elders, we admire her girth, her fissured bark, and marvel at the warty growths studded with twigs, the fungus growing out from her side. She is magnificent.

Here lies a limb that came down in a storm many years ago. A luxurious mantle of mosses, lichens and fungi covers it. The rotting wood, once as hard as rock, crushes to powder under the light pressure of my fingers. From my open hand, I pass it to the wind who takes it and returns it to the earth.

I realise in this moment that I am at peace with death. One day I shall also lie down on the soil, under a shroud of green, and let the fungi feast on me, recycling my physical body into atoms of carbon, into stardust. There is peace in this forest. There is life and death. All is as it should be.

> *Lay your head where my heart used to be*
> *Hold the earth above me*
> *Lay down on the green grass*
> *Remember when you loved me.*

I shall have this achingly beautiful Tom Waits' song 'Green Grass'[3] played at my funeral.


## GRAIN TESTS

*Daisylea, 11 May*

It's cold and rainy again today. I make a nettle frittata and a salad with the funnel-shaped violet flowers of ground ivy peeking through the crisp, green leaves. These tiny flowers make me smile and bring me joy. I realise how much I have missed colour in my food during the dull brown-food days of winter.

In the afternoon Matt and I plant some test beds of einkorn, emmer, spelt and bere barley, each about 2 metres square. I am intrigued to see which ancient grains might have grown in Scotland. Next year, when I start growing vegetables again, I'd like to have some grain as part of my longer-term plan for living off the land as much as possible. It's occurred to me that I might never want to go back to shopping in supermarkets. I love eating local food and generating so little waste. I read a paper that said barley was the chief cereal crop while emmer wheat was a dominant grain in several Scottish Early Neolithic rectangular house structures.[4] Stuck inside, I am teaching myself to identify more of the local grasses, as I'll pick their grains at the end of the summer. Between rain showers I pick the plethora of primrose flowers from the southern slope. Géza starts the ferment of another primrose wine. The new organic cotton jeans I ordered last week have arrived. I am down another dress size.

## HEDGES

*North Berwick, 12 May*

It's 12 May today which in the old Julian calendar was 1 May. May Day (or Hawthorn Day, for hawthorn flowers are known as 'the may') was traditionally when this ancient tree first comes into flower; its bridal-white bloom outlining fields and lanes.

I'm out on the world's edge at low tide, picking sea spaghetti, being careful to cut only one frond from each button. After the month since I was last here, most of the buttons have developed two strands. I cut off one of each pair. I can see where I picked previously by the short, cut ends and I can also see if other people have been harvesting here. I am very aware that it would be hard to forage sustainably if a dozen other families were after the same resources.

As I drive back through the country roads, the hawthorn hedges are blossoming . . . or not. There are fewer flowering hedges than ever nowadays because hedges are so severely scalped in the autumn with mechanical cutters. It's neater, I suppose, but it makes me furious. Cutting away the old wood so savagely is catastrophic for the local ecology.

Many species produce their flowers on last year's old wood, not on the soft new spring growth; no flowers mean no pollen or nectar to feed bees and other pollinators. When there are no flowers, there is no fruit to follow and without fruit, there is no bird food. Without food there are no birds. The world would fall eerily silent, except for the hum of mosquitos who thrive on blood rather than pollen. Long-distance seed dispersal ceases and fewer forests grow. With fewer trees, there is less oxygen and more $CO_2$. All this, just to make the hedges a bit tidier?

I love hawthorn so have been trying to do some unsolicited planting in the gaps. Tradition has it that hawthorn is for the heart, for grief, for the broken heart and for shock. There is plenty of clinical evidence to show that hawthorn extract dilates the arteries to reduce high blood pressure. By strengthening the heart muscle, it helps to prevent and improve the heart's recovery in cardiac arrest. I collect the leaves and flowers and dry them for tea. Other years I would make a hawthorn berry gin. I prefer it to traditional sloe gin recipes as it is not as sweet. It's dryer, like a very fine sherry as hawthorn is more like a wild apple than a plum. Haw brandy is also a good antidote for an aching heart.

My favourite hawthorn recipe is old-fashioned haw ketchup. Haws are boiled in vinegar with onions, garlic, ginger, spices and a little brown sugar, and then puréed through a sieve. The result is a thick tangy ketchup that goes with everything! This year I will have to substitute honey for sugar, wild garlic instead of onions and hogweed, Scots lovage and wild fennel seeds for the spices.

I pick rosebay willowherb shoots for supper. They are long, green and elegant with tasselled tops and look so beautiful steamed with young hops tendrils. The hops are delicious, similar to young green beans (I admit I am really missing garden vegetables). I eat them with crispy dry-fried hogweed shoots and venison fillet served with my rich, dark hawthorn ketchup sauce.

# CHAPTER SEVENTEEN

# THE FISH COURSE

*'Many men go fishing all of their lives without
knowing that it is not fish they are after.'*

Henry David Thoreau, *Walden: or Life in the Woods*

## CURING FISH

*Daisylea, 16 May*

I have been gifted two beautiful trout that Bob caught this morning.
One is huge, it must weigh about 2.5 kilos, the other about 1.5 kilos.
I am delighted as, living inland and not having a river fishing permit, I
haven't had fresh fish since I started this wild food year. After gutting
them and cleaning off the scales, I cut off some fillets from the chunky
end to cook and eat fresh. I am going to cure the rest of it as a gravadlax and then smoke it. A close approximation to smoked salmon!

My inspiration for this is the lovely Gill Meller. The first gravadlax
I ever made was from a recipe in his cookbook *Gather*[1] using a 'cure'
of salt, sugar and rhubarb as the acid that cures and preserves it,
paired with rose petals and fennel seeds. This time, I am using the
sea buckthorn juice I collected from the coast just before Christmas.
I line the dish with some soft, sweet cicely leaves, their aniseed

aroma already wafting up from the crushed stems. I sprinkle over a little sea salt with a few fennel-like Scots lovage seeds and lay the fillets skin side down. On top I sprinkle more salt and lovage seed, the bright orange sea buckthorn juice, and some fresh green spruce needles which, at this time of the year, taste of lemon-citrus pine. It's allowed to rest for twenty-four hours in the fridge before the cure is rinsed and patted dry.

For supper I roast the trout steaks simply, on a tray covered with a deep, protective coating of fennel fronds. As the fish oil seeps through they crisp up and create a delicious crust. I make mayonnaise by whipping an egg yolk with old, mushroom-flavoured oil from the pickle jars, plus a little grated horseradish root. I dug the root this afternoon so it is fresh and potent. Grating it once again generates far more tears than even the fiercest onion! A simple salad of violet leaves, crunchy elm seeds and lemony beech leaves with a mushroom 'soy' dressing and some tiny hard-boiled quail's eggs makes it complete. It feels like the healthiest, freshest meal I have eaten in the last six months.

## SMOKING

*Daisylea, 17 May*

The trout fillets are ready for smoking after twenty-four hours of soaking in brine and twenty-four hours of drying (after rinsing off the cure).

I'm sure that smoking began accidentally when overlooked food was left overnight beside the embers of a Palaeolithic barbecue. Waking up hungry, after a night on the mead, our ancestors found the smoked remains of last night's supper and became addicted to the flavour. It must have been a tremendous bonus then as smoking helps to preserve food so that it lasts longer – a great boon in the days before fridges.

I own a vintage 1950s or '60s metal food safe that I found on eBay at a bargain price. It is a rusty cream enamel with a bright red door, and four wire shelves inside. It has circular vents covered in mesh in which I have made some little flaps to control the airflow. With the addition of a small metal maze to hold the smouldering sawdust, it makes the perfect cold-smoking cabinet. I love the smoky taste of food whether it's venison sausages, cured pigeon breast, smoked eggs with swirling patterns that look as if they've been fired in a sawdust kiln, or venison 'bacon' that's been soaked in a juniper berry cure. In a past life I'd also have smoked aubergines and chocolate!

After eight hours, the trout fillets are done to perfection. Thinly sliced with a salad of freshly picked greens, they make a most excellent brunch.

## MUSHROOM MEDITATION

*Westfield, 18 May*

I am sitting in front of an enormous chicken-of-the-woods fungus growing out of an elderly cherry tree. It is stunningly beautiful; bright orange on the top with sulphur-yellow pores underneath. It will make delicious 'chicken' curry and 'chicken' nuggets – the texture almost identical to the real thing – but right now, I'm just gazing and marvelling at the myriad forms that life takes on Earth.

## ROOTING AROUND

*Kinross, 29 May*

My mother has had to have a minor operation and I'm collecting her from hospital today. I need to stay overnight until we're confident she can manage on her own. I'm sure she thinks I'm a bit crazy but she takes me in her stride! The only wild salad vegetables in her garden are sheep's sorrel, dandelion leaves and a small amount of willowherb sadly past the tender stage. She keeps offering me forbidden foods, confused by my diet but, with foresight, I have brought supplies. She is eating the contents of a tin of baked beans mixed with a handful of raisins and a spoonful of hot curry powder, which has been micro-waved for two minutes. 'It's easy!' she says to my raised eyebrows.

I can imagine the chagrin of chefs – both domestic cooks and res-taurateurs – having just got their heads around vegetarians, vegans, the gluten-, nut- and dairy-free, and then I come along singing, 'Wild food only, please!' There'd be curses in the kitchen.

It's about 9.00 p.m. but still broad daylight outside. I'm hungry as I've spent the last four hours trying to tame part of Mum's garden. I admit to a dual motive – it is chock full of dandelions. It's been a warm day and all the flowers have turned to clocks. I think they look beautiful with their gossamer helicopters poised for take-off on the slightest breeze, translucent in front of self-seeded harebells and chives, competing for ground space with tangy, lemony sheep's sorrel. But most gardens around here are tidy, orderly affairs, and the neighbours may not appreciate 20 billion new dandelion plants next spring. I stuff handfuls of the downy whirligigs, their tiny seeds suspended beneath them, into a paper bag to release later. I'm a big fan of guerrilla gardening in the right places.

It's not the seed I'm really after, though, but the long earthy roots. I persevere until I have a canvas bag full and at least one corner of the garden tamed. My mouth waters as I dig, especially when I extract a particularly thick but still juicy root from the ground. I have grown to love these. Despite the current hiccups and the need to find a supply of fat, I live like a queen.

# ANGELS

*Kinross, 30 May*

I wake up early when I hear my mother moving about. Then I snooze until 7.00 when I get up for a drink of water. The kitchen floor is gritty under my bare feet, so I reach for a broom. At eighty-two years old, with a health condition that causes terrible bone pain, it's hardly surprising my mother has allowed things to pile up a bit. Junk mail, old catalogues and empty envelopes are everywhere. Before I know it,

I've gone into full spring-cleaning mode. Somewhere around eleven, I suddenly realise that I'm almost faint from exertion that has been fuelled only by a glass of water and a cup of strawberry leaf tea.

I'm used to the feeling of low-level hunger much of the time these days, very aware that my calorie intake is regularly well under the recommended amount. Yet I'm surprised that I don't feel ravenous. My appetite is still small. Despite feeling that I am starving sometimes, I still struggle to eat very much at all. Is this because my stomach has shrunk?

This month I've tried to eat a dairy-free, vegetarian diet. Apart from green leafy vegetables, I have mainly been surviving on eggs as they are in season. I eat a hard-boiled egg now, mashed up with some chopped lemon-tasting sheep's sorrel.

Although our ancestors travelled when the food seasons changed, I have had to stay inland during the time of year when they would have moved to the coast, where there is more food. Now, knowing how my body feels during these long periods of fewer calories and no fats, it dawns on me that I will have to eat more fish. This will be a challenge. I've fished a few times but only ever caught one small sea trout, so assume I'm rubbish at it.

Sometimes, angels appear when summoned.

An hour later, Mum's friend Robert appears. We're chatting when Mum suddenly remembers that he fishes. I explain the situation and, as luck would have it, he is going fishing on the Bank Holiday and would be happy to give me some of his catch – if he's lucky. Fingers crossed.

Meanwhile, I am going to get my own rod, weights and flies from Falkirk car boot sale and learn about the intricacies of catching fish. Like every organism they have their individual preferences and habits!

Back home in the evening, supper is hogweed tempura made with an acorn starch batter. It tastes delicious, but I still go to bed hungry and light-headed.

# BANK HOLIDAY MONDAY

*Rigmoss Heath, 31 May*

I'm up at 6.00 for a cup of hawthorn leaf tea. With a slab of cold nettle frittata in my basket I'm soon off out. I need to pick the last of the St George's mushrooms – before the heat dries and cracks them.

It's a misty morning down in the valley and I can see low-lying fog tracing the river. A light coating of smirr is in the air. 'Smirr' is a marvellous Scots word describing the superfine drizzle that barely dampens your skin. Above the silver wisps, the sunlight is golden and already hot, drying and warming the earth. It is so peaceful, although – as there is no wind – I can distantly hear the roar of the motorway picking up. Lockdown is over. Once over the crest of the hill, the only sound is a cuckoo in a distant clump of pines. I find rings of St George's mushrooms up here; the biggest is 5 metres across – probably about thirty-three years old. In optimum conditions, they widen annually by 15 centimetres (6 inches).

Back home, I sit on the warm wooden deck sipping watermint tea and cleaning mushrooms to make soup for lunch. I press the shavings well into the earth under clumps of grass, hoping one day there'll be a ring on my lawn. House martins are swooping on emergent midges. Two of them seem to play with a white feather. They drop it, and then dive to pick it up, taking turns. I have never seen them do that before: do birds play? Behind me, early wasps are licking the wooden boards. I idly wonder how many centuries it would take for them to wear the oak away in pursuit of cellulose to build their cone-shaped, papery nests.

The sunshine heating my bones makes it easy to stay rooted in the present moment. I find that foraging demands close attention to the micro details of plants and fungi, and the ability to read the macro moods of weather and habitat. It commands me to be present, in liminal space, where neither yesterday nor tomorrow exist.

I get a text in the afternoon from my mother; Robert has caught a trout and is still fishing so hopes to catch another one later. Massive relief!

I know this feeling is short-lived, though. This year has taught me that I can never be complacent; I have to think ahead to the next month, not just the next meal. Besides the current problem of fats, I have a new gnawing anxiety about the summer. The shelves are looking bare and there are gaps and empty jars. I have run out of chestnut flour, there are only two handfuls of hazelnuts left, and about 100 grams of dried bilberries.

On the plus side, there are still some frozen wild mushrooms, a kilo of acorn flour and plenty of jars of pickles, but these don't make a balanced diet! I drive back over to Kinross to collect the fish.

Supper is fresh trout, of course. I stuff the belly with wild thyme and a few bog myrtle leaves and bake it in a clay pot in a nest of scrubbed dandelion roots. When I lift the lid, the steaming fragrance is exquisite. I take the fish out and return the roots without the lid to let them crisp up and serve it all together with a chickweed and sorrel salad – plus about twenty other species of odd leaves and petals. I eat a much bigger portion than I would if it were meat. I think that's the ghrelin brake off – a testament to the fat content. It is a living dish, rich with the flavours of field and river, so nourishing and filling.

# PART FOUR

# SUMMER

# CHAPTER EIGHTEEN

# TRANSHUMANCE

*'Shepherds know many mysterious languages;*
*they speak the language of sheep and dogs,*
*the language of stars and skies, flowers and herbs.'*

Mehmet Murat Ildan

## CHA-CHA-CHAGA

*Daisylea, 1 June*

I'm sitting in a warm, sheltered spot entrained with nettle, heart to heart. Nettle and I have been deep in conversation. Of course, this isn't a human conversation. Meditating silences the chatter of my mind, creating a liminal space where our spirits meet and converse. Someone who's never had this experience might call it 'imagination' but I know the difference.

After breakfasting on sautéed chicken-of-the-woods mushroom with a fried egg and a chickweed salad, I drive down to a river valley in the Scottish Borders. There is a stretch here where chaga fungus grows on the old birches. It seems to like the microclimate of low-lying dales where frosty air lingers, its stillness undisturbed by even the slightest breeze during the winter months. Luckily, there is no evidence that anyone else has found this spot and there are still many cracked black protuberances thrusting out of the silvery bark on many of the birches. The current popularity of medicinal mushrooms has put a lot of pressure on this wild fungus. Wild food doesn't scale and remain sustainable without mindful practices and land management.


## RUN DOWN

*Daisylea, 3 June*

My skin has become dry and itchy in places, and every time I wash my hair, an awful lot of it seems to fall out. In fact, I've noticed silver hairs cast aside everywhere. To start with, I put it down to a natural summer moult. I'm not so sure now, though. Last Saturday a cold sore tried to appear. I was picking honeysuckle blossoms off their stems, from which Géza was going to make mead, when I felt its telltale tingle. Within seconds, a red lump started to appear under my lip. We've lived together long enough, me and this virus, that I know its evil ways! I immediately knocked it back. A 1,000 mg tablet of L-lysine and a smear of propolis ointment did the trick, and the lump disappeared in less than an hour. However, it did highlight that my immune system might be a bit low. And now I come to think of it, some days I have woken with a mild sore throat or elevated glands which quickly resolve once I get going. This is a little disturbing as I'm usually as strong as the proverbial ox.

This morning I have woken thirsty – a seemingly unquenchable thirst – and realise it's not water that my body wants but fats.

I lazily google 'effect of lack of fat in diet' to confirm my suspicions.

'Fats are essential in our diet and it's recommended that our total fat intake should be around 25–30 per cent of our total energy intake,' says one cyber nutritionist. 'Most adults should eat at least 60 grams of fat each day,' says another. Hunger, fatigue, aching joints, susceptibility to colds, dry skin and brain fog are listed as the side effects.

Last night, I felt especially weak and fatigued. Supper had not been one of Matt's triumphs. The last of the brown meatloaf; squidgy purple blobs of defrosted chicken-of-the-woods, cooked in elderberry must – which tasted bitter; steamed dark green sow thistles that still felt spiky in my mouth. I tried hard but felt like a child forced to eat a bad school dinner. I just couldn't chew. An hour later I went to bed in a wave of wobbly fatigue, only to wake up this morning with this thirst.

For the first time in years, I am overwhelmed by the temptation for greasy fast food. I find myself in the car, heading to the nearest fish-and-chip shop, without any concern for the sacrifices I've made over the last seven months. I am craving fat so badly, it is worth it. I am starving.

It's closed.

I am so relieved and somewhat ashamed of my momentary weakness.

I'm eating eggs as they are abundant right now, but there are no fatty seeds, nuts or plant flesh. I have two handfuls of unshelled hazelnuts left to last until the autumn. There are no cultivated Scottish avocados or cashew nuts, let alone wild ones. During the last two months, with the resurgence of greens, I have thankfully eaten far less meat.

Now I feel I need more than I'm getting but I'm too shy to beg Bob or Robert for more fish so soon after their last donations.


# A PASTORAL DAY

*Achray Farm, 5 June*

I am finding out – as many observant foragers have before me – that in practice it is much harder to find food in hot summer months, once the lush abundance of the spring has passed. Tender, succulent wild vegetables are producing flowers and seeds, so their leaves have become tough, fibrous and tasteless. Eggs have hatched and flown away. Seaweed has reproduced, become slimy and lost its flavour. The stored starch (glycogen) that gives oysters their fresh sweet taste turns to sex gametes – their reproductive cells. Spawning changes the taste and the texture of most shellfish. So before the summer yields fruits, berries and nuts, the forager is reliant on collecting shellfish, fishing, hunting or eating dairy products to gain enough calories.

Fuelled by scrambled duck egg, fried chicken-of-the-woods fungus – it's lasting a fair few days – and some smoked trout with a salad of greens, I drive out to Brig o'Turk where my friends Maisie and Nicola live, on the quest for milk. I'm having a day out with their goats: placid mums, frisky kids and a stiff-legged old nanny. Each one has a very distinct personality. They cheerily follow Nicola out of the gate to the hills as if she's an alpha doe herself.

She keeps these goats because they help to close the permaculture loop. Permaculture is an approach to farming based on cyclical, holistic systems and emulating nature; a farming method very close to my heart, for it is truly sustainable and regenerative. These hardy animals eat scrub, weeds, many invasive plants, and woody plant material. They convert this into protein-rich milk and provide nutritious manure to fertilise the soil.

Loch Achray nestles in a majestic valley. The mountain peaks of Sròn Armailte and Ben A'an to the north, with the range encompassing Ben Venue, Stob an Lochain, Beinn an Fhògharaidh and Creag Innich curving to the south. Wild goats were recorded in the fourteenth century in Inversnaid, a seven-hour hike from this farm. There are somewhere between 3,000 and 4,000 in Scotland today, including a feral herd that lives on the slopes of Ben Venue. Goats may have arrived with Neolithic farmers around 5,000 years ago and these are the descendants of numerous escapees over the centuries. They have to be managed – their population has remained the same since the late 1960s – or woodland and sensitive habitats would never have time to regenerate. As with deer, culling is necessary to retain the right balance. Although it can be an emotive topic, without an alternative apex predator humans have to take that role if we want to maintain woodland.

While animal husbandry – the catch-all term for herding and domesticating animals – isn't foraging, it is a method of sourcing food that goes much further back than farming. We think humans have been domesticating herd animals for around 11,000 years. First with sheep and goats, and later cows. In the British Isles, the ancient Celts were famed for their dairy produce some 3,000 years ago, with evidence of trading dairy exports, like butter, to France. Butter was buried in bogs to keep cool and is still sometimes dug up by archaeologists.

The success of *Homo sapiens* at colonising all parts of the globe has depended on our ability to eat almost anything. However, despite a long and universal history, a growing number of Westerners now avoid dairy products. An opinion I often hear is that it's unnatural to consume another animal's baby food. Yes, we are the only species that does that, but it is also 'unnatural' to cook food, eat microwave meals, add artificial flavouring and preservatives and drink Coke. As I drive home, delighted with my milk, I wonder how dairying started. I suppose people must have noticed that baby humans and baby animals were nourished the same way. If a mother couldn't breastfeed, her infant would still thrive if given animal milk and simple processing like making kefir, kvass and kumis helped adults digest it too.

After the winter I've had, I completely understand why people began to keep animals. A steady supply of meat without the uncertainty or risk of hunting. Most early herds were probably semi-wild with herders and shepherds following the natural migration of animals from summer pastures where the grass is rich and lush, to winter shelter.[1] This is called transhumance and still happens, in Europe, in the Alps and some Mediterranean countries. In Transylvania, long-distance 300-kilometre transhumance treks, between the summer and winter pastures, can take six weeks in each direction.[2] On the Norwegian coast, there are still some areas where, after the winter, shepherds bring their sheep down to the coast. They race to be the first to chew tender bladderwrack shoots with obvious delight and sip seawater, before heading to the alpine slopes for the summer. Of course, this is dying out as a practice but I can imagine that it's a life filled with satisfaction although hard, physical work too. It's strange to think of milk as seasonal, but wild cows (extinct now) would usually calve between May and June. So before humans started to manipulate the bovine breeding season, milk was abundantly available throughout the summer months from May to September/October when the calves were weaned.

I'd love to have spent the summers in alpine meadows among fragrant herbs, wildflowers and grasses living in a simple wooden *shieling*, a summer hut; passing my time milking and turning milk into butter, cream and cheese. All northern Europeans made simple cheeses: Scottish crowdie, Norwegian surost, French Valençay and Greek feta. Bigger, cooked cheeses such as Swiss Emmentaler were made in the valleys – a 120-kilo cheese is far too heavy to carry down the mountain!

Nowadays, I do think that large-scale dairy operation in which the cows are kept indoors all year round and separated from their calves is cruel and unnecessary. The waste output from these intensive methods is also unsustainable. But small-scale organic farming with the animal's welfare at heart is different. We cannot go back to a Palaeolithic way of life, hunting and gathering. There are just too many of us; farming is here to stay.

Animals have fertilised Earth's soil, recycling the gift of plants, since the first land animals evolved. Does modern farming have to be so industrial in scale? I feel sure that if we stopped rearing cattle in feedlots, intensively dairying, and filling the soil with chemicals, and returned to animal husbandry the old-fashioned way, so much of what and how we eat would be better. We would enjoy a relationship of respect and mutual benefit – an honourable trinity of human–animal–soil.

We walk back along the dusty road with the herd, under the hilly slopes of Dùn nam Muc. The goats get plenty of roughage and variety here, such as the tips of bilberry bushes, bog myrtle, young trees, willow and juniper scrub. Here these happy, amiable goats are in their element and I am very grateful to them all for their gift of excess milk.

Lunch starts with a snack of nettle crisps. They are delicious, a wild version of kale crisps. A roast venison with a startlingly manic-red sauce made of freshly picked farm jostaberries, a side of nettle frittata, fermented wild garlic pickle and the prettiest herb and flower salad of cleavers tops, wild marjoram, coriander fronds from her herb bed, dotted all over with tiny heartsease violets. It was all cooked as a surprise by Maisie. I am so impressed and grateful. This is the first wild meal that someone else has tried to make for me. No mean feat! I'm so grateful I'm not going to quibble about the home-grown organic jostaberries!

# CHEESEMAKING

*Daisylea, 6 June*

I get up and have breakfast. St George's mushrooms, dandelion greens and a venison kidney. There is a lot to do today as I am about to embark on making cheese with 15 litres of goats' milk from Nicola. Yesterday evening I added some kefir grains, leaving them in overnight to inoculate the milk. In Scotland, all milk is pasteurised, so my first task was to reintroduce some bacteria; kefir does this really well. As the poor grains have been sitting in the fridge for seven months, I have given them plenty of time to recover!

I've been making cheese for years and experimented a lot with vegetable rennets. Rennet, containing chymosin (the main enzyme responsible for coagulation), is the enzyme found in the stomach of a baby cow or goat that causes milk to curdle. Once the curds are separated from the whey – the liquid part of the milk – they can be strained to make soft cheese. Some curds are also cooked and pressed to make hard cheeses. However, some plants also contain enzymes that will curdle goat's and sheep's milk, and occasionally cow's milk. These are not as strong as chymosin from animals so usually I just make soft cheese: labne, cottage cheese and cream cheese. As I'm on a wild food diet, I am pushing the boundaries of the vegetable rennets to make some hard cheeses that will keep until the end of November as, sadly, my diet precludes them until then.

I divide the milk into three 5-litre batches. I add boiled nettle juice rennet to one, fresh sorrel juice to another and ground thistle seed solution to the third. I leave them on the beer mat to keep warm. The beer mat is just a heated pad I bought second-hand years ago and it's put in good service. It keeps fermenting beer, yoghurt and cheese warm, doubles up as a warm foot pad for cold feet under my desk, and is pressed into service as a panel heater for the hen house when the temperature drops. I add towels on top to keep in the heat and leave it alone. After a few hours, I check on the pots. The nettle has made a perfect deep curd. I cut it into cubes whilst still in the saucepan then put it on the stove to reheat and cook a little. The sorrel has made fabulous green curds! The thistle needs a little longer as the curd looks very fragile, so I cover it up again to incubate some more.

After gently cooking, I ladle the curds into forms to drain. Traditionally, these forms are little baskets or pots with holes fired into them. I use old metal scale weights to apply pressure, helping to force all the whey out of the curds. I then wrap the curds loosely in wilted leaves and leave them on a little wire rack in my cheese safe to start their journey to maturation.

I skipped lunch and there's a lot to do, so supper is simple. I enjoy smoked trout with a big green salad of dog violet leaves, gorse flowers, dame's rocket and cuckoo flowers – picked from the scrubland above the dump – plus vetch shoots, European lime leaves, and chickweed from the top of Hillhouse. There was also a lovely young 350-gram chicken-of-the-woods mushroom on one of the oak trees as well. I get home to find that Géza has found a 2-kilo mushroom near Linlithgow Loch on a forage with Matt. All the 'chickens' are coming out together!

More welcome gifts this evening. Four trout and a leg and shoulder of venison from Bob's brother Norrie who's clearing out his freezer, along with six duck's eggs, eighteen quail's eggs and some hen's eggs. It's like the seven days of Christmas! Géza cracks open a bottle of elderflower mead. It's been such a satisfying day. I get so much pleasure from the process of making things and I particularly love the alchemy of cheesemaking as I watch the milk thicken, then split into chunky curds. Craft and handwork absorb me in a similar way to foraging. Darning the threadbare soles of my woollen socks, for example, has the same quality. I could just throw them away and buy new socks but the hour spent focusing on those tiny stitches is a form of meditation. The time used making and repairing my things makes me even more grateful for what I have in this life. In turn, this gratitude creates a feeling of abundance, even in the most simple life.

## WINGING IT

*Daisylea, 10 June*

My cheeses are slowly ripening. I watch them like a hawk in case mould should spoil them. Not having a cool, dark cheese cave, I have to keep them in the fridge with the vegetables and there is not much air circulating around them. The experiment with milk was a one-off event for the year so it would be truly tragic if they were to spoil. I am alternating them between the fridge and a small wood and mesh cheese safe: the former, too cold and the latter, too warm. Every other day I paint them with a brine made from salted whey. This helps the right moulds to grow and keeps the black ones that might spoil the cheese at bay.

I must admit to being very tempted to sample my wares. A cheese binge would sort out my fat cravings in no time!

Matt has cooked lunch using the venison hearts. We have kept the offal because it is a waste not to. He marinaded them overnight in a mix of mushroom ketchup, pickle oil, sea buckthorn juice, fresh wild thyme, wild marjoram and salt. Sliced thin and fried in the pan they are tastier than I expected, served with chicken-of-the-woods, minute quail's eggs and another lush salad of wild greens. I'm so full that I skip supper later, just snacking on Mark's defrosted smoked mackerel pâté, spread on thin acorn crackers.

# CHAPTER NINETEEN

# THE MERSE

'*Merse: Noun, Scottish.* **1.** *Low level ground by a river or shore, often alluvial and fertile.* **2.** *A marsh.*'

Collins English Dictionary

## HARVESTING DAY

*Tyninghame, 13 June*

As sure as night follows day, so tender leaf gives way to flower. On land, the plants' energies are deployed creating ethereal flowers. Leaves become bitter to taste and papery to chew. Once-juicy stems are now hard and hollow. Tough fibre and indigestible cellulose are required to hold aloft the heavy seed heads that will follow, as the blooms fade. I adore the flowers; their colour and beauty are food for the soul. But food for the body they are not! Their scents lend flavour but not substance. There is little to eat.

The herbivores agree. Deer migrate to the cooler, higher mountain slopes, where the grass is still sweet and lush. Many of our hunter ancestors followed them, later joined by nomadic pastoralists herding their goats and sheep to green summer pastures. However, for many foragers these sunnier days herald a return to the sea. After fuelling up on oyster mushrooms in pesto, the estuary is my chosen destination.

As I fork off the farm track onto the narrow path through the grass, the merse comes into view. The heat creates a shimmer like a desert mirage and my heart leaps. After months of lockdown this sight is as welcome to me as an oasis of water in the desert. Down on the merse, you cannot step anywhere that is not food. Acres of it! The flat mud pancake, intersected by treacherous channels, is vibrant green. Here and there, a haze of pink thrift and white sea wormwood drift into view. Around the edges, the plants jostle for space. The bank I am descending is untouched by salt water, so it is thronged with yarrow and sorrel that don't like saline conditions. Both of these were born to be eaten with fish. I can think of no greater seaside treat than eating freshly caught fish, its cleaned gut stuffed with yarrow leaves, baked until tender on a flat rock heated in the fire and served with a simple, tangy sorrel sauce, or perhaps with stone-baked mussels with sugar kelp crisps toasted on a stick. The memories make my mouth water. All thoughts of work and life are abandoned as the hedonist in me focuses on the pure pleasure ahead: discovering what feral foods nature has decided to gift me today.

I ignore the yarrow and sorrel and cross the ditch, fatally stocked with poisonous hemlock water-dropwort. It circles the edge of the merse like a moat full of piranhas. Hemlock water dropwort is one of the most dangerous plants in Britain. It starts growing in Earrach, earlier than many of the other plants. When the country-side is emerging from winter and still in muted browns and greys, its spookily-luminous green stands out sharply. It is not afraid to be seen and noticed in a hungry landscape as no one would dare to eat it!

Immediately after the ditch my feet land on silverweed, which loves a slightly raised mound where the sand has blown up over the decades. Its leaves are grey-white with a hint of chartreuse and cling to the ground. I ignore it now but make a mental note for the winter. The loose sand will make it easy to prise out the swollen tubers and if I take it from here this will not cause problems. Sand dunes, on the other hand, are a vital sea defence and digging roots out of them would destabilise them; it is the weeds and the grasses like marram that hold them together. Roots need careful ecological consideration when harvesting, and the landowner's permission. Historic records show that silverweed was a valued famine food in the Outer Hebrides. Extracting them from the machair, a unique and fertile, low-lying, grassy plain habitat, kept more than one family alive.

Finally, I am down on the merse. The first 20 yards, rarely reached even at a high tide, are thronged with grasses. Over the years my eye has honed its skills. I may need reading glasses now as I peer at books and a computer screen, but I can spot a clump of sea arrowgrass at a hundred paces. A stretch of grass is never just one species but to most people it appears as a monotonous green expanse. Sea arrowgrass is a particular shade of green, quickly confirmed by the way that its leaves overlap at the base, almost plaited. It reminds me of the way that the fronds are arranged on the tropical 'traveller's palm' tree. Earlier in the season you can find tiny young new shoots by looking for its flag – the dried, erect brown stalks that have survived over the winter and to which a few seeds still cling. Unlike sea plantain, the seeds of which are attached directly to the stem, each tiny arrowgrass seed is attached by a stalk. It's only a hair's breadth but it's enough for my eye to pounce on it and sure enough, parting the decaying brown reveals fresh green shoots at the base, emerging anew from the mud.

I harvest two large handfuls, about 200 grams overall, being careful to leave a few leaves on every plant so that it can carry on growing. This will last a month, kept in the fridge. Sea arrowgrass isn't a vegetable so much as a herb. I love the expression on people's faces when I give them 'grass' to eat. They put it into their mouths a little warily, but as they start to chew their faces light up, eyes suddenly animated with surprise. A chuckle. A disbelieving shake of the head or an astonished 'Oh!' – it tastes almost identical to fresh coriander. Snipped like chives or spring onions into a salad or used in a curry, it is completely interchangeable with the limp, supermarket herb that yields its pungency to hothouse cultivation.

*

I did a lot of research before I started eating this delicious arrow-grass. Advice from a friend was to only eat the white part at the very base of the stalk, because sea arrowgrass contains hydrogen cyanide: a poison. I disagreed. While it is right to be cautious, natural poisons are highly over-hyped in the fear department and very under-represented in nature as a whole. I would never eat a plant I couldn't identify 100 per cent, or thought was dodgy, but I do know that scientific research which studies individual plant compounds does not always reflect the reality of nature's larder.

*Triglochin maritima* is the botanical name of this grass-like plant in the Juncaginaceae (arrowgrass) family. It's always worth knowing the one botanical name of a plant as there can be many common names: sea arrowgrass, shore arrowgrass, seaside and common arrowgrass. Its botanical name helps to differentiate it from *Triglochin palustris*, the marsh arrowgrass of freshwater inland marshes. Wikipedia – still quoting a reference from 1929 – also states, 'This plant is toxic, as it can produce cyanide. This species has been known to cause losses in cattle, with green leaves being more toxic than dried material.' Scary internet science!

Going in deep, my investigations of published papers reveal that arrowgrass contains some cyanogenic glycosides called taxiphyllin and triglochinin, the latter averaging up to anywhere from 0.3 to 3.8 grams per 100 grams of dried grass. It is found at high levels during the new growth of leaves in the spring, and in the late summer of a dry August. It also varies according to where it takes up residence. It peaks on freshwater sites at 3.8 grams but on salty sites it drops to 0.3 and doesn't exceed 0.9 grams. This tells me that the cyanogenic glycoside content varies greatly. It is more concentrated at times when the plant is vulnerable: when its tender, young shoots are so appealing after the winter, and during dry periods when water is scarce and, no doubt, the herbivores are hungry again.

However, containing cyanogenic glycosides doesn't mean that the plants contain actual hydrogen cyanide. These are natural plant chemicals that *can* convert to hydrogen cyanide if they need to. I also learnt that the 'hydrogen cyanide generating potential' in partially submerged sea arrowgrass is only one fifth to one half of the value obtained for stunted plants on dry, caked ground. So the toxicity is much lower when the plants get wet regularly and much higher when there is drought and over-grazing.

Plants are not stupid. They have been doing chemistry for around 3,500 million years. They are master alchemists! Plants have a vested interest in this science, as they can't run away. However, most self-respecting plants do not go around fully armed with toxic chemicals all the time. In some cases, this tactic would harm their own tissues, and what a stressful existence to be constantly armed. So what most plants do is to assemble the building blocks of a defence system – in this case a poisonous gas – and activate the defence system with a 'trigger' enzyme when attacked or munched. When the right enzyme, in this instance β-glucosidase, activates the cyanogenic glycoside it makes hydrogen cyanide.

Primarily this is veterinary research as farmers are worried about grazing cattle on poisonous plants. So most of the studies on arrow-grasses have been done with cows in mind and not humans. Cows do not have stomachs like ours. They have a *rumen*. Unlike us, their food isn't broken down with acid but rather composted by bacteria. This is a longer process and requires more time, hence the multiple sacs in the rumen. When a cow eats arrowgrass, the triglochinin is broken down by a chemical reaction with the water in its rumen by microorganisms, and this reaction produces the hydrogen cyanide. Horses, who don't have a rumen or multiple stomachs, are rarely (if ever) affected by plants containing cyanogenic glycosides. Their digestive system does not easily convert glycosides to free cyanide.

For a cow, a fatal dose of fresh sea arrowgrass would be around 0.5 per cent of the ruminant's body weight if eaten in one sitting – it's not cumulative. On that basis, if a 70-kilo person had the digestive system of a cow, they could be in trouble at 350 grams, if they had picked this grass from a freshwater marsh at the start of spring or the end of a dry, parched summer. A packet of cut chives in a supermarket varies between 20 and 30 grams. So your lethal dose – if you were a 70-kilo cow-person – would be around seventeen 20-gram packets (or eleven

30-gram packets) eaten in a single sitting. I guess for someone who *really* loves coriander . . . But that's irrelevant as humans do not have bovine rumens. I suppose if you drank eleven cans of Red Bull in a row or ate seventeen deep-pan pizzas in one sitting, you'd be pretty ill. I think this is the trouble with a lot of 'social media science'; without context or wisdom to discern the truths behind 'facts', we sometimes miss the big picture. This is when errors occur and are then repeated so often online that we frequently believe things that aren't accurate.

Mindful of this I put the two handfuls into my basket and carry on walking across the merse.

As I cross the flat expanse, I feel my bare feet bounce a little. I have left my socks and boots behind a rock to be collected on the way back. The plants underfoot now are succulents, protecting themselves from the harsh, dry saline environment by storing plenty of water in their tissues. Not only are they soft underfoot but they are also crunchy, moist and deliciously tasty – with just a hint of salt – as I absent-mindedly chew on them. I love going barefoot; it grounds me directly to the earth, bringing back the freedom of my Kenyan childhood, and heightens my awareness of the land beneath my feet. Each footfall now lands on lunch. Rosettes of wild plantain, branching bunches of sea blite, buds of sea aster. After the dry leaves of land plants in their summer mode, these taste fresh, crisp and deeply satisfying. As I jump the channels where the tide has encroached into the merse, carving narrow passages that undercut the rootstocks along the fragile edge, I am careful not to slip. Mud squidging between my toes is one thing; being knee deep in it with the feeling of sinking even further is another.

The bay where the sea and the river meet comes into focus. Here you cannot tell the one from the other. The mud flats are now studded with spikes of vibrant green that look like miniature saguaro cacti from a Western movie. Marsh samphire. As much as I love it I cannot understand why this has become the only marsh vegetable represented in supermarkets. I don't often visit them but have occasionally seen samphire in the summer, lonely in a clear plastic box, flown in from Israel. Around me are acres of merse brimming with native, local, in-season salt marsh vegetables.

Using my hand shears I cut a bagful, careful to leave plenty of spikes. They are annuals that will produce seed for the following year's harvest. There is nothing careless in the way that I harvest. A greedy free-for-all approach will decimate the marsh. Judicious thinning allows the neighbouring plants to grow larger and more healthy. What nature gives so freely comes with a requirement for reciprocal respect.

Along the edge of the promontory as I thread my way back, I cut some sea wormwood; curly and as white as bleached bones in the sun. Crushing it between my fingers releases the most intense, heady fragrance. I use it as a herb and a little goes a long way. Sea wormwood is related to wormwood of absinthe fame; mugwort that aids shamanic flight; Sweet Annie used to treat Lyme disease; and southernwood. Traditionally these Artemisias were used to treat malaria and parasites. Sea wormwood would also make a good insect repellent but I mostly use bog myrtle on my skin, preferring the fragrance. It reminds me of the West Indian bay tree that was used to scent linen – another childhood evocation. I have little need of garden insecticides as, by avoiding chemicals and creating wild copses for nesting, it is full of bug-eating birds. However, there are a few roses that grow in a bed that separates my home from the wild jungle below, and sometimes they need the help of a wormwood spray if the wasps aren't doing aphid patrol properly.

The final plant that I harvest today is orache. Well ... plants plural. Spear-leaved orache, narrow-leaved orache and Babington's orache all intermingle where the beach meets the marram grass. It is hard to tell one from the other sometimes, but they are all unmistakably members of the goosefoot family with their splayed arrow-shaped leaves and silver-white powder coating. Steamed with a little butter, they are a heavenly vegetable – not dissimilar to spinach but without the 'iron' overtones. Picking them is immensely satisfying as they grow thickly, a few feet deep in places, so it takes no time at all to harvest a bundle. Although they shrink down considerably when cooking, I have enough to last the week and, being used to harsh coastal conditions, they keep very well in the fridge.

The walk back feels longer under the weight of the basket and I'm tired by the time I get home. However, plants are best prepared when they are fresh, so they're all rinsed and prepped straight away.

Matt has been making *mysost* from the whey left over from creating the nettle, thistle and sorrel cheeses. Waste not want not. The whey boils down evenly on the induction hob until a crystallised paste is left, whipped into softness. This salty yet caramelised spread is like a sort of Marmite cheese. Great on acorn crackers and, dehydrated, sprinkled as a savoury seasoning over food. I finally put my feet up – with some oatcakes, mysost and freshly pickled samphire – before falling asleep on the sofa in a tired but contented coma.

# CHAPTER TWENTY

# SUMMER SOLSTICE

*'Very generous things, plants. We don't deserve them, really.'*

Christopher Hedley, Medical Herbalist

## SUMMER SOLSTICE

*Cairnpapple Hill, 21 June*

The solstice was at 4.30 a.m. and marks the longest day of the year. Today was busy and long; on Zoom at my computer. Focusing on those with chronic illness, listening and being truly present for them, uses both mental and emotional energy. Walking up Cairnpapple Hill this evening, the light still feels like mid-afternoon. The air is clean and I am acutely aware of the oxygen. Climbing the slopes above the respiring beeches I can breathe again.

The sky is clear, and the view stretches out to the North Sea in the east, the mountains of the Highlands to the north, and Goat Fell – the highest peak – on the Isle of Arran in the west. It's a special place connecting us to our ancestors some 5,000 years ago. Twenty-four large post holes stud the henge, which is the circular indentation of an earth enclosure that surrounds a ditch. They probably once housed ancient oak trunk pillars, spanned by massive wooden lintels.

Scotland's 'Woodhenge' rather than a 'Stonehenge'. In the centre were hearths, possibly used for ceremonial fires as people gathered here on the hill.

I wonder what spiritual significance or emotional connection our indigenous ancestors had to the land. When you stand on Cairnpapple Hill at dawn, on the spring and autumn equinoxes, and face the east, you see the sun rise first over Traprain Law, then Arthur's Seat, then Huly Hill in a straight line. Some people believe paths – used for millennia – that join prominent geological features, celestial bodies at significant times, and ancient monuments, demarcate a sacred landscape that developed a powerful ancestral significance. The 'Lothian Line' joins three of these natural equidistant 'sacred sites': Cairnpapple Hill, Arthur's Seat and Traprain Law – the latter hillfort the home of mythical King Loth.

The place name for our county, West Lothian, may come from Lugus – a pan-Celtic warrior god and the Celtic god of trade. Other versions of his name are Lug, Lugh (Irish), Lleu or Llew (Welsh), and Hlot or Ljot (Norse). Another theory is that Lothian is named after King Lot (Loth), the king of Lothian, Orkney, and sometimes Norway in Arthurian legend. In Gaelic, the pronunciation of Lugh sounds like Loth. Whether King Loth was named after Lugh, or whether he was the god himself, has been lost to the mists of time.

Cairnpapple was an important place. There were five phases of major use with several building additions. It ended up as an enormous cairn with concentric rings of pits, ditching and banking. From an archaeological perspective, ditches are practical things usually dug for defence or drainage but we don't know the influence of religious beliefs. Some hypothesise that the ditch, which is – impractically – inside rather than outside the earthen rampart, was a torus to channel energy.[1] If you believe that the Sun God Lugh (colloquially Loth) sent rays of energy down to Earth, then at the equinox – a significant, hence powerful time – it's not inconceivable that you might dig a circular irrigation-style ditch opening to the sunrise in the east, to trap or concentrate that energy. Or even to corral and return the sunbeams to the east, to start a new day.

Philip Coppens, an ancient history journalist, writes:

*[Loth] played with the land that he had created at the beginning of
time, perhaps by 'walking it', following the tradition of the Australian
Dreamtime. What other name could be given to this land than the
land of Loth — the Lothians? The three sacred hills of the Lothians
were there to reveal the power of that sun god, and life was to be lived
accordingly.[2]*

The site spans both Bronze Age and early Christian ritual burial and
cremations, their traces found in the various cairns. Two stone axe
heads from Wales and Cumbria were unearthed, along with beaker
pots, a bone pin, club and a ritual mask. Who were these people, and
what did they do up here on this windswept hilltop?

We will never know, yet I feel deeply connected to them
through the land.

The fields up here have been grazed for centuries, creating a habitat
known as ancient grassland. It is in full bloom, delighting my soul.
Tiny wild pansies — or heartsease as I know them — peek through the
short grass, sporting purple petals behind bright yellow, with dark
markings vaguely reminiscent of miniature faces. In herbal medicine,
they rebalance dry conditions of the body. Heath bedstraw cascades
down the western slope in a froth of white. Tiny heath speedwell,
once known as *thé d'Europe*, lifts its tiny, soft, violet-blue flowers above
the clover, vying with the red spangles of sheep's sorrel in flower,
untidy anthers of sweet vernal grass, and the poky brown flower of
field woodrush.

Lying on the grass, under the warm sun, I am nose-to-leaf in a
minuscule world throbbing to the vibration of industrious bumble-
bees. Brome grass flowers flutter like wind mobiles, while fescues
arch over them. Dark brown plantain heads strike a puritan note
against the riotous, dancing parade of bird's-foot trefoil in yellow
headdresses.

I pick heath speedwell, heath bedstraw and heartsease for herbal tea – to capture this long summer's day in a solstice cup. I am feeling so much better than I was three weeks ago. My skin is no longer dry and my hair shines healthily again. The sunlight filters through to my bones and I slowly feel my energy return.

## GIANT ROOTS

*Daisylea, 28 June*

I'm drooling over photos of big roots. A new book arrived today, *People's Plants: A Guide to Useful Plants of Southern Africa*, about the edible and medicinal uses of South African plants.[3] In it are pictures of smiling people holding roots as thick as forearms and cradling tubers the size of babies. I'm in awe and very jealous! We have nothing this size in the British Isles. My lawn has lots of wild carrot, about to come into bloom, but I know from bitter experience that their roots are thin, fibrous and tough. This year, one has escaped into a herb bed dug into a fine tilth, weeded, and prepared for roses, daylilies and herbs. This intruder's foliage is four times the scale of its lawn relatives and my mouth is already watering at the thought of the enormous, juicy carrot monster that it may be hiding under its frothy leaves.

One of my favourite scenes from the comedy series *Blackadder* is when the servant Baldrick invests all of Lord Blackadder's money in a giant turnip.[4] Its hilarity has now taken on a deeper meaning for me. To the medieval peasantry, who were often hungry, the possession of a ridiculously enormous, swollen tuber would have induced ecstasy!

I dig up the giant wild carrot. Sure enough, the roots are as hard as stone. Oh, well. I chop up the foliage instead and use it as a substitute for parsley. Supper is baked trout with sorrel and field mint sauce, oyster mushrooms with chopped wild carrot herb, and steamed willowherb shoots that are only just the tender side of woody.

# THE COAST

*East Lothian, 29 June*

My new discovery is that goat's-beard buds are delicious! Reminiscent of tall, elegant dandelions but with leaves on their stems like a hawk-weed, they love the sandy soil along the coast. I gather their seed heads to spread them around, doing some stealth gardening. The late spring has also affected the coastal plants. The oraches are a month behind and the samphire is not as branched as this time last year. The grasses, however, have been growing fast to catch up and are heavy with large grain heads. I pick a few kilos of samphire, some narrow-leaved orache and sea blite. Walking back through the woods, I collect lady's bedstraw for my next cheese experiment as I've heard that there *might* be some more excess goat's milk available soon.

I carry on down to Barns Ness. Here is a most beautiful sandy wildflower meadow. In the sunny afternoon it's ablaze with the vibrant blue of viper's bugloss, bright yellow potentilla, and patches of purple creeping thyme in full bloom. I was hoping to find some fairy ring champignon mushrooms but it is too dry, so I just enjoy the walk. Following the path round, I ascend a steep mound and the dune heath habitat changes. A narrow deer path winds its way between a forest of elder trees in full bloom, the air so heady that with each breath I am inhaling pure elderflower. It's a sensory heaven. I make a mental note to return in the autumn when they are laden with juicy purple-black berries – the main ingredient of my pontack sauces and elixirs that bring flavour to the whole year. Protected from the deer by a skirt of spiky gorse, this fragrant corridor is sheer delight as I walk the narrow path, thigh-high in the flowering grasses whose seed heads shine silver in the warm peace of the evening sun.

Old, lichen-encrusted blocks of granite are stacked skilfully in a wall that snakes along the brow of the hill. The sudden rumble of a loud truck on the other side reminds me of the road signs I saw earlier for a cement works. Curious, I look over the wall. I shouldn't have. It's shocking. Such complete and utter devastation that it sears the core of my being. The bare pit is so vast and so deep that the raped earth is no longer even screaming. The contrast could not be greater between this idyll of nature on one side of the wall and the desecration on the other.

I am still reeling from the shock of that gaping wound in the earth at the cement works.

I google the company behind it. They do have a published environmental policy. I read that in May, their cement plants changed over to bags containing 50 per cent recycled plastic that can be further recycled (if builders do decide to sort their waste rather than just chucking it all in a skip as usual). But this plant produces 1 million tons of cement a year!

I have to commend them for having an environmental policy at all, but the irony is not lost on me that on 18 February they ran a competition 'to win two bee hotels – providing solitary bees with a comfy home, nutritious food, and a refreshing water supply, as well as 10 packets of wildflower seeds to sow at home'.[5] Ironic because the cement works is an example of the habitat destruction which is affecting bee decline. On one side of the wall an ancient meadow, and on the other, a massive open gash in the earth's surface, now stripped and completely devoid of habitat. The company's press release about the bee hotel competition states:

> This February Tarmac is spreading the simple message 'bee kind' to help raise awareness of the UK's declining bee population, which is having a hugely negative impact on the environment.
>
> With over 250 species in the UK, bees play a vital role in pollinating more than 180,000 plant species and crops. However, factors like climate change, pesticides, diseases, **loss of wildflower meadows and other habitats**, are causing a dramatic decline in bee numbers – these pollinators need some love.

They clearly do understand the issues. Reading more on their website, I am glad that they're thinking about sustainability such as what fuel and bags they will use, spreading seeds occasionally and installing the odd beehive.[6] Is it in proportion to the devastation already wreaked on nature? No, of course not.

Humans have to have houses, I get it, as well as schools, hospitals, workplaces, roads and runways. But surely we can cut down on the use of cement? However, I remember when we built our house, we wanted to stand it on small concrete pads and not a large concrete slab foundation. The engineers wouldn't let us. It was painful watching the mixer lorry pour it in.

I find it difficult to eat this evening but take a little soup Matt has made from fish bone stock, with wild carrot roots, fennel flowers and sea salt.

## ELDERFLOWERS

*Linlithgow, 1 July*

As soon as I wake up I make some marsh woundwort tea. I'm covered in weals, bitten to distraction by fleas. For the first time ever, they've infested the ferrets. Before breakfast, I clean out the entire hutch and run, liberally dusting everything with diatomaceous earth – an ecological alternative to chemical 'cides'. Marsh woundwort is the closest plant I've discovered to an antihistamine and is brilliant for insect bite reactions. I never intended to have a pet, but when I met Marley the ferret, who needed re-homing, I fell in love and she never left. Getting to know an animal intimately teaches you about other forms of intelligence, knowledge and consciousness. Perhaps for some people it's an easier first step to take before understanding plant intelligence. The whole of nature, the living world, is infused with cognitive agility. All you need to do to become aware of it is to stop and watch, observe and notice, and still your monkey mind for an hour.

I'm amazed at how telepathic I've become with Duffy, Marley's daughter. When she was heavily pregnant with her first litter a strange thing happened. I had been out all day and looked in on her as soon as I returned. I noticed she had started labouring; I stroked her head, then took my hand away to give her the peace and quiet that most animals need at this time. She grabbed my hand and pulled it back into her nest. She didn't want me to leave and would repeat this whenever I tried to sneak away. Her labour took several hours longer than I expected when, finally bracing her back paws against my fingers as leverage, she squeezed out the first kit in the early hours of the morning. Ferrets are very protective and not afraid to nip anyone who comes too close. My hand was Duffy's exception, always pulled in to share the nest, and she let me handle the kits from the moment they were born. I swear I often know what she is thinking and I think it's mutual!

It's a late brunch of cold roast venison with oyster mushrooms cooked with wild garlic and orache in a rosehip reduction and mushroom ketchup although Géza is eating a Hungarian *babgulyás* (bean stew) with fried chorizo that smells amazing. We're then off out to Linlithgow picking elderflowers. Géza makes a huge batch of elderflower wine every year. After they have matured for five or six years they are excellent, especially as he has perfected the technique of not making them too sweet. I'm also picking honeysuckle flowers as the buds open daily. Honeysuckle mead is a house favourite.

Later, back home, we both pick white clover from our glorious edible lawn. I'll dry it for tea (the red clover has gone brown already). The dog rose hanging over the rough-sawn pergola is also laden with delicate pink petals. They are already falling like confetti in each breeze, so the pressure is on to collect them before they go. With delicate flowers, you normally get about 150 to 200 grams of dried petals for each kilo of fresh blooms, so we have to pick a lot to keep us in herbal tea for a year.

I am down another dress size now.

# CHAPTER TWENTY-ONE

# FLOWERS AND FRUIT

'The fairest thing in nature, a flower,
still has its roots in earth and manure.'

D. H. Lawrence, *Pansies*

## FORBIDDEN FLOWERS

*Hillhouse, 2 July*

Did plants create flowers to entrance us as well as the bees? I am lying on the grass in the sunshine at the back of Christina's house, watching baby Maya asleep on the rug, in a little white sunhat under a parasol. Just over three months old now she has filled out into a good-natured, chubby cherub full of smiles, with a calm, even temperament. It is fascinating watching her intelligence develop and her consciousness unfurl like the overhanging peonies. I love the sweet intimacy of mother and daughter, despite the current lack of speech! She is spark out in the drowsy heat, her eyes shut but her eyelids quivering as if she is dreaming. The small garden's borders are in full bloom and their perfume hangs heavily in the air. I wonder if she dreams of giant flowers and butterflies? It is hot and I'm watching bumble bees at eye level drowsily exploring the daisies in the grass. The garden is beautiful although, unlike the bees, we can't live on flowers. For lunch, I pick some daisies and decorate a field mushroom and nettle frittata, hidden under a heap of lightly steamed samphire.

Back home, in the cool of the late afternoon, I pick the open heads of old-fashioned cabbage roses. I have been growing some of a heady-scented old variety for a company that make botanical extracts. They are one of the few plants in my garden that aren't wild. Then more elderflower, some valerian leaves for salads, but I leave the foxgloves behind. As pretty as they are, these are toxic; they yield the drug digitalis that can slow your heart right down!

As I sit with Foxglove, she whispers on the evening breeze. 'These herbal teas you're making with all the flowers, they look so innocent, don't they? Who would have thought what power they could have?' She draws herself up to her full height as she speaks, towering over me.

The foxglove is, of course, correct. We tend to think of herbal teas as gentle infusions. Yet, at the right strength for a specific condition and constitution, they can be as strong as any other medicine. For gastritis, take marshmallow leaf to coat and calm an inflamed gut lining. Add meadowsweet to balance the stomach acidity and chamomile to soothe the irritation. Balance it with a little liquorice root to harmonise the blend. For swift relief from dysentery, boil bramble leaves and stem bark into a decocted tea.

The name 'foxglove' came from 'folk's gloves', the folk in question being the fairies. Sadly, 'magic' was the reason often used to persecute people like me, with herbal knowledge and a sensitivity to the other-than-human world, as witches. Some accusations were by clergy protecting a patriarchal religion; 90 per cent of those accused of demonic possession were women. Sometimes accusations of witchcraft were a form of revenge, one way to get back at a friend or neighbour for a perceived harm. Much of the oppression was about power – a deadly misogynistic persecution. In Scotland, historians have identified about 3,837 people accused of witchcraft between 1563 and 1736 (when the Scottish Witchcraft Act was repealed).[1] There were probably more than this, as the information appears mainly in trial records. Around 67 per cent were executed, usually by strangling or burning at the stake. Of those identified as witches, 84 per cent were women. Why *are* witches usually women? A third of them were my age and a third came from the Lothians. It's chilling.

Edinburgh University's online Survey of Scottish Witchcraft and their interactive map gives an astonishing amount of detailed information.[2] Less than a mile down the road from me, here in West Lothian, a witch called Andro Turnbull lived in Hillhouse Cottage. He was detained in Linlithgow on 2 May 1617, the day after Gaelic May Day, Beltane, but there the record irritatingly peters out.

As I walk down the lane to pick goldenrod along the burn, I remember and am grateful for the freedoms that we enjoy today. It is easy to forget how privileged we are to have freedom of expression, the right to roam, the right to vote. It was only when I was twelve, which doesn't feel so long ago to me, that British women stopped having to get permission from their husband or father to open a bank account! There are laws to protect us from prejudice, yet it still exists – some of it blatant, some of it very subtle. It targets race, religion, class, gender, sexuality, politics, dress, accent and many other areas as we try to shoehorn each other into the normative. In this age of polarisation, debate becomes vicious very quickly. Are we less tolerant or does social media amplify our differences in a way that far outstrips traditional media? Not everyone fits into a convenient formula and perhaps if more of us re-examined the world through the lens of queer theory, 'to startle, to surprise, [and] to help us think what has not yet been thought', to quote American theorist, David Halperin,[3] we would be more tolerant of all the differences between us.

The flowers have so much to teach us about variety. Their diversity has developed because of their need to work in partnership with animal pollinators. Evolution is the new revolution.

# FRUIT

*Torphichen, 4 July*

Matt was out this morning with a local botany recording group known as the Foliage Fraternity and has returned with wild strawberries.

A member of the group noticed the plants sprawling across a sunny corner, warmed by the worn, lichenised churchyard stones in Torphichen Preceptory. Matt already knew that they grew there and tried to distract the group with an orchid. To no avail. They swooped on the fruit like a flock of hungry pigeons and he feared they would never move on. But, when he went back after the walk was over, there were so many yet undiscovered that he has come home with a full kilo of wild strawberries.

I cannot even begin to describe how delicious they taste. I haven't had fresh fruit since 22 April when the last of the windfall apples ran out. Luckily, green leafy wild vegetables contain high amounts of vitamin C but even though wild violet leaves have five times the vitamin C content of an orange (per 100 grams), there is just no comparison when it comes to the flavour and texture of fruit versus leaves!

I want to cram them into my mouth by the handful in a frenzied orgy of delight. It takes all of my self-restraint to divide them into two bowls, drizzle birch sap syrup over them and take two spoons from the drawer. I eat slowly, savouring each mouthful, with a smile on my face to rival the Cheshire cat. A thought creeps in: if the strawberries are ripe, then the blaeberries are not far behind them!

After eating, I find a small tub and pull on my wellies. It's hot and dry but blaeberry picking often requires standing in ditches. Sure enough, on the back road, there are tiny purple globes peeking out from under the leaves of the bushes that cling to the high bank, backing onto the gorse hedge whose flowers have disappeared over the last month. Many are not yet ripe but I blissfully pick around 80 grams, oozing fructose in the warm sunshine with buzzing bumble bees for company.

The Scottish blaeberry is a wild bilberry, a diminutive relative of the blueberry. It is a fraction of the size but makes up for its lack of bulk with an intense flavour that vastly out-competes its watery sibling. Over the next few weeks it's going to be really important to check all the fruit patches almost daily.

Supper is wild strawberries again. This time with a naughty scoop of home-made elderflower ice cream. I could not resist making the tiniest portion from the first of the elderflowers, a little birch sap syrup and some of the excess Achray Farm goat's milk with carragheen gel. I gave the rest of the tub away. Temptation is too hard to resist when you know that something exquisite is close at hand!

## SUGAR

*Daisylea, 5 July*

I found one of my son Callum's old school notebooks when I was tidying up this morning. I read it over a cup of herbal tea and some cold venison with samphire, chicken-of-the-woods and oyster mushrooms. Callum must have been about eight or nine years old and studying 'Chemistry in Nature', judging by the title. He's written:

> *Plants build up their substance in the process called photosynthisis [sic]. This is a chemical combination of carbon dioxide and water to form water and sugar. Essential to this process is a catalyst called chlorofil [sic] and is active [activated?] by sunlight. Plant sugars are formed into starch and cellulose. Starch and cellulose are all carbohydrates. In man, sugar is absorbed by the blood and the sun's warmth is released to give him energy.*

I love that last line, 'and the sun's warmth is released to give him energy'. It's a good reminder that starch is really winter sugar for giving us vitality in the cold weather or monsoon rains when a plant's life force has gone back below the ground. In the warmer months or dry season, plants are stashing sugar as cellulose. This provides fibre but is pretty indigestible. On average, the tender leaves we eat contain 10 to 12 per cent cellulose, depending on how tough they are.

Pure sugar is rare in nature and seldom in season, yet sugar is now served up every day of the year. In the wild calendar of Western Europe, it is only in season during the summer months as a component of seasonal fruits. The first wild strawberries appear in Scotland at the end of June, followed by wild raspberries and gooseberries in July, then bilberries, cranberries, rowan, blackberries (bramble) and crabapples into the autumn, with sloes, hawthorn and rosehips still lingering on the bushes at the start of the winter in November.

Where would I get sugar out of season? Perhaps honey. The hives are full by the end of the summer and the bees live off the stored honey during the winter. You might only find a trickle left in the spring. Perhaps tree sap syrup, but only if you'd invented a sturdy enough pot to boil 10 litres for hours to get just 100 ml of birch sap syrup. It's so precious that you'd dispense it just a teaspoonful at a time. (Incidentally 'birch sap syrup' autocorrects to 'bitch slap syrup' so I've learnt to be doubly careful posting anything about it on social media!)

The truth is that sugar is a seasonal product and should only be available for a limited amount of time – mainly as fructose – during the summer and autumn months, when we are at our most active. So even the 'allowed' RDA* of 30 grams a day all year round is completely out of season in the winter and spring. The consequences are bleakly clear: a growing epidemic of corpulence and diabetes.

I'm reading a lot about sugar in the news these days as the major player in the obesity crisis. Specifically, processed sugar from sugar cane, sugar beet and corn. It's hidden in many of the processed foods that people eat: from bottled and canned drinks, to microwave meals, cakes, biscuits and sauces, not to mention chocolates and treats. The thought of them makes me feel mildly nauseous.

It occurs to me that in nature, on a foraging diet, sugar is impossible to come by in the volume that we eat today. In the not-so-distant

---

* RDA stands for the government's Recommended Daily Allowance.

past, the principle of seasonality applied just as much to sugar as it does to every other food that we eat. However, it's now available all day, every day and everywhere, from the twenty-four-hour petrol station to the cinema foyer, positioned by the till to remind us that we might need a quick fix to fuel our addiction whether we're driving or watching a movie. And it is highly addictive. This once rare treat hits the body chemistry like nothing else.

As a forager, my main source of sugar occurs naturally in fruits, but just how much could I find to eat and for how long?

I try to imagine a twelve-strong tribe gathering berries. They'd certainly eat a few mouthfuls on the spot. After all, who can resist picking a tasty strawberry and putting it straight into their mouth! Perhaps they would collect some to take back to the camp. This would be a pleasurable way to pass a morning but it's unlikely they'd pick more than a small basket each of tiny berries. Wild strawberries are a fraction of the size of modern strawberry cultivars. They take time to harvest, they're not all ripe at the same time, and the plants are spread out over a hillside — not packed densely into one area in regimented rows. If Matt and I picked a kilo of wild strawberries in one go we'd feel triumphant.

Back at camp, they'd share their finds with other members of the tribe. A feast of berries has to be eaten straight away as they don't keep. Some of them become mouldy in just one day without a fridge. Perhaps, in a bumper 'mast' year when berries are prolific, they'd lay some out on stones in the sunshine and dry them into 'raisins', with the squashed ones at the bottom of the basket forming a strip of fruit 'leather'. The sugars would preserve these for quite a while if they could resist the temptation to eat them!

Realistically, say four of the tribe each pick a basket of black-berries to share, that's four baskets amongst twelve, so a third of a basket each. I'm estimating that each person gets through 10 kilos of berries per year, across all the wild berries. A plastic punnet of blackberries in a supermarket is 200 grams so 10 kilos is the equivalent of fifty plastic punnets of berries per year. Assuming most of those are consumed across the four months from June to

September, that's an average of 83 grams – under half a punnet – of berries per day over a 120-day period. I calculate the sugar content of a daily ration of blackberries: a daily sugar intake of 4 grams for 120 days. Currently, our government advises a limit of *30 grams of sugar a day* for 365 days of the year. There's a massive discrepancy between our sugar intake now (mainly refined) and our ancestral sugar intake from fruit!

There are the tree fruits as well: the main ones are cherries, plums, apples and pears. The wild versions that our ancestors would have known were not the big juicy fruits of today. Bird cherry and damson plum are small with a larger stone than cultivated varieties and they ripen on the bush or tree. Crabapples, pears, quinces and medlars are usually small and hard until bletted (softened by the first frosts). These keep better into the cold months – I have found quite edible crabapples in December – and can be used to supplement food in winter. However, even if I doubled my 4-gram-a-day fruit sugar intake, and extended the season to the end of December, my intake would still be under a third of the current RDA.

Occasionally, an intrepid forager ancestor found and raided a wild bees' nest for honey. There is rock art evidence that wild honey was collected as long ago as 40,000 years, with straw or pottery hives made from around 7,000 BCE. According to the British Beekeepers Association, bees in most modern hives can produce on average 27 kilos of honey in a good season.[4] The Natural Beekeeping Trust estimates that in a tree hive, wild bees will produce between 15 and 22 kilos.[5] Traditionally, in the wild a third is left for the bees, so a yield of 10 to 15 kilos is the most common, and for my theoretical forager tribe that's about a kilo per person or three jars of honey, perhaps in clay pots, to ration over a year. We've no idea how many wild hives our ancestors would have found and taken each year. The nests are made high in trees and the bees will defend them. It's a dangerous business.

Regardless, eating sugar out of season, even when it's within the 'daily allowance', has a disastrous effect on our bodies. The funny thing is that I actually don't crave sugar at all, despite wondering how I was going to feel without even the occasional chocolate treat. More importantly Matt, who checks his blood sugar weekly due to inherited diabetes, has found that his levels have consistently stayed in the normal range since March.

## DRYING BERRIES

*Torphichen, 6 July*

Matt checked Torphichen again and picked another 400 grams of wild strawberries. We should really dry some in the trusty dehydrator for the winter months ahead, but the thrill of eating fresh fruit is just too exciting to exercise self-control.

I wonder about going up to Inverness on Saturday. There's a woodland I know full of wild bilberries, lingonberries and cranberries. It's a long, wasted drive, however, if they're not yet ripe. I would prefer to keep my petrol use low and my food miles local.

There are a lot of blaeberries accumulating in the fridge now, from various forays out to nearby bushes. It makes sense to dry some for snacks to eat once the berries have passed.

After fried scarletina bolete mushrooms for lunch, with a venison 'Bob-burger', and a salad of vetch shoots that taste just like pea tendrils, I pack the dehydrator. Berries on the bottom layers and flowers on the top ones. Trays of white clover, interspersed with dog rose, eglantine and cabbage rose petals, honeysuckle, elderflower, mullein flowers. I'm capturing the essence of summer for herbal teas later in the year. I set it to a low heat so I don't burn off their volatile oils. Nevertheless, some always escapes. It smells divine.

## MUSHROOMS ARRIVE

*Torphichen, 8 July*

Two days after the last pick and Torphichen yields another 600 grams of wild strawberries. That's 2 kilos in total so far from that sunny churchyard corner. The bilberry total in comparison is just 240 grams at this point – but they are just at the start of their season.

I have my favourite brittlegill mushrooms called 'charcoal burners' for breakfast, cooked up with wild garlic and wild carrot leaves. Although the wild garlic is dying back outside in the heat, the succulent juicy stems have kept incredibly well in the fridge. Not having learnt my lesson last month, I dug up another wild carrot yesterday, chosen for its glorious, abundant thick foliage. However, although the root underneath was about the size of a domestic carrot, it was so woody that even the small lateral roots were inedible. I'm so disappointed. I'm really in the mood for a juicy roasted carrot.

Recently I've been longing for large chunky, crunchy vegetables: carrots, courgettes, gherkins; the wild world in Scotland does not yield such delights. There is all the foliage that I separated from the root, though, and it makes a perfect substitute for parsley – fresh and dried.

The charcoal burners have just come out this week, but when you're looking hard, there are actually mushrooms all year round and not just in the autumn. The brittlegill (Russula) family are easily identified by their mainly chalk white crumbly stems and brittle gills, that shatter like flaked almonds at the mildest touch. They also have coloured tops in a wide array of colours: from ochre yellow, scarlet, claret, burgundy, purple to green and, in the case of the charcoal burner, silver, grey, pink and purple all together in one cap – giving it the appearance of a dying coal. Of course, there's always one person who is the exception to the rule, the black sheep of the family. In the brittlegill family, the charcoal burner is the only one that has flexible rather than brittle gills!

## MATT'S BIRTHDAY

*Bathgate Hills, 10 July*

A jar of wild honey arrived in the Saturday post.

Despite my rootless past, I, who have never fully belonged

anywhere, have found my 'tribe' through my love of the natural world. In three years' time, I will have been in Scotland for a full half of my life. I feel as though I have finally put down roots. As with the plants, these roots allow me new growth, but it is rootedness in my community that causes the blossom. A flower is nothing, if not appreciated by the eye of a beholder – whether bee or me.

This afternoon I make acorn and cranberry cakes to spread with the gifted honey. They are birthday cakes for Matt. I offer one to Géza who accepts just a half 'to try'. He rarely eats with us now, saying he doesn't want to deprive us of our hard-won finds when he can so easily go to the supermarket! This is one downside of having different diets as I have always enjoyed the camaraderie of shared mealtimes. Early evening in the Bathgate Hills, we both go out and pick even more wild strawberries. We also fill a huge basket with charcoal burners, along the lane running down past the 'tribute stone circle' above the old silver mines.

## LADY'S MANTLE

*Daisylea, 12 July*

The sun is blazing down and all the flowers are in bloom: roses, yellow fennel, common hogweed. The 'lawn' is a mass of snowy white clover. I pick and dry them for teas in the winter.

Today I also pick a basket of lady's mantle leaves. It's rarely eaten as it doesn't have much taste and is very dry in the mouth. A consequence of the rapid weight loss since I started my wild food year is that the skin on my stomach, arms and legs is looking baggy. Lady's mantle leaves have some unique properties and I'm going to make an infused oil to tighten everything up.

The botanical name of lady's mantle is *Alchemilla vulgaris* – from the medieval Latin word *alchimia* and Arabic *alkemelych* meaning 'alchemy'. Our ancestors believed that dew from the leaves – that seemed to magically appear – could turn base metals into gold. It actually exudes beads of excess moisture through a process called 'guttation'. When the plant has already had enough water, and can't get rid of it by evaporation, it pumps the excess out through hydathodes – special water pores on the leaf margin. My Swiss cheese plant also does this if I give it too much to drink.

Lady's mantle's 'magic dew' looks like tiny pearls clinging to the serrated edge of the velvet leaves. They are sectioned and, turned upside down, reminiscent of a panelled Elizabethan cloak – an embroidered billowing over-*mantle* embellished with pearls and jewels. As a cosmetic, the leaf extract was thought to tighten, soften and moisturise the skin. A member of the Rosaceae family, lady's mantle leaves are certainly high in shrinking, tightening tannins. In Eastern Europe, this plant was known as the 'virginity herb': if a young lady thought she might be compromised on her wedding night, she would crush some leaves and pop them up inside her and her new husband would never know the difference!

There is no mention of this use in the UK in the older herbals that I've read. Perhaps British girls were beyond reproach! However, when you get to my age, lady's mantle is the perfect alternative for corrective cosmetic surgery. As well as making a fabulous anti-wrinkle eye cream and sorting out the chicken skin on your ageing neck, if you bruise the leaves with a rolling pin and bind them over your breasts every night, they will, according to the herbalist John Gerard, 'turn the dugs of an old maid into the paps of a maiden'. He also wrote in 1597, 'it keepeth downe maidens paps or dugs, and when they be too great or flaggye, it maketh them lesser or harder'.[6]

I bruise the leaves lightly and put them into a large jar, then cover them with sweet almond oil. As I'm not eating this, I've treated myself to the oil instead of using lard as in the old days. They will be left to infuse for the month before straining off the leaves. I then weigh the now vivid green oil, add 30 per cent of its weight in beeswax, and warm it gently in a bain-marie over hot water until the wax has melted. Off the gas so they don't evaporate, a few drops of rosemary essential oil act as an antioxidant, and it's poured into jars to set into a soft salve. Priceless!

# MIGRANTS

*Daisylea, 13 July*

Suddenly summer swallows arrive, swooping around the house, looking for nesting sites. The house martins have chucked their first brood out of the nest under the eaves. Perhaps they are planning a second. The still-fluffy youngsters sit on the gutter, cuddling together.

The grasses are flowering too and so great is the profusion of vegetation that the jungle completely hides our little stream, and you can't see a single house. Standing on the rickety wooden bridge, I could be forgiven for thinking I'm somewhere tropical. The ancient einkorn wheatberries have germinated and are now bearing small heads of grain. So einkorn would have grown in Scotland!

I'm still eating huge salads at the moment, even though many of the leaves are starting to get tough and bitter. Today I found some Good King Henry from the Amaranthaceae family related to fat hen, orache and quinoa. It tastes similar to spinach. I steamed the leaves to have with crispy wild rabbit, pulled off the bone, mixed with a little egg and fried. I adore these fresh greens and my appetite has grown as much as the plants have!

# BAREFOOT

*The Meadow, 14 July*

Overnight my mind has been tumbling like a hamster on a wheel pinned to the back of my brain. I find that, while I'm asleep, my brain carries on thinking about my patients, formulates their herbal prescriptions, writes poems, and ponders the big questions of the universe. Sometimes I wake exhausted but often I am more clear-headed then than at any other time of the day, my head full of answers to the challenges I face. It's now 5.45 and the sun is hinting – from behind Cairnpapple Hill – at the dawn of another golden day. In this quiet light I go outside and lie, face down, on the thick white mat of creeping clover that passes for a lawn. I have been longing to do this for days. It is cool, comforting and the smell of Gaïa is both sweet, verdant and slightly spicy as I inhale deeply. There is no barrier between us. No tarpaulin, rug, plastic, rubber, sole, tyre or other insulation.

A startled bumble bee still asleep outside its nest waves a leg at me. Its Fuzzy-Felt fur traps air and acts as insulation, helping it regulate its temperature and cope with cold mornings. However, without the warmth of the sun on its wings, it can only buzz at me. It cannot fly away. I make herbal tea freshly infused from the lawn and eat wild strawberries. Both are ethereal foods for the soul.

I have a friend who walks barefoot *all* the time. I get it.

This evening I fly to Poland for the long-awaited field trip with my friend, Łukasz Łuczaj. He is a professor at the Faculty of Biotechnology at the University of Rzeszów, where he heads the Department of Botany. Łukasz is a huge champion of meadows; he harvests unendangered ancient seed mixes every year, encouraging others to create new wildflower habitats. He has invited me on a field study to survey Polish meadows and to investigate some of the wild foods.

Although more people in the UK are planting them again, over the last century we have lost 97 per cent of our hay meadows because of industrial farming, urban sprawl and poor land management practices. Currently, just 1 per cent of Britain is still home to traditional meadows and grassland pasture.[7] Three quarters of these are less than 3 acres in size. That's just one and a half times bigger than a football pitch. You could fit seven and a half meadows into the Amazon Distribution Centre in Dunfermline alone!

I'm also keen to go as he has invited me to stay at his home. Pietrusza Wola is in the Dynowskie foothills of the southern Carpathians. Here Łukasz has created a wild garden on 17 hectares of land (nearly two of the aforesaid Amazon distribution centres). Just like the rewilding strategy behind my own 4-acre garden, he is creating as many habitats for native flora and fauna as possible. Part is ancient woodland set aside as a 'reserve'. There is managed coppice, a wooded meadow, and wildflower meadows. He's dug out three ponds and even scattered giant blocks of concrete from a dismantled bridge to create rock-like habitats. I am looking forward to seeing his progress and trying some traditional Polish foraged foods.

# CHAPTER TWENTY-TWO

# A POLISH SUMMER

*'Never say there is nothing beautiful in the world
anymore. There is always something to make you wonder
in the shape of a tree, the trembling of a leaf.'*

Albert Schweitzer, *For All That Lives*

## FIRST DAY IN POLAND

*Pietrusza Wola, 15 July*

I wake to a brilliant blue sky. Breakfast is a cup of marsh wound-wort tea and a handful of walnuts. Nut trees are abundant in southern Poland, especially walnuts. While they're not native, they are common self-sown feral trees and many people have a stash of autumn-ripened walnuts in their loft. I try cracking them with a stone on a quern and miss every third nut that skates across the floor! Having rationed nuts so carefully during the Scottish winter, it is wonderful to have the luxury of eating as many as I like.

Outside, in the garden surrounding Łukasz's traditional wooden cottage, the sun is already warming the land and insects are busy. Wildflowers are in full bloom in riotous profusion. Grapes burst out of the hedgerow: hard, green and yet to ripen but cheek-to-cheek with red raspberries that, ripened to perfection, are devoured by my hungry mouth! Elegant evening primroses and wild carrots are happy together on a bank of sandy soil surrounded by daisies – their 'day's-eyes' fully open to greet the sun. Spiky viper's bugloss corners the blue and purple patch with cornflowers and knapweed – the odd red field poppy peeking through. Everywhere is a cacophony of colour.

In the far corner, there is a loud humming. A swarm of ferociously busy honey bees, sucking the sweetness of a million white mulberries. This mulberry tree is the tree of Eden in this Polish paradise. I quickly learn that the bees do not like sharing with the greedy. They appear to have an in-built five-minute timer and exceeding their time limit results in a nasty sting. Twice! I learn fast.

At 2.30, the sky grows black and the heavens open. I sit in the protection of a little porch surrounded by a torrential downpour that reminds me of the East African monsoons of my childhood. I'm picking the seed heads off Velcro-like cleavers to make 'coffee' as Łukasz has never tried it. After toasting the bobbles to a nutty-brown, I boil it up in his hammered copper Turkish coffee pot. Delicious.

After the rain, we go for a drive, stopping to pick black pods of the bigflower vetch (*Vicia grandiflora*) growing wild along field edges. I shell them as Łukasz drives, popping out the little lentils inside. Early humans ate wild lentils *Lens culinaris* (aka *Ervum lens*) at least 13,000 years ago, judging by remains found in Greece's Franchthi Cave. Humans lived in this cave around 40,000 years ago. In Britain, we find *Vicia tetrasperma* (aka *Ervum tetraspermum*), the lentil vetch. I can see from the botanical names that they are related. These Polish bigflower vetches are even larger than our lentil vetch. I'm impressed.

The long grass is full of fat Roman snails. Łukasz explains they're illegal to gather out of season but he has some frozen ones for me, collected in May. I try to look grateful. I truly am when we find a wild cherry tree festooned with the most delicious red cherries. I spend the rest of the afternoon exploring his land.

For supper I cook slices of roe tenderloin with wild garlic,

juneberries, chanterelles and a scarletina bolete. Łukasz doesn't have
any fat saved up so I sear the meat in a hot pan, then sauté it in a little
water. A heap of fat hen and gallant soldier leaves are steamed as a
side and we garnish the dish with fermented saffron milkcaps. I am
very reassured. With sacks of nuts and the generosity of nature there
is plenty to eat under this warm, European sun.

## OUTWITTING THE BEES

*Rzepnik, 16 July*

Wild cherries for breakfast. A treat!

Round the back of the house, the path to the forest winds past
huge piles of logs, beckoning. I walk between two large clumps of
heart-leaf oxeye daisy. Its enormous golden flowers remind me of
elecampane. A million hoverflies and butterflies swarm adoringly
around it. I'm as captivated as Maya the first time Christina wound
up her musical crib mobile. I have never seen such a profusion of
butterflies. Not just in number, but in species variety as well. Brown
ones with thick cream and thin orange bands; sienna brown with
cream bands and delicate tracing; dusty suede brown with orange
checkerboard; fawn with brown and cream bullseyes; orange with
brown splodges; fluorescent lime green; whites with delicate green
markings and black with a 'mantilla lace' effect. Poland still has about
160 butterfly species compared to barely sixty left in Britain.

Later, down in the valley I dig wild garlic bulbs. There is pleasure
in the rhythmic task of stick-digging until the long white bulb pops
out of the rich mud. When hunger drives me in, I prepare a casserole.
Roe chunks stewed in wild garlic bulbs and roots, ground ivy and
yarrow as flavouring herbs, walnuts, juneberries, chanterelles and
brook thistle – with yucca flowers from a neighbour's garden.

I'm rapidly learning the way of the bees. The best method to
pick mulberries is to wait for the shower of rain that always heads
over at around 2.30. The bees can't fly with wet wings, so have to
sit for a while until the sun comes out and the raindrops evaporate.

While they are patiently waiting, half-hidden beneath the leaves they've crawled under for protection, I work fast and pick a big bowlful of creamy mulberries. I respect the bees but can't help feeling triumphant at outwitting them. The fruit is the sweeter for the victory – silly!

## NEW DISCOVERIES

*Rzepnik, 17 July*

Today Łukasz is running a wild food workshop and has gone to Rzepnik early. I feast on nuts and berries, have a cup of cleavers coffee and put a packed lunch together. Then I walk the 2 kilometres to the village. I'm impressed that there isn't one scrap of litter. Unlike Britain, where the verges are now full of drinks cans and polystyrene takeaway boxes thrown out of people's cars – ugly and a danger to wildlife.

Rzepnik is built around the church of St Paraskevi, graced by a 450-year-old ancient oak 'Jagiellon' – the Royal One. At the workshop breakfast is under way. Nettles, comfrey, sow and cabbage thistles finely chopped, mixed with batter, then fried to make wild herb fritters. They smell delicious but I resist! Tea is brewed from rosebay willowherb, raspberry, horsemint and meadow geranium.

Later, in the woods, I come across a new plant I have never seen before – the Dutchman's pipe. A fascinating plant as it doesn't photosynthesise. Instead, it is parasitic on fungi that are connected to, and getting their nutrients from, the surrounding trees. A thief! The woods are dry so there are not a lot of fungi but I find a display of *Trametes gibbosa* fungus – the 'lumpy bracket' – perched on a stump. It looks as if it's covered in deep green velvet. I am entranced. Leaving the shelter of the trees, I discover there is no shortage of insects in Poland. The profusion of horse flies and other biters love my unacclimatised Scottish skin. I crush tansy and rub its oil into my hair to deter them. With necklaces and bangles of bruised ground ivy I must look like a woodland sprite.

In the long grass behind a mud track in the middle of which are the sculpted tracks of a wolf, we stop to catch green grasshoppers. I haven't eaten them since I was a child in Malawi. We also add European paper wasp larvae to the lunch menu. They build small open nests every year in Łukasz's garage, each containing a few dozen juicy larvae. Like wood ants, they taste a little of lemons. Black and red stinkbugs, more formally known as Italian striped bugs, are fried – they taste vile!

In the afternoon, we visit a riverside habitat where ancient weeds of cultivation still grow among the stalks of wheat. Tuberous pea, sporting deep pink petals, and rye brome – both eaten in Polish famines. Nearby is mauve-flowered devil's-bit scabious and greater burnet whose thick black roots were eaten by Siberian Yakuts after boiling to remove the tannins. There is meadow cranesbill and heath bedstraw – neither edible – that add to the beauty. I admire a dazzling black and white striped butterfly – the scarce swallowtail – prancing over a patchwork of marsh thistle, Himalayan balsam and dodder. Down towards the river, plants scramble in a mixed-up jumble of luxuriant growth: soapwort, dark mullein, tansy, black horehound, bramble, fat hen, prostrate and curly topped knotweeds, competing with bushes of lavatera backed by elegant goldenrod. Tufts of wiry grasses and tough woolly burdock stud the hard, sun-baked track.

Opposite, towering over the silverweed, is bulbous-rooted chervil – the star of the show. It's a scary-looking plant – a dead ringer for its relative the poison hemlock. Venomous-looking, purple-red blotches mark the lower stem and its toxic leaves look spookily similar. I've never seen 2-metre-tall poison hemlock though – certainly not in Scotland. However, in their first year they have a tender, non-toxic, edible root. Łukasz's friend Wojtek explains that the best harvesting period is from early June (once the leaves have died back), through to September (before the chunky tubers start sprouting underground, losing their flavour). Sometimes dubbed the turnip-rooted chervil, this starchy root gets so large that rural folk cultivated it, in blight years, as an alternative to potatoes. I want to rename it Baldrick's chervil!

# A TASTE OF THE EAST

*Rzepnik, 18 July*

This morning is a rush. I was too tired last night to plan today's food. I slice a little wild boar loin into chunky bacon-like strips and quickly fry it in its own fat with wild garlic. As soon as it's cool, I wrap it in leaves to take with me. I'll add some berries or salad leaves to it later. Grabbing a handful of walnuts and some dried mulberries – high-calorie snack food – we head up to Rzepnik village.

Breakfast at the camp is flatbreads over an open fire. Łukasz fills them with a chopped wild herb mix of nettle, chickweed, dead nettle and thistles to make a filling, turning the flatbread into a pie-like calzone – an Armenian recipe called *zhingyalov hats*.

Lunch is Georgian *pkhali*. They are superb. A simple blend of minced, squeezed, boiled plants: nettle, brook thistle, white dead-nettle and ground elder, with an equal amount of walnuts. The mixture is shaped into balls and left to dry a little. They're traditionally decorated with pomegranate seeds but the saskatoon juneberries look just as pretty. Łukasz learnt how to make them directly from Georgian villagers when he was documenting their wild vegetables. I share this passion. This is knowledge we may all need again one day.

# IMMERSION

*Pietrusza Wola and Targowiska, 19 July*

It's 5.00 on a Monday morning Polish time, though only 4.00 back in Scotland. The air is misty and cool, the world outside my window still damp from yesterday's gift of rain. Towering, magnificent birch sentries herald the approach of the forest just 50 metres from this small wooden clinker house, nestling in a vibrant meadow. Although the world at large has not yet woken, it soon will, as a few birds have started their serenade. The house still sleeps on. I can hear the heavy rhythmic breathing of Łukasz down the corridor and a house marten – a relative of the Scottish pine marten – stirs in the roof space above me, scrabbling against the boards as it rearranges its nest.

I should be tired but I'm wide awake. Snippets of yesterday's conversations still swirl around my head, like the mist on the mountains drifting between the pines. I feel nature's presence strongly this morning. The complexity of life outside my window is infinite, and the intelligence in 'the system' is awe-inspiring. The indigenous peoples of this Earth did not worship nature because they needed to invent a god, or gods, to explain what they didn't understand. No. They sensed, saw, heard and honoured the innate intelligence of life that pervades our planet. They didn't think humanity had accidentally evolved in an inanimate world of objects. Living in deep connection, cloaked by the life of the world, how could you not realise her animating power or recognise that it breathes through all living things?

Lost in thought, I pause, absent-mindedly scratching yesterday's bites. I think every blood-sucking insect in the Carpathians has smelt my thick, iron-rich Scottish blood from miles around and feasted on me. I drink from a water bottle that I filled with a crushed marsh woundwort plant. Its green leaves and purple flowers make gentle, foamy bubbles at the edges as it slowly begins to ferment. It's the closest wild herb I know to a natural antihistamine and the itching will soon subside.

Every plant has a gift for us.

Arsesmart certainly does! Later I find this fiery, mouth-burning, peppery plant in the middle of a track where the mud churns up into a moist ridge, winding through the damp, shady part of the wood. It has knobbly red knees along the stem, jointed as are all Polygonum knotweeds or buckwheats. Its name, *Persicaria hydropiper*, means 'water pepper with leaves like a peach tree'!

I pick several handfuls of the divinely tasty leaves of the brook thistle. *Cirsium rivulare* means 'thistle that loves growing by a stream'. Brook thistle isn't native to Scotland but I wish she was. The fresh flavour and texture are superb and the young leaves aren't spiny. There are water caltrops floating on the large pond, a sort of water chestnut. Names can tell you so much. It is called this as its tough, diamond-shaped seed casing comes to a lethal point at every corner, reminiscent of the weapon, a caltrop – a small, spiked piece of metal, with sharp points sticking out at different angles. Roman soldiers, who used the name *tribulus* ('jagged iron'), would throw them on the ground to slow down advancing armies. Japanese samurai had *makibishi*. You don't want to get one stuck in your foot!

The woods here are infused with the scent of ginger wafting up from a low-lying plant that's colonising the ground – asarabacca, nicknamed European wild ginger. Although its foreign relatives are used as a spice, it rarely is, as without drying it is very cathartic. At the back of the house I discover a row of daylilies – each edible bloom only lasts twenty-four hours.

Here in the Carpathian woods, the sun has now dispelled the mist, and a golden glow suffuses the air, bringing everything to life. The peaceful silence is interrupted, not by the rising hum of commuter traffic, but by the chirping of grasshoppers, the warbling birds and the hum of bees around the berries. Knowing the heat of the day will rise in a few hours and sap my energy, I slip back again into the woods.

After brunch, Łukasz and I – with a picnic of sliced venison, walnuts and dried berries – set off on a circuitous journey via a field of potatoes stocked with supper – fat hen, field-pennycress, grains of barnyard grass and wild green bristlegrass. I spot the distinctive seed pods of the tasty cress, shepherd's purse, named for its upside-down, heart-shaped pods resembling a ram's scrotum from which money-bags were made. Eventually, we park on the fringe of a forest near Targowiska. On the edge of a swamp that beavers are busy remodelling, we find a clearing full of wild blackcurrant bushes and tuck in. Łukasz really wants to show me the victory garlic, a broad-leaved Eurasian species of wild onion. Unlike bear's garlic and most wild leeks, it lasts long after the spring has passed. The swamp's mosquitoes are busy biting me so I chew garlic leaves, spit, then smear the green juice over my face and ears. It seems to deter them. We find dung beetles on the path back which Łukasz thinks are edible, but we spare them, as we have no container. A last-minute reprieve from the insect-eaters!

Heading south towards the Carpathian range – bear forest country – we stop to admire milkwort on limestone heath grassland and an acre of golden *Telekia* flowers. By the early evening, the circuit of southern Poland complete, we find ourselves waist-deep in a field of betony, greater burnet and crawling slow worms. Here is a plant now that I don't recognise with huge clouds of fluffy cream blooms. It is shining meadow rue, beloved by marbled white butterflies, sandwiched between agrimony and wild angelica, the latter covered in a host of tiny orange bugs.

Back after an amazing day out, I braise slices of venison tenderloin in a dry, oil-wiped pan, with wood sorrel, roasted Solomon's seal root, a dandelion salad and cleavers coffee. Łukasz goes one better and cracks open a precious bottle of wine – *Chateau de Łuczaj 2018* – made from his own wild grapes!

It seems so much easier to survive in the wild here compared to Scotland. What drove our ancestors out of the sunny countries?

## THE CARPATHIAN MOUNTAINS

*Kiczora, 20 July*

We breakfast on wild boar and snail stew with lots of steamed greens and Solomon's seal tubers. It has been very useful having stew on standby to reheat, just needing the addition of the fat hen and pennycress picked yesterday. Up in Łukasz's woods the fungi are finally starting to appear. A clump of delicate, white *Ramaria* coral fungus and a few stinkhorns (aptly named *Phallus impudicus*) that I smell from a mile off.

Late morning, Łukasz has something special to show me. The pagan oak Dąb Poganin at Węglówka, nearly 10 metres in girth, one of the five largest oaks in Poland. It is astounding. I'm immediately drawn to placing my hands on it. Unlike many ancient trees, this one is incredibly healthy and its life force is palpable, surging up the tree under my hands. I am in awe.

We're on our way to visit several meadows in Kiczora. The etymology of this Wallachian name comes from *chicera*, meaning 'overgrown mountain'. I realise how apt this is when I spy the profusion of wildflowers spilling down the hillside, bordered by wild cherry. My head barely above the grasses, nostrils filled with the scent of a hundred flowers, I climb the hill. Delighting in the plants, I speak their names out loud, greeting each one as I step into their space. I'm reciting the magical words of my own incantation invented for the Great Meadow Spirit:

> *Tufted vetch, hairy vetch, yarrow, calamint and chicory,*
> *purple crown 'n' yellow meadow vetch, field poppy and betony.*

> *Bird's-foot trefoil, big-flower vetch, black thyme, meadow salsify,*
> *dark 'n' dense-flowered mullein, scentless mayweed and agrimony.*

> *Greater knapweed, viper's bugloss, oxeye daisy, wild carrot,*
> *meadow cornflower, evening primrose, wild angelica and soapwort.*

> *Devils-bit 'n' field scabious, common hogweed, rough hawkbit,*
> *meadow fescue, valerian, dodder and brome.*

I haven't been in a meadow like this since I was a child, fifty years ago. It is truly alive. The bobbing flowers and pregnant seed heads of the grasses sway in the warm thermals that ripple over the lea in waves, as if we were standing in a fragrant ocean. Gently rocked to the music of a thousand hoverflies and bees.

As I sit in the grass at the top of the hill, catching my breath, taking notes and drinking in the view, a striking five-spot burnet lands on my hand. This stunning moth, barely the width of my grass-stained finger, has five vermilion-red spots on each graphite-grey wing. The sheer abundance of butterflies is because there are so many species-rich meadows concentrated in this area. By contrast, a report – 'Our Vanishing Flora' – published in 2012 by the wild plant conservation charity Plantlife¹, highlights the loss of wildflowers across Great Britain. It found that a staggering 97 per cent of wildflower meadows have disappeared since the 1930s. Everywhere in Europe, we see the decline of meadows – due to overfertilisation, abandonment or urbanisation – yet here in Kiczora paradise still reigns.

Breathe.

It is possible to feel both profound sorrow and joyous elation at the same time in a meadow.

After dozing in the sun for a while, happy as a child hidden in a grassy nest, I explore the top of the hill. A few wild strawberries hiding in the shade still sport some flavour-packed fruits, but not for long. At each level, the mix of plants has adapted and changed. It is dry on the top of the hill and yellow with tansy, agrimony, lady's mantle and St John's wort. Along the treeline, we gorge on wild cherries and raspberries. Neither the sloes nor the elderberries are ripe but, at the bottom once more, I glimpse exquisite wild carnations in full pink peeking up amongst the fragrant wild mint.


## TIME FLIES

*Back to Krakow, 21 July*

Fuelled by nut pancakes, we're heading north on a circuit that will dog-leg back to the airport in Krakow. To add to my collection of Polish giants, we visit the Christian Oak at Januszkowice. It's right next to a small builder's yard. Ironic when yesterday's Pagan Oak was in a churchyard! The ditch behind it is full of field bindweed, its pink and white flowers like Brighton rock candy, climbing over serrated-leaved tormentil and 'prehistoric' horsetail – the Tatra Highlanders used to eat their young shoots. Hiding behind them is Japanese knotweed trying meekly to disguise its invasive status.

I inadvertently step on a wasp's nest hidden in the grass. They are furious and swiftly plant a double whammy sting on the back of my hand. Luckily, there is plenty of plantain growing on the dusty path, to chew into a soothing poultice.

We make a whirlwind stop *en route* to visit Łukasz's friend Dr Wojciech Szymański, known as Wojtek. He wrote his PhD on the efficiency of collecting wild foods. His garden is bustling with pots of all different sizes in which he grows an impressive collection of nettle *Urtica*, arrowhead *Sagittaria* and chestnut *Castanea* species, and a stunning black-centred *Oxalis* that I fall in love with. Sadly, time is too short and there are still so many things to talk about.

My head is full as Łukasz drives me to the airport, crossing magnificent open gypsum grasslands, full of fumitory, rattle and sickleweed. Sickleweed is a new edible 'carrot' for me – there is none recorded in Scotland. All too soon, my Polish summer is over and, clutching my snack box of nuts and dried berries, I race for the flight home.

# CHAPTER TWENTY-THREE

# GRASSES AND GRAINS

*'The moment one gives close attention to any thing,
even a blade of grass, it becomes a mysterious,
awesome, indescribably magnificent world in itself.'*

Henry Miller, *Henry Miller on Writing*

## BACK IN SCOTLAND

*Daisylea, 27 July*

Back home, an hour behind Poland, I wake early and cannot get back to sleep. I get up – Gaïa is calling, whispering on the dawn wind.

Outside now, the grass and soil under my bare feet and between my toes, breathing the cool air deeply, I feel the presence of love. Vegetal love. Not – this morning – from me towards the trees, shrubs and herbs, but from them to me. We have so much in common. Holding a leaf in my hands I marvel again at the liquids that run through our veins. Green chlorophyll with its molecules of carbon, hydrogen, oxygen and nitrogen revolving around a *magnesium* ion. The red haemoglobin of blood, the same molecules revolving around *iron*! The leaf's mouth-shaped stomata opening and closing, intaking carbon dioxide and releasing oxygen. (Scientists don't like to call it breathing!) My lungs inhaling oxygen and exhaling carbon dioxide. We are each giving the other the kiss of life in a perpetual planetary Yin-Yang cycle.

For food, oxygen and life itself, we humans utterly depend on the plants here on Earth. The plant kingdom *is* the 'mother' in 'Mother Nature' because mothers give life. Neither humans nor our animal kin can photosynthesise to create sugar and carbohydrates, nor can we create oxygen. Even the carnivores must eat the herbivores that eat the plants. We cannot turn the vast energy of the sun into food every minute of the waking day while simultaneously pumping oxygen into the atmosphere. Our dependence is critical. If nature cut the umbilical cord that connects us, none of us would survive.

I'm entranced, bewitched, devoted! This is my summer of love.

It may sound strange to think of nature as *a lover*. It's not just a sentiment; it comes from thinking a lot about my relationship with the land and it is the *quality* of the relationship that I'm examining, not eco-sexuality. We glibly bandy about the phrase 'nature-lover' but for our very survival, we need to rediscover the depth of our relationship with Gaïa with the intimacy of an adoring spouse.

Britain, we hear, is a nation of 'nature-lovers'. Over 8 million Britons belong to conservation organisations to save animals, birds, woodlands, etc. and yet the Natural History Museum's Biodiversity Intactness Index[2] shows that because of centuries of farming, building, industry and population density, only 42 per cent of the UK's biodiversity remains intact (the global average is 77 per cent).

But Britain also has one of the lowest levels of nature connectedness,[3] despite our love of nature documentaries and millions of nature preservation memberships. We are global leaders in destroying the natural world, guilty of nature-loving from our armchairs.

You can't have a relationship with a lover that you don't *spend time with* or it falls apart. We need to be *givers*, as well as takers, or the relationship quickly becomes one-sided, even abusive. If people don't respond to nature exactly as they would to their beloved, how will we make the connection necessary to change our lemming-like rush to self-destruction? If you cherish Earth like a wife, would you still douse her with chemicals? How do we introduce people to this beautiful world so that they too are enraptured? Or do we depend only on trying to persuade them rationally that current levels of consumption and pollution are not in their best interests? In my experience, it is only passion that changes the world. I wish I had the answers.

## COUNTING CALORIES

*Daisylea, 28 July*

Hungry, hungry, hungry. There is food in the house but I just don't fancy mushrooms or meat today. My body says enough is enough. I am missing nuts, berries and the lush greens of spring – now that the plants have turned their attention to flowers and seeds – and I'm suddenly craving fats and carbohydrates again. I mention this in a social media post. Lots of people who see it make suggestions as to what I could eat, but none of the ideas involve fats or carbs. There just aren't any around here in the wild at this time of year.

NHS.co.uk states that, 'As a guide, an average man needs around 2,500 kcal a day to maintain a healthy body weight. For an average woman, that figure is around 2,000 kcal a day. These values can vary depending on age, size and levels of physical activity, among other factors.'[4]

I try to work out my calorie intake for some of the things I've been eating this year. Each of the following values relates to 100 grams of the food in question.

| | | | | | |
|---|---|---|---|---|---|
| Acorn flour | 501 Calories | 54.7g Carbs (54.7g net carbs) | 30.2g Fat | 7.5g Protein | |
| Burdock root (boiled, no salt) | 88 Calories | 21.2g Carbs (19.3g net carbs) | 0.1g Fat | 2.1g Protein | 1 cup is around 125 grams — 110 calories. |
| Chanterelles (raw) | 38 Calories | 6.9g Carbs (3.1g net carbs) | 0.5g Fat | 1.5g Protein | 1 cup is around 54 grams. |
| Dandelion roots | 45 Calories | 9.2g Carbs (5.7g net carbs) | 0.7g Fat | 2.7g Protein | 1 cup is around 25 calories. |
| Chicken egg (hard-boiled) | 155 Calories | 1.1g Carbs (1.1g net carbs) | 10.6g Fat | 12.6g Protein | 1 cup chopped boiled egg is 136 grams. 1 large egg weighs around 50 grams. |
| Chicken egg (poached) | 143 Calories | 0.7g Carbs (0.7g net carbs) | 9.5g Fat | 12.5g Protein | |
| Field mushrooms (boiled) | 28 Calories | 5.3g Carbs (3.1g net carbs) | 0.5g Fat | 2.2g Protein | 1 cup is around 156 grams. |
| Field mushrooms (raw) | 22 Calories | 3.3g Carbs (2.3g net carbs) | 0.3g Fat | 3.1g Protein | |
| Hazelnuts | 628 Calories | 16.7g Carbs (7g net carbs) | 60.8g Fat | 15g Protein | 1 cup of chopped nuts is around 115 grams — 722 calories. |

| Hen-of-the-woods mushroom (raw) | 31 Calories | 7g Carbs (4.3g net carbs) | 0.2g Fat | 1.9g Protein | 1 cup is around 70 grams. |
|---|---|---|---|---|---|
| Oyster mushrooms (raw) | 33 Calories | 6.1g Carbs (3.8g net carbs) | 0.4g Fat | 3.3g Protein | |
| Sweet chestnuts (boiled) | 131 Calories | 27.8g Carbs (27.8g net carbs) | 1.4g Fat | 2g Protein | |
| Sweet chestnuts (roasted) | 245 Calories | 53g Carbs (47.9g net carbs) | 2.2g Fat | 3.2g Protein | 100 grams is around 12 nuts. |
| Trout (dry, cooked) | 150 Calories | 0g Carbs (0g net carbs) | 5.8g Fat | 22.9g Protein | 1 fillet weighs 143 grams on average (can vary wildly). |
| Venison tenderloin (broiled) | 149 Calories | 0g Carbs (0g net carbs) | 2.4g Fat | 29.9g Protein | |
| Walnuts | 654 Calories | 13.7g Carbs (7g net carbs) | 65.2g Fat | 15.2g Protein | 1 cup is around 100 grams or about 50 walnut halves. |

I can quickly see that if you take meat, nuts and eggs out of the equation, it's a pretty low-calorie diet – around 800 calories. Eggs are highly seasonal and don't keep well. Nuts are seasonal and do keep well but they are heavy to carry – although they can be cached and hidden in hope for a return journey later in the year. It surprises me that the starchy roots of dandelion and burdock are so low-calorie. The only multi-season calorific foods here are game and fish. I should emigrate!

## CURRY

*Daisylea, 30 July*

I spend several blissful hours on the sunny merse this afternoon. The mainland vegetables are really getting dry and stringy now that they're focusing on seed heads, so I'm thrilled to stock up on succulent samphire, sea plantain, sea aster and blite.

While I've been away at the coast, I've left some red deer stewing meat and some quail's eggs in the smoker cabinet. The meat has been sitting in the sun for most of the day, so needs to be cooked immediately. As I've picked sea arrowgrass seeds and they are still fresh and pungent like green coriander seed, I decide to make a curry.

I grind some of the sea arrowgrass seeds along with those of dried hogweed. They are from last year although this year's seeds are ready to harvest already now that the flowers are fading. Some bog myrtle goes in too – I often use that like bay leaves – and a pinch of sea wormwood, a pungent, bitter flavour. I toast the mix in a dry non-stick frying pan until it's brown, turning it from time to time so it doesn't catch and burn. I then add a little water to prevent everything sticking and fry the cubes of red deer in the spices. As it's simmering, I finely chop some hot dittany and water pepper. I use the leaves sparingly; it's not called 'arsesmart' for nothing and it's the closest wild plant we have to chilli in Scotland!

## GRASS GRAINS

*Daisylea, 31 July*

I've got my eye on the grasses that are ripening down in the meadow. It's been a very long time since I had bread.

There is a narrative about eating wheat that goes, 'We've only been eating grain since the beginning of agriculture some 10,000 to 12,000 years ago.' We tend to think of wheat as a 'bad' product of agriculture and advocates of a *true* Paleo diet eschew grains.

This is a false construct. In fact, according to all the papers I have been reading recently, archaeologists have found large amounts of starch granules on Middle Stone Age stone tools in Mozambique, proving that early *Homo sapiens* relied on grass seeds, such as sorghum grass, at least 105,000 years ago. They also ate the African wine palm, the false banana, pigeon peas, wild oranges and the African 'potato' *(Hypoxis hemerocallidea)*.[5]

The Paglicci grinding stone, from southern Italy some 32,670 years ago, shows that people were eating slender wild oat *(Avena barbata)*, various grasses (Poaceae), acorns and several other unidentified species at the time.[6] In the Haua Fteah limestone cave of northern Libya, a grinding stone was in use around 31,000 years ago, to mill barley *(Hordeum vulgare)*, goat grass (genus *Aegilops*) and a further thirteen unidentified species.[7]

At the archaeological site of Ohalo II in Israel, during the Late Glacial Maximum around 23,070 years ago, ancient humans utilised at least 142 taxa, plus a variety of mammals, birds, rodents, fish and molluscs.[8] Of the small-grained grasses the most commonly prepared was brome *(Bromus pseudobrachystachys/tigridis)*, followed in descending quantity by wild barley *(Hordeum spontaneum)*, foxtail *(Alopecurus utriculatus/arundinaceus)*, alkali grass *(Puccinellia* cf. *convoluta)*, smooth barley *(Hordeum glaucum)*, seaside or Mediterranean barley *(Hordeum marinum/hystrix)* and also wild emmer wheat *(Triticum dicoccoides)*.[9]

I haven't even begun to add up the quantity of species we have eaten this year yet, but it must be several hundred. It just goes to show how inventive humans can be, and have always been, in trying out different foods.

In the post today, a friend has sent me some deer fat, some lacto-fermented wild garlic powder plus some crystallised sycamore syrup. Fergus's timing is perfect, as we ran out of sycamore crystals a week ago. The fat is extremely welcome.

Tomorrow, if it is fine, I'm going to harvest the first of the grass seeds and make some bread. Tonight I am going to grind acorns.

This evening, Matt brings a sheaf of cocksfoot grass back to the house. Examining the seed heads meticulously, I notice slim black fingers poking out of the grains. I instantly recognise this tiny fruiting fungus. Ergot! The whole batch has to be thrown away.

Ergot is the precursor of LSD; and the drug ergotamine, that stops haemorrhagic bleeding, is also made from this fungus.[10] In the Middle Ages, no one associated this cereal-loving mushroom with the madness and illness that follows eating infected rye. Called St Anthony's Fire, the resulting ergot poisoning makes you go mad whilst also constricting your blood vessels so that eventually, your hands and feet get gangrene and drop off. There is no way that I'm experimentally eating ergot bread, pasta or cake!

# CHAPTER TWENTY-FOUR

# LÙNASTAL

*'Live in each season as it passes;*
*breathe the air, drink the drink, taste the fruit,*
*and resign yourself to the influence of the earth.'*

Henry David Thoreau, *Walden: or Life in the Woods*

## LÙNASTAL

*West Lothian, 1 August*

Lùnastal (or Lughnasadh) on 1 August celebrates the start of the harvest season with the offering of the first fruits and now overlaps with Lammas Day, a harvest festival tradition originally from the south. The day was celebrated in many ways: a visit to a holy well, feasting, marriages and handfasting, fairs, riding the marches, horse racing and athletic contests like tossing the caber. There's the Burryman, who parades South Queensferry with every millimetre of his clothes covered with sticky burdock burs bestowing good fortune, while women return from the shielings to court and marry. This is a period of intense gathering, running throughout August to the end of September, closing with Celtic Mabon on 22 September and the

Christian harvest festival on the Sunday closest to the full Harvest Moon – this year on 23 September.

The wheel of the year turns again. We're now halfway between the summer solstice and autumn equinox and the grass heads are arching down, a sign that they are ripe and ready for me to harvest. Cocksfoot, like wheat, stays upright. I had my eye on this for some time as potential grain until the ergot infection.

I think that Lùnastal – not the summer solstice – is the true midsummer in Scotland, before the approach of autumn. We've just finished picking the wild strawberries that have given us 4 kilos of their tiny fruits from just one patch. Native raspberries and feral gooseberries have finally ripened and we've had fruit every day this last week. Now my attention turns to the seeds and grains. I should have scythed the meadow before Lùnastal to prevent the pioneer plants – dock, nettle, thistle and hogweed – from seeding to help more varieties of wildflowers become established. However, during our first inroads into the brush, Matt noticed the large heads of cocksfoot grass. I agreed to leave it uncut to gather as grain. This might have made flour or even a substitute for rice.

The parts of the herbs that I gather for teas and medicines are changing. I'm rushing to finish picking all the leaves before they start to yellow; the flowers before they turn to seed; and I'm already gathering ripened seeds from nettle and sea arrowgrass. The hard fruits like hawthorn berry and crabapples, as well as roots, will wait until October at the end of autumn.

Lùnastal is the start of the period when we need trade and travellers, arts and crafts of which Lugus is the patron. Towards the end of summer, our old tribes gathered to help each other harvest the food stocks needed for the winter. Through the post, parcels of food from my friends all show how typically we foragers squirrel away bounty from previous years. It's an all-hands-on-deck communal effort to gather everything that is ripe and store it before the fungi start their job of recycling.

Rab's family have been busy on the farm with the year's second cut of grass for winter silage. After the dry heatwave at the end of July, the nights leading up to Lùnastal have hummed with the buzzing of harvesting machinery and tractors. Further afield, the winter barley has just been cut – about two weeks late this year due to spring's slow start.

I have had to get new jeans; I never thought I'd be a size 12 again.

## JACKPOT

*Alderplace Forest, 8 August*

It's a very early start today as I'm taking Matt up to Alderplace Forest in Argyll and Bute. It's super dry down here in West Lothian and I can hear the mushrooms calling me from where they are nestling in damp cushions of old moss in Alderplace Forest. Sadly, Géza can't come as he's injured his leg – he's gutted as hunting fungi is one of his favourite pursuits – but he's shared his Google pins for one of the forest's inner sanctums. It's going to be a long day out and I've made some Georgian *pkhali* for lunch and taken some smoked eggs out of the freezer.

Leaving Ceum nan Seangan (the Path of the Ants) behind us, we take the Tri Drochaidean (Three Bridges) trail and quickly find mushrooms nestled under birches and pine. I test the difference between the inedible false chanterelle (only found under the pines) and the tasty true chanterelle (found under both). If you tear open the former, it is coloured inside whereas chanterelles are white under their yellow jackets. However, the real test – which you can't experience from reading a book – is the texture. Handling a false chanterelle is like pinching an old lady's flabby cheek, whereas squeezing a true chanterelle is like pinching a baby's chubby bottom!

I have a third ear when it comes to mushrooms. I swear I can hear them calling. We quickly leave the trail and labour uphill, spread out, moving from clump to clump. I listen out for the occasional snap of a twig to locate Matt. Near the top of the rise, I come over a crag and before me is a verdant mossy dell. It is hooching with chanterelles, just quietly growing and getting on with the business of being fungi; a veritable golden jackpot. Their sheer number amazes us both.

After an hour of picking, we call it a day. There are still plenty of mushrooms, but each of us now has a fully laden, heavy basket and I know we shall eat for a month. By the time we get back to the car, our arms ache from the weight and our faces from smiling. Mushrooms securely stowed, we have a picnic. It is the perfect day: no rain, no midges – the biting vampires of Scottish summers – plenty of mushrooms, plenty of baskets, plenty of help and joyful hearts!

By the time we get back, I'm done in but it's the right sort of weary. Aching calves. Happy heart. It's good to be hungry. Good to be tired. A light supper of . . . fried chanterelles, followed by a small dessert of fresh raspberries and blackcurrants with a drizzle of birch sap syrup, hits the spot.


## READING THE NEWS

*Daisylea, 10 August*

Breakfast is pretty yellow chanterelles, rehydrated chestnuts and succulent samphire from the coast – it stores exceptionally well in the fridge. I am avoiding eating any more fresh eggs as none of the wild birds are laying any more. But my four hens don't seem to have got the message that this is no longer the nesting season so I'll be giving them away.

I found some beautiful grisette mushrooms up at Beecraigs yesterday, hiding amongst the ferns, and have eaten a big plateful for lunch. My belly is full, sated, when Géza comes home with supermarket sticky fried chicken wings. They're not something I would usually be attracted to, but something about the sweet-spicy smell has me drooling. Thinking of sweetness, I'm kicking myself for poor timing as all the local berries will ripen while I'm away on holiday.

In a few days time I'm going up to the beautiful Applecross peninsula for a week. This is one of the oldest inhabited places in Scotland, as humans have lived here for at least 9,500 years. Middens – the archaeological name for rubbish dumps – and cooking sites show they ate shellfish, especially limpets, as well as red deer, birds, cod, mackerel and haddock. I thought it would be the perfect place to challenge myself to a holiday far from my wild food stores!

At the computer, writing up my notes from yesterday, I get distracted. The news makes sobering reading. The sixth assessment report of the Intergovernmental Panel on Climate Change (IPCC) has been published today.[1] It only comes out once every seven years and assesses the reports, surveys and studies of thousands of scientists around the world. The basic conclusion is that we're running out of time to prevent extreme weather events from disrupting our lives. Scientists reacting to the IPCC report predict that if we don't act now, by the time the next report comes out in 2028, it will be too late. I read about the issues in more depth, and from different angles, instead of going outside for a walk.

As global heating reaches 1.5 degrees centigrade, a significant number of people will face major problems with food supply as global production struggles. Warmer temperatures, increased humidity, wildfires, loss of glacial meltwaters, changed rainfall patterns, drained rivers, and more frequent drought will reduce the yield of most key crops. I feel quite heartbroken thinking about it. Some people think warmer temperatures will be good for crops (like soy) and will lengthen northern growing seasons. Sadly, any advantages will be cancelled out by the overall damage.

I remember reading Rachel Carson's environmental science work, *Silent Spring*,[2] at the age of twelve. I was shocked and saddened. The world's population had just reached 4 billion in 1975. Now, with the world's population expected to reach 10 billion by 2050, global food production needs to increase another 50 per cent over the next thirty years, to feed everyone. An extra 7,400 trillion calories will be needed every year by 2050. With current farming methods, we would need to cultivate a new land mass twice the size of India.

A survey I come across finds that 63 per cent of Britons want to buy more products in season and to lower their carbon footprint, but apparently only 33 per cent currently shop seasonally.[3] Alarmingly,

44 per cent admit to being 'clueless' about which season fruit and vegetables are ripe in. A third think you can grow avocados in Britain and Ireland – you can't – and 17 per cent think button mushrooms can only be cultivated in the autumn – instead of all year round.[4]

I realise there need to be massive changes to current agricultural practice, both crops and livestock, to prevent major food supply issues, with rising prices and shortages. And an awful lot of education.

The IPCC report makes for tragic reading. Climate scientists believe humans are changing the climate in an 'unprecedented' way and making 'irreversible' changes. The UN secretary general, António Guterres, says, '[The IPCC report] is a code red for humanity. The alarm bells are deafening, and the evidence is irrefutable: greenhouse gas emissions from fossil fuel burning and deforestation are choking our planet and putting billions of people at immediate risk.'

Sadly, it's not just on land. Reading more reports I discover that marine biologists working for the US government's National Oceanic and Atmospheric Administration (NOAA), have found dead zones in the ocean. One map shows a critical area in the Gulf of Mexico along the coast of Texas and Louisiana, from Houston to just south of New Orleans.[5] Apparently, agricultural run-off – the pesticides, herbicides, other agrichemicals and manure from farms and livestock operations – has created oxygen depletion in the sea. This makes it impossible for marine animals and plant life to survive. The US Coastal Hypoxia Research Program has also found that, in summer, low oxygen levels and high acidity along the Pacific Northwest coast of Oregon are now the new normal.[6]

To boil it down: *not* buying organically grown food contributes to killing the oceans.

I wonder at the role that wild food could play in all of this? There never seems to be a shortage of nettles!

Supper is pretty similar to breakfast. Chanterelles and chestnuts, with sheep's sorrel leaves instead of samphire, some oak-smoked venison 'pancetta' topped with slices of a fresh button porcini that I found in Alderplace Forest. Pudding is fresh blackcurrants and raspberries again, this time topped with a little tart. The pastry case is acorn and chestnut flour bound with water and a little melted deer fat. The filling is blackcurrants in honey, all caramelised and gooey. What a treat! But although my stomach is happy, my soul is saddened by the state of the world.


## RED SUNRISE

*Daisylea, 11 August*

I wake up at 5.37 a.m. as warm light infuses the room. The first red sunrise! This is a stark reminder that summer is coming to a close, because here in West Lothian red sunrises herald the start of autumn. The old saying goes:

> *Red sky at night*
> *Shepherd's delight*
> *Red sky in the morning*
> *Shepherd's warning*

There are certainly plenty of red-sky warnings as I browse this year's environmental reports. I am very careful not to read the news today!

For supper I have steamed samphire and wok-smoked mackerel, with a wild herb salsa dressing. I wonder how long we will continue to be able to catch mackerel off the Scottish coast.


## WORK DAY

*Daisylea, 12 August*

I am still resolved not to read the news. Instead, when I wake up, I sit in the armchair by the window, overlooking the valley, and meditate under the red dawn.

The main meal of the day is steamed sea spaghetti with chante-relles in a creamy sauce, made of powdered dried oyster mushroom and acorn starch, with sliced reedmace shoots.

## SUMMER HOLIDAY

*Inver Mill, 13 August*

On holiday! I'm going up to Applecross, where humans first lived in Scotland, and taking Matt with me – leaving Géza to hold the fort. After one cup of 'lawn tea' to welcome the new day, I thrust myself into my usual last-minute panic packing. I put everything I think we will possibly need into the van. Wicker baskets (to collect foraged food), mesh bags (for storing said finds in the fridge), cool box (for fish), smoker, dehydrator, fishing tackle, collapsible crab pots, forag-ing knife, walking boots, wellies, rocket stove, firewood, firestick, frying pan . . . everything but the kitchen sink!

I also take on holiday my four nettle, thistle and sorrel cheeses – to keep them brined and prevent them going off in my absence!

We are hoping to live off the land up on the west coast but just in case I also take a leg of venison, a bag of dried feral apple, some bere barley and acorn flour, a small tub of deer fat, some wild honey, a small bottle of birch sap syrup and a bag of samphire. I also take one bottle of mushroom ketchup, one bottle of hawthorn ketchup and one of elderberry pontack – three of my favourite Elizabethan preserves for adding flavour – plus a jar of blackcurrant jam dated 2016.

We're finally off. Our first stop is Inver Mill in Perthshire where Matt takes the low path along the river while I take the high path through the old pines. There I find the first biggish ceps of the year – two beauties that together weigh 250 grams – plus a haul of small, firm pine boletes, lots of grisettes, some larch boletes and various brittlegills. There are not many greens in the wood to col-lect – mainly just wood sorrel – and I easily get distracted watching a fascinating black and orange sexton beetle. Laying my head on the moss to watch him crawl around is like entering another world on another planet, taking in the terrain from my new beetle-perspective. I quickly come back to reality when something bites me on the chin. Ouch! That was uncalled for.

Within half an hour, it looks as if I've been smacked in the face with a golf ball. Luckily, plants are not fond of insect invasion either. They not only produce essential oils to deter them, but can also emit scents to attract their predators and, thankfully, they have soothing compounds that heal. I find some hedge woundwort, chew it into a poultice and drink some woundwort-infused water to calm down my 'sting'.

A few detours later, I call a moratorium on mushroom hunting as it's 5.30 and still Perthshire! Eventually, two hours later, we're over the Cairngorms and I ask Matt, now driving, to pull into Lay-by 97. I know from my past adventures that, just over the crash barrier, there is a very fruitful wild raspberry patch stretching down the hill.

One hour and a tub of raspberries later, we pull into the car park at Lingon Forest.

Supper is a medley of fresh wild mushrooms, torn into pieces, and cooked in an old steel frying pan over the rocket stove and garnished with wood sorrel; what more could anyone want?

I doze off in the back of the van, listening for a while to owls and the whispering of trees, before falling into a sleep coma. Matt, in his tree tent hammock, is slumbering somewhere deep in the woods, rocking on the breeze.

## ENZYMES

*Lingon Forest, 14 August*

I wake up in the back of the van, cosy but stiff. Pulling on my clothes, I go outside to find somewhere to pee. I see a gap between two bushes at the edge of the car park and slip through it. Just two steps in there is a small stream to cross, an easy leap, but I stop. There, sticking out of the bank, is a large, fresh pine bolete mushroom. Or I should say 'was' as it doesn't take me more than a few seconds to twist it gently, prising it out of its snug hole in the crumbly soil. I don't even have my knife with me yet, so grip it by the firm-fleshed cap to avoid accidentally rubbing any loose dirt into the stem. I leap the stream and, at the base of a Scots pine, I am immediately accosted by a *pair* of pine boletes. Smaller than the first, these are perfect conjoined twins that are also clamouring to be my breakfast! I ferret about a bit further and find parallel ranks of old pines nestling in thick, moist moss and decaying pine needles; this is just the sort of habitat that fungi love to fruit in. I gather as many grisettes as my hands can hold and go back to the van. I wish I'd brought a bag with me.

Within minutes, I'm cooking up the mushrooms in a frying pan over a low flame on my portable stove. Matt must have smelt them on the wind as he reappears, bleary-eyed and hungry. Sprinkled with a little wild garlic salt, they are naturally delicious. The freshness and immediacy of this meal gets me thinking. I know little about fungi enzymes and make a mental note to find out more. I know that plant enzymes activate at the point of picking or grazing. A bulb of garlic, still encased in its papery wrapper, doesn't smell much of garlic. However, peel it and crush the cloves, and immediately it releases its pungent aroma and ramps up its taste. After chopping and crushing, I leave it for five minutes before putting it into a frying pan, to increase the flavour. This is all because of the enzymes.

Garlic, as with so many other plants – and possibly fungi too – undergoes a catalytic conversion. Most plants are far too sensible to hang about with powerful or toxic chemicals permanently in their cells. Perhaps, like in humans, it would damage them in the long term. So they store a lot of their chemicals in an inert form. An enzyme can quickly activate these 'passive' chemicals, usually released at the point of attack, to convert the chemical into an 'active' one. Garlic (*Allium sativum*) stores its secret weapon as the passive chemical *alliin*. When crushed, an enzyme called *allinase* converts alliin into *allicin* – a super-smelly, strong-tasting animal and microbe repellent that also has powerful antibacterial, antiviral and antifungal properties. This is hugely useful at the point of attack but eventually, herds of deer move on and insects fly away, so after some hours the enzyme stops working and the allicin degrades. Plants are at their most bioactive at the point of harvesting. Usually, by the time that 'fresh' vegetables get to a supermarket, their enzymes have long since stopped acting and, cut from their roots, they have begun the process of dying.

I ponder this a lot as the food that I eat on the road, from forage to fork, is as fresh as you can get it and the plants and fungi are still alive when they hit the pan, pumping out enzymes and medicinally bioactive; this is presuming I haven't been so stupid as to pick anything toxic, as this bioactive phase also applies to poisons too. What I am eating must be at its bioactive peak!

With breakfast finished, I 'wash up'. While on the road, this means picking handfuls of the long, dew-covered grass, curling it into a coil, and using this to wipe out the pan, plates and cutlery. I dry the steel frying pan thoroughly over the flames of the stove. This will prevent it from rusting and its baked oil patina will remain non-stick for a long time.

Grabbing my basket, containing a tub and some waxed cotton bags, I head up the hill with Matt to see what's there; I'm intent on finding berries. The bilberries have ended, so I'm only expecting to find a few stragglers, but the lingonberries will be nearly ripe. Matt has never seen them before so I'm delighted to find some to show him. There are few places I know in Scotland where wild lingonberries grow. Luckily, being too sharp and sour for most people's taste, they are rarely picked.

However, before I get to the main berry patch, I want to harvest juniper berries. This most excellent spice is fantastic for cooking venison and I have almost completely run out. It takes me another hour to reach the juniper spot because I am distracted by a spur of larch and birch wood that I haven't really explored before. The deep moss is inviting, larch boletes are calling, and a previously undiscovered bilberry patch reveals ripe fruit, still lingering on the slope down to the loch. I pick 400 grams of bilberries and a big bunch of bog myrtle, then set off again only to find that the junipers are dead, and the forest beyond them has been clear-cut; razed to the ground as far as the eye can see. Ouch! My heart sinks.

The joy of the day helps me to ignore this vandalism. One wonderful thing about foraging is that every time you go 'wild shopping' it is memorable. Our finds of wild food form a mental map. They not only personalise the landscape but also expand our bank of memories. I often find myself saying things like, 'Géza, do you remember when you stopped to pee in Griffin Forest and we found that giant porcini? Go about 500 yards down that path . . .' or, 'Turn up the track by Rab's field where I found that bumper haul of field mushrooms ten years ago.' I certainly don't remember supermarket trips in the same way! The feral apple tree on the bank of the Avon river will stay in my grateful memory for ever, as the tree that saw me through the winter of my wild food year.

By mid-afternoon, the lush, green country above Inverness yields to winding paths through dramatic mountain passes on the road west. Waterfalls hurl themselves down rock faces like suicidal bungee-jumpers. My breath catches around every stomach-sinking hairpin corner, stunned by the power of this ancient landscape revealing itself peak by peak. The mood of the mountains is constantly changing. One minute a high *beinn*, swathed in clouds, glowers down at the rounded *meall* at its shoulder. The next minute, a soaring, craggy *sgùrr* pierces the sky. Each Gaelic name for a hill or mountain speaks volumes about its shape, size, colour and history.[7]

Around 5.30, we reach the bottom of the feared Bealach na Bà (Pass of the Cattle). Before it was built, in 1822, the only way to get to Applecross, a peninsula girdled by mountains, was by sea. This single-track road zigzags alarmingly up from sea level to 626 metres (2,054 feet) and closes once snow falls. This cut off the community for most of the winter until 1975, when a coastal road was built to the north.

I have to get Matt to drive, as my nerves cannot cope. When I was twenty-five years old, an oncoming truck on a narrow, windy, coastal road ploughed into me, nearly sending me down a cliff to my death. I survived but I've found driving along narrow parapets, particularly those without crash barriers, a wee bit challenging since then. When I do open my eyes, however, the views are stupendous.

Driving up to the cottage I've rented, we're greeted by three chunky horse mushrooms, and 20 metres from the front door lurks an opportunistic porcino. '*We won't see you starve!*' it tells me.

Supper is quick. Smoked mackerel with fried tawny grisettes, which are delicate and don't keep as well as most other fungi. I also make some mushroom soup from the Inver Mill larch boletes. They need eating up as they weren't refrigerated while on the road.


## ABUNDANCE

*Applecross, 15 August*

A short walk on the first morning, and Gaïa soothes all my survival worries. Feral fuchsia bushes, bearing ripe green berries like dangling earrings, line the pebbly, southern shore of the bay. Most fruits go from green to red or purple, but the fuchsia likes to be different. The thin purple fruits swell to plump green, streaked with purple-brown, on their journey to perfection. Their taste is a cross between a fig and a grape. Matt disappears inside the bush like a bear while I quickly fill a 2-litre bucket from the edges, despite some well-meaning holidaymakers who worry that I'm trying to poison myself. Only one of the four is adventurous enough to try one. A smile spreads over his face as he munches, 'Well, I never,' he says, but his friends won't try them despite the fact that I am obviously not dead and in excellent health!

After lunch we go mussel hunting. The tide is out in the bay at Sand, overlooked by the Mesolithic rock shelter where our ancestors lived. It is an eerie but powerful feeling to pull mussels off the rocks and roast them on hot stones in exactly the same way as they did, some 9,500 years ago. I climb up to the shelter. Under the immense rock awning the craggy walls are blackened; the soot of ancient fires has become fused into the very stone. I place my hands where the Ancient Ones have been before me. I can feel the past like a very fine, almost invisible fishing line. I sense a light humming, vibrating and stretched taut thread, imperceptibly reverberating through the millennia. This connection creates a different perspective of time and I feel deeply at peace.

Later, up on the scrubby coastal grassland, sipping from a flask of larch bolete soup, I'm looking out to the islands, under the watchful eye of An Garbh-mheall (the Rough Rounded Hill) under Sàil na Cloiche Mòire (the Foot of the Great Rock – although *cloiche* can mean testicle as well as stone). The dung of grazing sheep has enriched the thin soil and today there is a huge crop of field mushrooms: 5 kilos to be precise! It is two days before the moon reaches the perigee – its closest distance to Earth – and most mushrooms dislike this, so will rush to fruit before it comes, or wait until after it passes. Why, and whether it is the effect of gravity, who knows? Matt has grown mushrooms biodynamically since 1995 and has observed this first-hand, year in, year out.

Supper is, of course, mushrooms. A grilled horse mushroom stuffed with other varieties, chopped chestnuts (defrosting rapidly), hogweed leaf, and some grated thistle cheese. Despite my best efforts to keep it cool, the thistle cheese has rapidly deteriorated and won't last until the end of November. I can't bear to waste it. I have scrubbed down the moulds on the sorrel and nettle cheeses and painted them with seawater. They are now on the porch to dry, perched on chopsticks to allow the cool sea breeze air to circulate and dry them. We also eat a salad of samphire and wild herbs with smoked pigeon and a little roast venison, with plenty of raspberries and wild fuchsia berries for pudding.

# MACKEREL FISHING

*Toscaig, 17 August*

We breakfast on charcoal burners with windfall apples found on the coastal road's verge, boiled sweet chestnuts, watermint and wild marjoram. Then off to remedy the food situation.

Having heard that fishing off Toscaig pier is a sure thing for mackerel, we head the 4 miles south from Applecross to arrive at 1.30 p.m., before the tide turns at 3.30. Perched on the rocky edge of Loch Toscaig, the incoming tide still ripples through the floating wracks, yellow from the summer's heat. In the distance, the Isle of Skye is silhouetted blue-grey on the horizon, behind the rocky hill that is Àirigh Alasdair (Alastair's shieling – his summer hut). The name conjures up a weather-beaten, craggy shepherd tending his flock, high above the inky deep water at the mouth of the sea loch.

It's time to put my newly acquired second-hand fishing rod to use. I plan to try out some mackerel lures that I've borrowed. The end of the pier is already partially occupied. Just what two novice fishers need, to be watched by a pro, but Nick, from Littlehampton, turns out to be a good and patient sort. I explain my ineptitude and that I have to catch *something* as we're living on wild food for a year. He doesn't comment on this madness but, summing up my lack of expertise fairly quickly, offers a quick lesson. It's just as well, as apart from how to tie a blood knot, I have pretty much forgotten all previous instructions!

Fishing requires patience but I'm not bored and my line-casting technique slowly improves. The sensations on the end of the line impart information: hit the bottom, snagged some seaweed, a nibble and so on. Soon Matt feels a fish biting, but I can tell it's small by the minimal strain on his line. He reels in an 8-cm long pollack that expires before we can throw it back in. Never mind, it can go towards supper.

Next up is a much larger cod that Nick reels in. It looks the same length as my foot. To my horror, he releases it and throws it back into the water. I'd have eaten that!

As if in sympathy the water yields a bite on my line. Reeling it in, I can see a flash of silver and black. A mackerel! I'm delighted. Just what I wanted. It's quickly followed by Nick reeling in his second line with two fish. A tiddler that he throws straight back in and a small mackerel. As he releases it I blurt out, 'Are you going to throw it back?'

'Why? Do you want it?'

'Yes, please! If you don't,' I reply. He snaps its neck and hands it over. Into the cool box it goes with mine.

Nick has two lines out quite far away with chunks of mackerel as bait, and tiny orange floats that mark their position. They're sunk deep and he's hoping for something a lot bigger than the fish I am after. I'm getting the hang of casting out, trying to avoid tangling my line with his. He then bags what, without my glasses on, initially looks like a baby shark – it's a dogfish.

'You want this?' he asks.

Matt pipes up, 'I like them.'

'You'll need pliers to get the skin off,' advises Nick. 'Keep hold of it with two hands,' he adds as the fish thrashes about.

'And what's the best way to kill it?' asks Matt, staring edgily at the wriggling mass.

'Put a knife between its eyes – that will sever the nerves in the brain and kill it quickly.' This is the part that I hate and I can see that Matt isn't relishing the prospect either. I carry on casting and leave him to it.

It's curiously calming, fishing. My mind has time to wander but it doesn't. It's trying to map this new underwater world. As the lead weight on my line bounces off the bottom of the sea loch I am gaining a sense of its geography. 'Nick,' I say, turning to my fellow fisherman. 'You've fished a lot. In the places you know very well, do you have a mental map in your head of the bottom of the sea?'

He immediately knows what I mean and nods. 'I do. And during low tide I walk around and look at the gullies and pools, see where the seaweed grows, note where it's deep and where there are rocks or channels. When the tide is in and I'm fishing, I remember all these places.'

'It's the same with mushrooms,' I reply. 'I have a mental map of where all the fungi mycelium is in the forest. I can see in my head how large it spreads around each of the trees and I know where the mushrooms are likely to come up. It's like the layers in an architect's drawing. You can switch them on or off and see below the surface of the soil.'

I swing the rod back and hurl the lead as far as I can once more. Then I let the spool run the line out, as deep into the water as it will go. I'm rewarded by this venture into the deep. The rod bends and I can feel it jerking. I've caught something again! And it's heavy. I've caught two mackerel, not just one! I have my picture taken with my fish: evidence that I didn't cheat and buy them from a fishmonger.

Matt has got his line snagged. It seems to have caught fast on the bottom. He's in a quandary; if he cuts it off, he'll lose the five-hook mackerel line. Nick comes to the rescue again and shows Matt how to wrap a towel around his hand, wind the line around several times and tug. It comes adrift and I breathe a sigh of relief. Last time Géza went fishing he managed to chuck the entire rod into the sea! Needless to say, he's never been allowed to live it down.

I take another turn. It's around 5.00 p.m. now and the tide is an hour and a half after turning. I can see the seaweeds clambering down the shore as it goes out. When the water gets shallower the mackerel depart, as they prefer deep water. Remembering the steps from throwing the javelin at school – it was the only sport I liked that didn't involve running or jumping – I take an unconventional run-up and cast the line as far as I can. I reel it back in, jerking the rod up and down to make the feathers on the hooks act like a shoal of small fish. Then suddenly, the rod is arching tensely and the line tugging like mad. I'm sure that I've caught something big. It's hard to turn the spool handle with my left hand and hang on to the rod with my right. The line is so heavy. I finally manage to haul it up and there, on four of the five hooks, are four perfect mackerel.

At 6.30 p.m., I've been fishing for five hours and am ready to call it a perfect day. Twelve shiny, fresh mackerel. Not a bad catch for a novice!

Supper is gutted, washed and grilled mackerel – as fresh as it gets. I fry some chanterelles – which are keeping well in the tiny fridge – with some fuchsia berries and lingonberries. Sprinkled with wild garlic salt, it's a delicious meal, although it took me so long to fastidiously pick out all the bones that I had to reheat it again.

## DINNER PARTY

*Applecross, 18 August*

What is harder than living off wild food day in and day out? Throwing a dinner party, of course!

Soon after we arrived here, I looked up Lesley and Thomas Kilbride. Lesley runs foraging walks in Applecross and is also a member of the Association of Foragers. She is an expert dyer using plants, lichens and mushrooms to dye the wool she hand-weaves with Thomas, near Fearnamore at the top of the peninsula. They moved to Applecross in 1975, before the road was even built over the top. They crofted, lived off the land, home-schooled and raised their nine children here. They both have a twinkle in the eye and a lifetime of stories. On impulse, I invite them both over to the Jam Factory, the tiny space that I've rented from the Applecross Estate, for dinner.

After a late brunch of 'biscuits' made from mashing up boiled chestnuts and frying them as discs until crisp, topped with a little of last year's home-made blackcurrant jam, I begin to plan the menu. Having come home with twelve mackerel yesterday, hot-smoked mackerel is a straightforward decision. Matt gets to work, using a rock to de-barnacle some mussels. I put him in charge of the smoker, set up outside, while I commandeer the tiny kitchen.

The final menu goes like this:

### To Drink

*White Rioja for Lesley and Thomas that I bought at the village shop for them. Matt and I drank birch sap, gifted by Lesley.*

### Nettle Leaf Crisps
*Made and brought by Lesley.*

### Surf and Turf Soup
*Mackerel and dogfish head stock with venison and
larch bolete gravy, strained to keep it clear as a
consommé, and reduced to intensify the flavour.
We added steamed mussels at the end, along
with tiny smoked larch bolete and horse mushroom buttons — halved lengthways — and a little
smoked salt. The result — a deep flavour of 'earth
meets the sea' with a surprisingly smoky depth
from adding just a few mushrooms.*

### Hot Smoked Mackerel with Samphire and Chanterelles
*Filleted mackerel hot-smoked using my Kelly
Kettle burner (as I didn't have any paraffin) to
smoulder oak chips in a tin smoker box from Bob.
Boiled samphire with a watermint mayonnaise.
Chanterelles, fried with wild marjoram,
watermint and garlic salt. A delicious green salad
of sweet cicely, chickweed and dandelion that
Lesley foraged, and a small piece of
dogfish liver — also smoked.*

### Rosehip and Fuchsia Berry Tart
*Blind-baked acorn shortcrust pastry, with a
smidgeon of ancient bere barley added to help it
bind. Scarlet Japanese rosehip 'shells' from the
edge of the wood behind the house — de-seeded
and thoroughly washed to remove the itchy
hairs — filled with feral fuchsia berries from the
shore. I made a treacly syrup of locally foraged
rowanberries, rosehips and green windfall apple,*

*cooked with wild honey and birch sap syrup, to*
*drizzle over the tart before baking.*

### Herb Tea

*A handful of flowers and herbs from home com-*
*bined with finds from the shore; honeysuckle and*
*fuchsia flowers, white clover, rose petals, water-*
*mint and rosebay willowherb.*

It is so nice to have company. When I was growing up in East Africa, we fed every traveller. Lesley asked me, soon after they'd arrived, if she could help as I was still cooking. 'Everything's in hand,' I replied. 'Just tell stories!'

## LEAVING

*Applecross, 21 August*

The last few days have gone by in a whirl. I have now become an 'expert' mackerel fisherwoman and we've smoked another dozen that I caught yesterday to take home. Fortunately I brought a big bag of sawdust just in case we were lucky. All the offcuts from the oak boards of our house are gradually going under the saw to make fuel for the smoker. Closed-loop recycling!

We leave Applecross at six in the morning to avoid other cars on the Bealach na Bà. It is foggy passing under the Meall Loch an Fhòir (Rounded Hill of the Lake by the Hayfield) and doesn't clear until we're out from the shadow of the giant Sgurr a' Chaorachain (Peak of the Torrent). I'm grateful for the magnificent, warm woollen blanket I bought from Thomas, now wrapped round my knees. He wove it using wool from the sheep on their croft, and Lesley dyed the yellow stripes that run through the grey with tansy. A precious thing.

It's a long journey down to Otter Ferry, on the Cowal Peninsula, to see Andrea, Lucy and new baby, Lucio. Longer than usual because the verges are sprouting fungi everywhere. They are like porcino

lookouts posted at regular intervals to lure us into every passing
wood. On the overgrazed, barren stretches of heather and bracken,
I make Matt – a quiet soul not known for his effusive conversation –
play the car game I devised, 'Desert Island Plants'. If you were
stranded on an island, which had a magical soil and climate where
anything would grow, but you were limited to just ten plants to provide all your needs for the rest of your life, which would you choose?

I always have coconut and nettle in the top two. They can both
provide food, cloth, string and rope. Coconut also provides 'water',
oil, sugar, thatching and logs. Nettle donates a variety of medicines,
from an antihistamine and an anti-inflammatory antiarthritic, to a
mood tonic and kidney restorative. And, if a Man Friday washes up,
it will keep his prostate healthy! It will also feed countless butterflies,
insects and birds.

The other eight on the list vary each time I play the game, but it
helps ease the long journey home.

## HOME AGAIN

*Fallen Tree Wood, 23 August*

I need to stretch, to walk, to breathe.

Down in the Fallen Tree Wood, the evening light has already faded
to dusk amongst the trees, but I know my way so well that I can find
it blindly in the gloom. A badger is just waking up but retreats into
his den as soon as he sees me. I check my mushroom spots. There
are a few scanty chanterelles, that's all. Then suddenly, crossing the
wood at a different angle, I find a baby bouchon mushroom – a perfect young penny bun. It is hardly visible in the dark, and not in an
expected place, but my hand reaches down as if it has eyes of its own
that can see in the dark.

The find feels like a present from Gaïa. A brief gesture to make me
smile. Tonight I feel the heaviness and physical pain of grief. One of
my patients in the clinic today was sad and I have taken on a shared
sorrow. I recall the first time I ever wrote a poem. My dearest friend's

son had been killed in a car accident. My then husband asked why, when I had never even met her son, did I feel it so heavily. I think grief is sometimes so great that it spills over from our individual hearts into a shared pool in the collective unconscious. Sharing the process of mourning relieves the volume and weight of it.

> *Come, my loved one*
> *to my house in the sun*
> *where I'll keep my sweet*
> *memories of you.*

I reflect on how much our physical condition masks the expression of feelings in our bodies. I am not just lighter in kilos now, but also lighter in spirit. For every kilo I have lost I feel younger by a year. But perhaps it is also that the person I glimpse in the mirror occasionally, more closely, matches the sprite inside now! Perhaps I have been carrying grief, locked into the matrix of my body. The flow of energy through me was blocked, and losing weight has removed the constraint. I only now realise how far I have come, how different I felt last year. I am less bound to the tangible as my being becomes ethereal. Emotions, feelings, memories: these are all energy and eating wild food is releasing them.

I sit on the dry fir needles with my back to a large rock. The woodland here is so quiet.

Hmm. The *woodland* is quiet but, from outside this haven, the sound of combine harvesters cutting the grass filters through the air to my ears. Then the clank of the big bucket on the front of a JCB excavating and moving rocks. Thud, grind, shudder, as it attacks the earth in the far distance. There is no silence any more. I slide further down between the two rocks, sinking into headphones of moss that drown out the noise. I gaze up at the treetops, protectively arching over me. Here I am at peace.

On the way home, I pick some chubby yellow chanterelles from their dance circle around the ancient beech, next to the towering Scots pine where a pair of grey squirrels has a very untidy, penthouse drey. This particular mycelium often keeps fruiting into November. I fry them for supper as soon as I return. At the point when we eat them, with some smoked mackerel from Applecross, they can barely have registered that they have left the earth.

'One of the penalties of an ecological education is to live alone in a world of wounds,' says conservationist Aldo Leopold in his book, *A Sand County Almanac*.[8] I get it. So often I feel intense joy and peace when immersed in nature, just the two of us together, but my profound sadness at her degradation and destruction always lurks.

There are new words to describe the eco grief shared by so many. One recently coined is *solastalgia*, first used by philosopher Glenn Albrecht in 2003. He describes solastalgia as the homesickness felt when you are at home, but your home environment is changing due to environmental damage.[9]

Biophilic communities, those with an innate love of living things, and groups of people dependent on the land or agribusiness, are particularly affected and experience a 'loss of certainty in a once-predictable environment', Albrecht explains. Solastalgia is often accompanied by a sense of powerlessness felt in the face of environmental injustice.

Whilst many old words still work perfectly for me, this philosopher's ideas challenge me to think anew. We do need to leave the Anthropocene – this era of massive human impact on the earth's geology and ecosystems – behind us. We need to develop, as he puts it, by employing 'creative thinking inspired by the science of symbiosis [that] can lead us into the *Symbiocene*, a new era that nurtures all aspects of being human in a world we share with all other beings'.

## MAGNESIUM

*Daisylea, 27 August*

There is neither red sky nor mist this morning. We've been having a heatwave that's prolonging the summer. Lùnastal is where autumn and summer overlap. Sometimes we just have alternate days at random. I wake up with leg cramps. This has been happening for a few weeks now. I think I might be low in magnesium.

The RDA for magnesium in adults is 400–420 milligrams for men and 310–320 milligrams for women. Chocolate, avocados, nuts (especially almonds, cashews and Brazil nuts), legumes, tofu, pumpkin seeds, whole grains, fatty fish, bananas and leafy greens are the best sources in food. I can see a problem here! No hazelnuts are ripe yet, I'm not near the sea to fish and apart from minimal leafy greens, there is *nothing* on that list that I can eat right now.

Magnesium also controls brain function. My memory right now is shit. Simple words are sometimes elusive. I forgot the name for a dandelion, for example. Or I might say dandelion when I'm looking at a nettle. I need to find more vegetables or I will have to take a supplement. I have taken no extra vitamins, minerals or other nutrients this year so I am reluctant to start now, but perhaps my brain is just having to work too hard?

It is bloody difficult to find information about the magnesium content of wild foods.

On one site I read that 100 grams of mackerel contains 60 milligrams of magnesium. Fresh mackerel weigh between 200 grams and 600 grams but average 350 grams – once the bones are removed. As I rarely eat more than one fillet a day, I'm probably getting 60 milligrams of magnesium from this rich, oily fish.

Wikipedia tells me that there are 13 milligrams of magnesium in 100 grams of chanterelles. That's a handful – but I need over 300 milligrams a day!

It is hard to find good-quality nutritional information. I recently tried to secure some funding to investigate the nutritional properties of wild foods, based on a common, qualified testing benchmark, but no luck yet. We might all need this information in thirty years' time!

Perhaps I need more nettle. It's too old to eat right now, but I could drink more tea. An article from Mother Earth News tells me, 'One recent study found that 500 ml of tea made with 20 grams of dried nettle leaves, steeped for thirty minutes, contains 76 mg of magnesium, which represents about 20–25% of men's and women's daily requirement, respectively."[10]

How on earth did prehistoric humans ever survive? What did our ancestors do without hair mineral tests and Google? Did they know that strange leg pains were magnesium deficiency? No. But they might have searched for plants to eat that made them feel better and probably, from experience, those high in magnesium: nettle, plantain, wild oats, horsetail. Did they drink herbal teas? In Tianluoshan they have found 6,000-year-old Neolithic tea roots (*Camellia sinensis*) planted in neat rows – evidence of cultivation.[11] The answer is, yes.

A long walk with Géza in the Vila Forest helps my mind escape. We come back with two baskets of porcini plus small, solid cow boletes and variegated boletes. He is always happiest when looking for mushrooms. The long walk also cures the mystery leg cramps and I resolve not to sit for long periods at my desk!

## A QUIET DAY

*Daisylea, 29 August*

I've got ninety days to go on my wild food diet and despite the hiccups along the way I am feeling great on it. It's a dull and misty Sunday morning. I'm sure the spiders have been busier recently as the low light level highlights dozens of webs around the window frame. Perhaps they too are preparing for the winter. As the fruits of summer trail to a close, the autumn berries must produce the last food for flies and hence a final arachnid feast. Or perhaps I've been slack on the housework again!

I scan the news headlines. I should start paying more attention if I'm going to re-enter the modern world soon. There are stories of food shortages and photos of empty supermarket shelves, and also shortages of ingredients needed by big-chain fast-food outlets. What has been going on? On the other hand Rest Less, a digital community, surveyed their over-fifty members about climate change. Roughly three quarters, 78 per cent, of people want the government to move faster than at present on climate change; and 65 per cent want it to happen faster even if it means that products and services become more expensive or more difficult to get hold of.

We are not a totally dinosaur generation, us oldies!

Yet like a housewife from centuries past, I have now packed the upper shelves in my kitchen full of jars of pickled variegated and cow boletes from yesterday's harvest. We have baked chanterelles, ceps and more smoked pigeon with wild fennel for supper and spend the evening shelling acorns and bottling rosehip purée. Yesterday my neighbour Allan dropped off six pigeons to smoke and Matt prepped them while Géza and I were out in the forest. The marinating and oak-smoke flavour really improved them.

## WORK DAY

*Daisylea, 30 August*

Breakfast is baked apples, mixed boletes (porcini, orange and brown birch, bay and scarletina boletes) with smoked pigeon.

It's a busy clinic day today, so Matt fixes lunch – a winning combination of salmon and chanterelles.

Supper is smoked pigeon again, fresh feral apple and pickled quince, alexanders and hogweed. After supper, we bottle the rosehip purée made yesterday. This is the wild forager's go-to substitute for tomato paste!

# PART FIVE

# AUTUMN

# CHAPTER TWENTY-FIVE

# NUTS, SEEDS AND HONEY

*'A seed neither fears light nor darkness,*
*but uses both to grow.'*

Matshona Dhliwayo, *The Art of Winning*

## PICKING NUTS

*West Calder, 1 September*

This year is a not bumper year. That would be a mast year – when the trees produce more nuts than usual and we have an Indian summer. Today I have left my basket at home despite my plans for harvesting. Instead, I've brought my canvas backpack. Carrying nuts is heavy work and I'm after hazelnuts from the trees that line the paths of West Calder Woods.

Nuts are hugely popular now and eaten all year round. However, once we ate seeds, nuts and grains for just a short period of time. We gathered them in the autumn and ate them over the winter. People only eat them every day now because global trade makes this possible. The popularity of nuts is a big environmental problem. I remember travelling in New Mexico, through the outskirts of El Paso on the edge of the Chihuahuan Desert, and being astonished to see pecan orchards growing in the dust. My friend Julie, with whom I was staying in her cabin perched up in the Gila Wilderness, was fighting a campaign to save the Gila river – one of the last wild, untamed rivers – from irrigation extraction. Nuts don't just consume huge amounts of water, the vast almond orchards of California also devour bees. They are imported in their billions to pollinate the trees before dying from toxic pesticides so that we can eat almonds all year round.

Here in Scotland, the ancient clans gathered together in the autumn to pick hazelnuts *en masse*. Large middens have been found with huge numbers of hazelnut shells in them. Wandering through the hazel grove today, picking the nuts and filling my backpack, I'm thinking about these clans. Foraging is hard enough when you're feeding just one or two people let alone a crowd. So, people spent most of their time in small family units. The nut harvest was a time when extended families were reunited in the common goal of gathering stores of valuable, portable food for the winter. The young and fit could flirt and pick nuts at the same time, before hauling home the heavy baskets. I would happily sit with the oldies in the last of the sun, cracking nuts and jokes. This evening I will be sitting around the table with friends, cracking nuts and possibly the same old jokes as if thousands of years have not passed.

The nuts I do find are beautiful and plump inside their puffed green sleeves that flounce at the cuff in a lacy edge. The younger ones will go into the blender, to be soaked overnight before straining to make hazelnut milk. The pulp will be carefully dried and ground to make flour for next winter. The older ones will be left alone to fully ripen and for the shells to harden – sleeves removed lest they decay and the mould disastrously spoils my stores.

The next day I am out again. Yesterday I noticed the hogweed seed on the turn from green to purple, signalling that it's time to harvest. Autumn is busy! I use the hogweed seed in curries, soups, chutneys and anywhere that I would otherwise use coriander. It tastes just like coriander seed, with a hint of cardamon infused in orange oil. As foraging becomes more popular, there is competition for mushrooms and berries, but rarely do I see anyone else collecting the edible seeds. Many – especially those in the carrot family Apiaceae – can replace spices or even, sometimes, add an entirely new taste sensation.

Plants reproduce by creating seeds that have a long shelf life. This is so they can wait for the right climatic and environmental conditions to start growing. Seeds come in different forms and we mainly talk about them in the following terms: seeds, kernels, nuts, peas, beans and grains such as wheat, oats and barley. In the northern hemisphere these are ready to harvest mainly in August and September. Some grass species make seed that can be gathered in late July. As our culinary skills developed over the thousands of years that hominids have been experimenting with fire and cooking, we found out pretty quickly that even indigestible grass grain could be ground up in a stone mortar, and cooked with a little liquid, to make a gruel or porridge. Or, that toasting seeds made them easier to chew and even tastier. From a human forager–farmer perspective, the ability to render seeds edible by cooking them, together with their long shelf life, was a huge boon, giving us a source of densely packed calories that won't spoil if they're not kept in an icehouse or a fridge. Our ancestors collected, dried and stored them – in the north to save food for the winter months and in arid areas to see them through times of drought.

Last month I picked a few bags of pendulous sedge seed. This will give me the basis of 'flour' to make crackers in the winter. It grows on the edge of my land. One plant rapidly became two, then ten, then fifty! At least it has some useful seed to exchange for the space it takes up.

When a seed drops to the ground in the autumn it has to hang around all winter, when food for the animals is scarce, until the spring when it can sprout. As a prime food target for countless hungry animals, they have to find ways to make themselves less vulnerable so that enough of them can survive. The main way that they do this is by being mildly toxic – or in some cases downright poisonous. All seeds could be poisonous so that all survive, but the plants always show incredible generosity. 'Mildly toxic' means *have a little but don't be greedy* – one of nature's central themes when it comes to food! Humans learnt that soaking pulses and throwing away the water removes many toxins.

The question of toxicity can scare those who are new to foraging, despite a variety of beans being widely consumed all over the globe. While it is sensible to avoid the attractive-looking 'mange-tout' pods on gorse and broom – as much as anything else because they contain chemicals that could affect your heart rhythm – people often agonise over how many of the young, tender, curling tips of common vetch or bush vetch they can eat. It's all a matter of quantity. Take canavanine that you'd find in sprouting clover: once the seeds have sprouted, canavanine falls from tiny levels to minuscule levels of toxicity. A 70-kilo human would have to eat 14 grams of canavanine to match the toxic dose for a mouse. That's between 700 grams and 1.5 kilos of alfalfa sprouts, based on 8–20 milligrams of canavanine per kilo. 700 grams of alfalfa sprouts is six times the size of the standard supermarket box; 1 kilo is nine boxes. I can't imagine eating two in one sitting, let alone nine. The only scenario where this could be a problem I imagine would be in juicing, which was not a traditional Stone Age activity.

Nature loves variety, seasonality and diversity, and humans evolved as omnivores. We are not supposed to eat large quantities of the same thing every day. Our system can cope with small amounts of natural toxins but once you start eating foods out of season – or overdosing on them – it is not the forager's way and I'm sure it's when many health problems begin.

Of all our native nuts, the hazelnut is the easiest to eat as it requires no preparation other than shelling. I can vouch for this as I crack the few that escaped my backpack under a heavy stone and cram my mouth full. Walnuts and sweet chestnuts can also be eaten straight after shelling, but I prefer to roast chestnuts to improve their flavour.

Healthy 'seed snacks' are a brilliant substitute for crisps and other less healthy snacks. They are also great as a crunchy topping for salads and bakes, and just as tasty. I used to love toasting cracked hazelnuts, pumpkin seeds and sunflower seeds in a dry frying pan. Once they began popping and browning I would place them in a dish and sprinkle over a little soy sauce. Just enough for them to hiss and absorb the liquid – not so much that they go soggy. Very addictive! I miss them.

## POWER CUT

*Daisylea, 2 September*

I wake at 4 a.m. and sleepily try turning on the bedside light. Click-click. Still no electricity. I am instantly alert. Shit!

The power went off at 7.00 last night and it won't matter how much the insurance company might pay out if all the food in the freezer spoils. No amount of money will replace a year of stored wild foods.

Trying to distract myself from looming disaster I scroll on my phone. Someone on social media has posted an arrow mark and asked, 'If you were an Australian Aborigine and saw a huge ➤ drawn in the desert sand, which way would you go?' The obvious answer is, 'right', although the simplicity of the question gives me pause. The answer is actually, 'left'. ➤ is the footprint of an emu, its toes pointing forwards. If you follow the direction it was walking you will go to the left!

This reminds me of the aboriginal tribe, Guugu Yimithirr, who I once read about.' They have no words in their language for 'in front of', 'behind', 'right' or 'left'. These four words describe the world as if it were centred around us. Instead, the Guugu Yimithirr always refer to the compass directions north, south, east and west. 'Come and sit down to the east of me,' they might say, or, 'Can you pass me that book to the north?' They locate themselves in relation to fixed points in the world around them. No matter where you are, inside a windowless room in a skyscraper or in a cave along the shore, you need to know exactly where you are in relation to the cosmos – the incredible computer of your mind recording your relationship to true north every waking moment. I spend the morning trying it and it does acutely heighten my understanding of place.

I wonder how much the language we use determines our vision of the world. Many other ancient tribes – in Namibia, Bali, Polynesia or Mexico, for example – used this form of linguistic geolocation. Even our Celtic languages had so many more words to describe how we relate to the land than English.

Despite last night's tasty stewed ceps and chanterelles, hot smoked salmon steak and a mixed green salad of wild rocket, chickweed, field mint and vetch, my brain feels a little 'buzzy'. It could be stress. Luckily the power comes back at 7 a.m., and, despite its being out for twelve hours, none of the food has gone off.

I join Matt and Géza in the kitchen. Géza is brewing coffee so Matt and I have some cleavers 'coffee'. I tell them my thoughts about the Guugu Yimithirr and spend the rest of the day trying only to use compass points in my speech. It's a challenge but makes me hyper-aware of myself in relation to my surroundings.

## CAULIFLOWER FUNGUS

*Perthshire, 4 September*

Lovely, delicious cauliflower fungus is definitely one of my favourites. My friend Lisa found one on her trip around the Highlands. I shared with her the location of my super prolific 'cauli spot' in the hope that she would find more.

Amongst foragers the sharing of locations, where we privately forage, is a gesture of immense respect and friendship. Years ago, when I lived in Perthshire, I had a neighbour who also collected fungi. After six years she showed me where she picked horse mushrooms. I knew then that she trusted me and we were true friends.

Our foraging places are often intimate spaces. They contain, not just sustenance, but personal memories of discovery and delight.

In our old brain, where foraging memories are stored, we never forget where and when we found the giant ceps, those jewel-red lingonberries, half a dozen cauliflower fungi all in a row. These are special and treasured moments, so we cherish and protect those places.

So, only true friends may enter. Those who we know will take care and not violate that space, those who are not greedy, who will not strip it bare for profit, who walk with light feet, give back to the earth, and share a deep love of the natural world. True foragers understand that generosity leads to reciprocity, as that is a fundamental law of nature.

In the concrete world, people forget that nature provides for us, and fear of scarcity breeds greed and selfishness. The loss of the nurturing relationship humans had with the plants, fungi and other-than-humans is at the heart of the threat our planet faces. The divorce of humans from nature is proving to be very expensive.

Our life depends on the trees and plants. Without them, there is no oxygen to breathe and no food to eat. We do well to be grateful and remember that.

Lisa is travelling back south again and coming to stay. I invite a few foraging friends over for an outdoor barbecue. This quickly turns into a small party.

I cook delicious food for us all, and everyone also brings dishes to share. Not one illicit morsel goes into my mouth. It was tempting, though! Instead, I drink elderflower mead and make mushroom kebabs, smeared with a hawthorn and honey paste, grilled over the coals. They are excellent.

## SUNDAY FORAGE

*Vila Forest, 5 September*

Having tidied up after the barbecue, I potter about and make a fruit pie with apple, brambles and greengages with an acorn flour crust.

After lunch, I take Lisa and Matt to Vila Forest. It is Sunday afternoon and, of course, there are loads of pickers as anticipated. I expect to find the forest has been picked clean, but it's a big place – even though Britain has fewer forests than anywhere else in Europe. This fact, at first glance, is hardly surprising given we're a tiny country, but in terms of percentage of forest cover we only have 13 per cent, compared to the European average of 38 per cent. Only half of our forests are native woodland with indigenous species, the rest is conifer 'battery farm' plantations. The Vila Forest is mainly plantation.

Lisa wants to find a porcino for the foraging course she's running, but I don't. With a freezer full of mushrooms, I am after the plentiful bilberries. And the blackberries – oh, my!

After a few hours, deep in the wood, I find one 'just hatched', faultless porcino. Here's a dilemma. I feel selfish keeping it as I know how badly Lisa wants one, but it is so perfect. In the end, just after I've decided to give it to her a second one pops up right by my feet. Problem solved! Nature is so generous.

Baked brambles with greengage pie. All it lacked was a little ice cream.

## BEES

*Daisylea, 6 September*

My friend Ella has given me honey from a wild bee swarm caught and hived in the spring. A fortnight ago, I remember hearing the mighty buzzing of wild bees in Strome Woods while picking mushrooms. Usually, honey is harvested at the summer's end.

The first nectar flow of the bees is between the middle of April and the end of May when the bees have been feasting on oilseed rape, fruit tree flowers, sticky sycamore and the mayflowers of hawthorn. The second is the main flow. This happens somewhere between the middle of June and the first week in August – entirely depending on the weather. Now, the bees are sustained by a plethora of summer flowers including red and white clover, rosebay willowherb, bramble blossom and their beloved lime tree ambrosia. Finally, somewhere between August and September, the highland bees harvest heather nectar. Once the weather starts to cool, the honey can be more difficult to extract.

Honey is one of the most nutrient-rich foods in nature and stored correctly it lasts for years. At 80–95 per cent sugar, honey is a dense, concentrated source of glucose and fructose. With the addition of bee larvae, which provides protein and amino acids, it gave early humans significant calories, especially when combined with plant foods and wild meat. Rock art from the Altamira caves (Northern Spain) shows that humans were collecting honey at least 25,000 years ago![2] Of such importance is honey that the Hadza people of Tanzania have co-evolved with a bird called the honeyguide.[3] It helps them to find hives full of honey in return for its share. It has the most wonderful scientific name – *Indicator indicator*.

Given its critical role in feeding humanity, it seems so ungrateful, careless and crazy that we are contributing to the honey bee's decline. Then there are diseases that cause hive collapse like the varroa mite, the small hive beetle and the Asian hornet. Interestingly, the varroa mite thrives in low hive humidity and struggles to reproduce in higher-humidity hives. I would have guessed, after living in African countries for decades, that global warming causes higher humidity and helps solve the varroa mite problems. However, according to the Met Office, although higher humidity is increasing over the ocean, it is dropping and becoming drier over the land mass – playing right into the hands of the varroa mite!

I don't think the answer is to stop eating honey and abandon the bees to their fate. I'm convinced that supporting small beekeepers helps to invest in the bees of the future. We desperately need this partnership.

All these thoughts of bees remind me of a powerful poem by Stephen Harrod Buhner from *The Secret Teachings of Plants*.[4] For me it doesn't just sum up the relationships we have between men and women, but between us and Gaïa herself.

Semen *is Latin*
*for a dormant, fertilized,*
*plant ovum—*
*a seed.*
*Men's ejaculate*
*is chemically more akin*
*to plant pollen.*
*See,*
*it is really*
*more accurate*
*to call it*
*mammal pollen.*

*To call it*
*semen*
*is to thrust*
*an insanity*
*deep inside our culture:*
*that men plow women*
*and plant their seed*
*when, in fact,*
*what they are doing*
*is pollinating*
*flowers.*

*Now.*
*Doesn't that change everything between us?*

# CHAPTER TWENTY-SIX

# MUSHROOMS

*'To me a lush carpet of pine needles or spongy grass is
more welcome than the most luxurious Persian rug.'*

Helen Keller, *Atlantic Monthly*

## TRICKSTERS

*Vila Forest, 16 September*

'Ella and the *Amanita muscaria*.'

It sounds like the title to a story, and in a way, it is. I am driving to
Vila Forest to look for blaeberries and penny buns. As we're driving
along, I'm explaining to my friend Ella that the sensory communication possible between humans and plants is also possible between
humans and fungi — albeit with quite a different character. I tell her
how fly agaric, the *Amanita* in question, always seems to know when
I am talking about it and will magically appear just to make a point.
'They have cellular intelligence,' mushroom expert Paul Stamets
says about fungi.[1] 'When you walk through the forest, they leap up
in search of debris to feed on. They know you're there.'

Before lockdown, I tell Ella, I went for a walk at Bracklin Falls. I
was teaching but it was hard work as there were few fungi that day.

After leaving the birch woodland, I walked down a dusty, dry path along the edge of a plantation wood. Tightly packed fir trees were competing desperately with each other in their scramble for sunlight. There was not a single mushroom in sight. So, needing to keep my group engaged, I told them a story about the fly agaric. That classic red toadstool with white spots.

When I ended the story, the group sat spellbound for a minute. Then the sun broke through the cloud cover. 'Oh, look!' said one, gesticulating and pointing behind me. 'Is that the mushroom you're talking about?' I slowly turned around. About 30 metres into the forest, a shaft of sunlight pierced the gloom of the dark conifers and illuminated a small dell. Right in the middle, on its own, was the largest fly agaric I have ever seen. Tall, regal, shiny, without a blemish. I swear it was laughing at me.

'*Here I am*,' teased the fly agaric. '*Did you call? I heard you were talking about me, so here I am!*'

Ella laughs. 'Do they really do that?' she asks.

We arrive at Vila Forest and park the car. With baskets and buckets, we walk up the dusty road. Soon the grassy verges turn to springy bilberry bushes with birch and Scots pine thrusting up in their midst. On the edge of the bank we spot the first mushroom of the day. It is a huge, single, freshly open fly agaric.

'*Hello!*' it says mischievously. '*Were you talking about me?*'

Ella giggles.


I spy a clump of three dirty cream-coloured mushrooms, with a suede-like texture, by the path. They smell of uncooked pastry. They are the miller mushroom. Millers dislike growing alone. They are especially fond of the company of two friends. So much so, that a fellow fungi fanatic, Dick Peebles, calls them 'the Holy Trinity'. Whenever I spot a miller, I usually find a chubby penny bun nearby.

The second of the miller's friends is the fly agaric. *Fly*, of course, has various meanings and many of them apply to this queen of the woodland: wily, clever, sly. They used to be soaked in a bowl of milk to keep flies down in a dairy: as the insects drank the milk the fly agaric poisoned them. Plus, the botanical part of the name *muscaria* is after Muscidae – the botanical name of a fly family.

You also 'fly' if you consume one of these, once past the sickness. That's the journey that muscarine and muscimol will take you on. They are a magical mushroom, and the basis of the Christmas story.

Once upon a time – how all good stories start – in the frozen far north, where icicles shimmer at night, there is a place called Sápmi.

Sápmi, also known as Lapland, is deep inside the Arctic Circle – next stop the North Pole – and it encompasses the northernmost regions of Finland, Sweden, Norway, Russia and the Baltic Sea. This is where the nomadic Sámi people have herded reindeer for at least 2,500 years, driven north by the Vikings.

When living in a food desert, whether through climatic extreme or urbanisation, everything that nature provides is seen as potential food. Humans have adapted to make the most of many toxic plants, rendering them safe through boiling, pickling and fermentation. In China, even deadly monkshood is turned into food through special processing. The Sámi detoxify the fly agaric by boiling and rinsing, boiling and rinsing, some three to five times to prevent sickness and hallucinations. Not all members of the Amanita family can be detoxified this way. Although these ancient peoples had never studied chemistry, somehow they realised that by feeding the mushrooms to reindeer – who love to eat them – and collecting the reindeers' urine to drink, they could encounter the numinous without the hangover and nausea! Or so the legend goes.

During the harvesting, young Sámi people would go on ahead to pick the mushrooms and lay them on the conifer branches, to be collected later. As the elders trekked up the path, they would see the glowing red caps of the fly agaric, with their snazzy white spots, nestling on the conifer trees, just like Christmas baubles!

The Arctic winter is deep and long. The polar night, eleven weeks of complete darkness, lasts from mid-November until the end of January. Imagine the Sámi *goahti* – a shelter of bent branches covered with peat and moss. Deep snowdrifts, blown in by the biting north wind, pile up and surround the shelter, almost hiding it from sight. The only way in and out is through the smoke-hole. Inside the warm goahti, a Sámi shaman drinks the fly agaric preparation and, leaving their body beside the fire, flies up through the chimney high above the earth. They see the spirits of the plants, animals and the magical reindeer – also flying on the effects of *Amanita muscaria*. The shaman seeks gifts of prophecy, healing and blessings to bring back to the tribe and, after flying around the world, returns with these gifts down the chimney – just like Santa Claus.

## DUNG DWELLERS

*Pentland Hills, 22 September*

After a lunch of venison and mushroom soup with a chickweed salad, I'm picking snowy waxcaps on the windswept fields that cover the Pentland Hills.

They like it up here where the grass is never treated with agri-chemicals. Noticing how the grassland mushrooms cluster around cow pats and sheep droppings brings home to me that mushrooms need ungulates. The waxcaps, psilocybe and dung roundheads on our grasslands, even our lawns, need manure. There are highly significant differences between the communities of fungi that live on different types of dung. If the dung goes, they go. We think of species loss in terms of bees, birds, mammals and occasionally plants, but we rarely think of the extinction of mushrooms, although their mycelium is the circuitry in the internet of life.

They slip away unnoticed except by a few. Am I the only one to mourn the dearth of field and horse mushrooms, the scarcity of giant puffballs and field blewits? Black holes appear where chemicals are sprayed and antibiotic-filled animal faeces no longer provide a host. The lights go out under housing estates, motorways and car parks as we pave the planet.

I wonder at the chaos we have set into momentum by killing off the mycelial web that connects all of nature's systems. What will happen if that crash reaches a tipping point? I can't dwell on it because I've imagined the consequences, and it is too terrifying to think about.

Australian eco-philosopher Glenn Albrecht notes that, 'The use of "cides", the killers of life in agriculture, wipe out soil symbiosis.'[2] I would add that they will also eliminate the fungal network that underpins one of the two *critical* communication networks of the plant kingdom. 'At micro, meso and macro levels of life, it is the bonds between symbiont species that maintain and perpetuate life and its health, including that for humanity. Dysbiosis is death. Symbiosis is life.'

I believe there is hope – certainly hope for Gaïa. There are far more terranascient spores from these ancient organisms filling the air than we realise. Just this one artist's bracket fungus (*Ganoderma applanatum*), here on the hill on this beech tree, can disperse 5.4 trillion spores in six months. A single giant puffball (*Calvatia gigantea*), fruiting in a field, will discharge 7 trillion spores. They are in the clouds, the dust storms and the foam that caps the ocean's waves. German researchers measured between 1,000 and 10,000 fungal spores in every cubic metre of air that we breathe and, in a thunderstorm, the concentration can increase dramatically from 20,000 to over 170,000 spores per cubic metre in just two hours.[3]

I expect they'll be back when conditions are right, given that fungi evolved to recycle all of nature's carbon forms and they have already learnt to eat oil. In 1988, concerned about the deterioration of the environment, American mycologist Paul Stamets bred a strain of oyster mushroom that was superb at breaking down oil. A research team contaminated soil at an experimental site in Bellingham with diesel fuel.[4] The scientists were aiming for concentrations similar to those of the *Exxon Valdez* oil spill that polluted Alaskan beaches: 20,000 ppm (parts per million). After four weeks, the section of the plot covered in wood chip innoculated with Stamets's mycelium had flourished. Unlike the control and treated piles, still dead, dark and foul-smelling, his pile was pale brown, fragrant and host to a bumper crop of mushrooms. Fungi-eating insects attracted birds that dropped seeds and, nine weeks later, colonies of plants were flourishing. Polycyclic aromatic hydrocarbons were now below 200 ppm.

They had just better learn to adore eating plastic and concrete!

Supper is a roast shoulder of venison – the last one in the freezer – with some roasted blackening brittlegill mushrooms, in a rosehip purée, gorse flower vinegar and feral green apple sauce. We eat it with a mushroom salad of raw beefsteak, raw penny bun, wild apple, bramble vinegar, and leftover hogweed shoot pickling oil.

The beefsteak wasn't from a cow. The beefsteak mushroom (*Fistulina hepatica*) is one of Gaïa's cellulose recycling team, found mainly on old oak trees in Scotland, and Géza has collected three today. I have seen the beefsteak on Spanish chestnut but there are few sweet chestnuts in Scotland – they are poor nut producers this far north. They have been designated a rare species on the red list of macrofungi in many countries. Like many macrofungi they live on dead and dying old trees. The premature removal by the 'Health and Safety Brigade' as soon as a tree shows the slightest evidence of infection poses a real threat to the existence of many tree-dwelling species.

One thing I find especially interesting about the beefsteak is that it can choose to be either a white rot fungus (breaking down *syringyl lignin*) or a brown rot fungus (acting on *guaiacyl lignin*) depending on what type of cells it inhabits.[5] It got its name because it looks exactly like a piece of raw meat or liver, even 'bleeding' a red juice when it's cut. The striated pattern and texture also resemble meat and it contains protein, with nine essential amino acids.[6] However, don't try to cook it like a steak. It is best cooked with other ingredients to help bring out their flavours: it intensifies taste rather like adding salt or monosodium glutamate, so it's great in risottos or stews. Today I am having it thinly sliced like carpaccio, with shavings of baby penny buns and paper-thin apple slices with a tangy dressing.

\*

Absent-mindedly chewing on far more apple slices than planned, I realise that it's not just the fungi and the plants that fascinate me. It's the interspecies dynamics that they have. I was brought up to believe that nature, 'red in tooth and claw', was all about survival of the fittest and competition. Yet, as if to set an example to all of us, it is far more about cooperation and symbiotic relationships.

The roots of a plant extend into a band of soil containing beneficial microbes. It is called the rhizosphere. Plants select microbes and maintain a species-specific rhizobiome, not dissimilar to our own microbiome. These microbes play a fundamental role in a plant's growth and health, and often help to defend them against pathogens. Plants communicate with them via phytohormones when stressed, and produce a multitude of secondary metabolites that have bioactive effects on the soil. There is also quite a bit of crosstalk signalling between species. Plenty of chat!

Nowadays, there is a lot of information available on how this system works. Current crop production is extremely damaging to the soil and its microbes. Scientists now realise there is an urgent need for the rhizobiome to be taken into consideration in modern farming practices. Saturating the earth with chemical herbicides and pesticides is suicidal, and it's not a slow death either.

A reference dose is an estimate of the quantity of a chemical that a person could be exposed to, every day for the rest of their life, with no appreciable risk of adverse health effects. According to the US Environmental Protection Agency, the reference dose for glyphosate for humans is 1.75 mg/kg/day.[7] So for a 75-kg person the reference dose would be around 131 milligrams per day.

I often find there's controversy around organic versus non-organic food. I think it comes down to one thing: do you want to poison yourself? I want someone to help me make a short video. My aim is for it go to viral. This is the plot:

*Scene: A dinner table.*

A family sits around the table waiting for a meal. I tell them I'm about to serve up a wonderful organic meal. One of them remarks that it smells delicious but they don't personally believe that organic food is any better than non-organic food. Another chimes in that they agree and it's just not worth the extra money. I just smile and say, sure, I can make it non-organic.

*Camera pans to steaming plates of food that look so delicious you can almost smell them through the screen.*

I place a plate in front of each person. They are looking at them with relish. Then, I place two little shot glasses in front of each plate. Each has a small amount of liquid in it. They look up, puzzled. 'What's this?' they ask.

'This one,' I reply, pointing to a shot glass, 'is your permitted safe dose of pesticide chemicals. This amber one is your herbicide. It includes 131 milligrams of glyphosate, often known as Roundup. Do please pour them over your food.'

*Camera pans to their faces. They sit silent. Not one of them moves to pour the chemicals over their food.*

That is how it works.

There are probably around 385 million cases of unintentional acute pesticide poisoning every year worldwide, resulting in around 11,000 deaths.[8] I don't think buying organic should be a personal choice; I think it should be mandatory for all food to be produced without harm to us, the soil, the insects,[9] animals and the biosphere. Anything else is discrimination. Discrimination by the rich against the poor. Discrimination against those confined to the food deserts found in both cities and rural villages. There are calories in the take-aways and corner shops but no actual nutrition.

Some argue that organic food production couldn't feed the world and people would die of starvation, but the current system of crop production is also death. Slow poisoning is just a different way to die. Once the soil is dead and the oceans have died, what are we left with? Remediation projects, using native plants and the bacteria helpers in their rhizobiomes, can restore old mining sites. Despite the harm caused to the planet, all is not lost. Pioneer plants are on a mission to heal the earth. Weeds like nettle, thistle and dock can break through concrete and oyster fungus will break down an oil slick. Any abandoned city lot soon reverts to the wild. Colonies of plants arrive to create soil once more and breathe life back into the air.

Plants can and will restore the wild along with their able fungal assistants. They give me immense hope.

# CHAPTER TWENTY-SEVEN

# AUTUMN EQUINOX

*'Mushroom tracks are elusive and enigmatic;*
*following them takes me on a wild ride.'*

Anna Lowenhaupt Tsing, *The*
*Mushroom at the End of the World*

## MABON

*McNees Wood, 23 September*

Mabon is the pagan harvest festival celebrated at the autumn equinox – this year 22 to 23 September. Like all the pagan dates, it spans the period from dusk to dawn. The long days of glorious summer light have shrunk back to equal the length of the encroaching darkness of winter. The world is in balance for a moment but poised for change.

Mabon heralds the falling of leaves, cold winter nights and the retrieval of woolly jumpers from bottom drawers to get *còsagach*. (This Gaelic word is now marketed as meaning 'snug, warm, cosy, sheltered' but ironically it comes from *còsag*, 'a damp, mossy crevice' – perhaps a tiny shelter from the savage elements.) The Christian harvest festival brought in to replace Mabon is on the Sunday closest to the Harvest Moon, which was the full moon two days ago.

However, winter is not here yet and before winter comes autumn, the season of plenty! I have two months to harvest enough berries, nuts, plants and fungi for my winter stores and the shelves are already mostly full of jars, tins and bags straining with the bounty of my hedgerow harvest. For a forager this is a lush time, and the knowledge that winter is waiting in the wings just focuses the mind all the more.

In this year of wild, I've noticed that my foraging pattern has changed. Once I was content to just go for a walk and while meandering about I'd pick a little of this and that in passing, for a salad or side dish. Now, every walk is with intent. I go at the right time, in the right weather, with a bag or basket, to a specific location where I know there is a very strong likelihood of harvesting a decent amount of whatever it is I need. I'm reminded that I've read of this in surveys of contemporary hunter-gatherer tribes. One person might do a recce but no energy is wasted 'faffing about', as my late father would say. But when the tubers are big enough, the fruits ripe, or the nuts starting to fall into reach, then a foraging party would be dispatched to bring it all back.

Wasted energy is precious lost calories, and we can measure foraging trips in calories spent. That's not as relevant when you're driving, but I'm also aware of 'petrol calories' and their environmental impact. Although my foraging range stretches to a 50-mile radius, I rarely drive more than 20 or 30 miles as most of the food I am picking is within walking distance of home. I seldom have to walk more than a mile and a half to find supper. Given the average calorie burn of 100 calories per walked mile that's a 300-calorie round trip.

Thinking in calories changes my perspective. My walks are no longer about garnishing a salad or making a foraged side dish, they're about survival; and it's even more crucial that I gather enough food as I am trying to cut down on meat. This is a problem. I wonder how much I need to harvest to replace the 300 calories from my walk, not even counting the calories needed for my metabolic rate?

The basal metabolic calorie calculator involves some old-fashioned maths! To calculate the amount of calories (kcal) I need to sustain my basal metabolic rate (BMR) for twenty-four hours, I need to do this sum:

BMR (male) = 66.47 + (13.75 × weight [kg]) + (5.003 × height [cm]) − (6.755 × age [years])

BMR (female) = 655.1 + (9.563 × weight [kg]) + (1.85 × height [cm]) − (4.676 × age [years])

Apparently I need 1,438 calories a day just to stay alive without moving or losing weight. There's more. The Harris Benedict Formula calculates the total calorie intake required to maintain my current weight *and* move around. I look it up and work out that I need 2,026 calories for today including my trip to McNees Wood.

I'm curious now. I've been happy to lose weight so far but . . . there is a limit and Matt is already skinny. Some research on wild foods explains the weight loss. I use 100 grams as the baseline for everything.

If I catch a tree flushing with oyster mushrooms at the right time, I can hope to pick 2 kilos. I look them up: they contain 33 calories and 3.31 grams of protein per 100 grams.

Digging up raw burdock root yields 72 calories raw with 1.53 grams of protein. Cooked it has 88 calories and 2.09 grams of protein.

Wild watercress grows in the stream. That has 11 calories (about a supermarket salad bag size) and 2.3 grams of protein.

I've got three ingredients now. At a push, I could just about eat 250 grams of oyster mushrooms in a single meal, with 150 grams of watercress and 150 grams of burdock root. That's quite a lot of food to fit in, but it would only give me 231 calories. If I ate the same for breakfast, lunch and dinner that would be 693 calories. An apple is 61 calories so I'll calculate eating three of them although they're still not completely ripe yet.

I'm up to 876 calories but still 1,150 short of my 2,026-calorie goal.

Hmm. I look up game meat: 100 grams is 150 calories and 30 grams of protein. Even eating meat three times a day, I will still be short. Could the research be wrong about how many calories our ancestors actually ate? I am actually feeling pretty healthy!

# TEMPTATION

*Daisylea, 24 September*

With Ella staying, I quickly realise that I have achieved the self-discipline (of which I have little) to stick to my wild food year, by *not* exposing myself to temptation. So far at home, with Géza having his own fridge, there's been little temptation to resist.

However, we find a gigantic hen-of-the-woods mushroom, just begging to be cooked with butter and cream. I am bad and allow myself one, naughty treat and fry this delicious mushroom up with some finely sliced onion in butter, adding a tiny dash of sour cream at the end. Seasoned with some wild garlic salt, this dish is sublime.

I feel very guilty – even though the bulk of the meal was completely wild – but the pleasure outweighs the guilt. After all, I convince myself, this wild food year wasn't to prove that I was some sort of female Bear Grylls. It was to show that, in a crisis, I could live healthily off a diet of just wild food. I could have avoided the 'treat' ingredients easily enough, given that I haven't touched them in ten months, but a forest-fresh tender maitake is just too rare and exquisite a find to be puritan.

We talk about the news over dinner. Food prices are going up around 5 per cent this winter but hen-of-the-woods, late-season nettle tops and tender chickweed are still free for all!

# CHAPTER TWENTY-EIGHT

# OCTOBER

*'Meanwhile the wild geese, high in the clean blue air,*
*are heading home again.*
*Whoever you are, no matter how lonely,*
*the world offers itself to your imagination,*
*calls to you like the wild geese, harsh and exciting*
*over and over announcing your place*
*in the family of things.'*

Mary Oliver, 'Wild Geese'

## MUSHROOM MAPS

*Beecraigs, 9 October*

It's Saturday and today there are only seven weeks left to go. I can't believe the end of my wild food year is in sight. I'm reminded of this deadline when I check on the state of the apples, going soft in their box. I really could do with wooden racks to help them last as this is the best way, without a lot of fridge space, to store them. There is an urgency to preserve food for the winter but the freezers are chock full already. The blackcurrants have come out and have to be dried or turned into a sugarless jam. At least they've made room for the large fallow deer joints that some friends have given me after a cull. The rest of the cuts, that won't fit into the freezer, I dump into a marinade as I'm rushing to get out of the house. Later I'll dry it to make venison biltong.

Surely all of this work no longer matters because in seven weeks' time I can eat anything I like. But I have grown used to this way of life now; I might not want to go back. Despite the occasional wobble, I am feeling pretty good, exceptionally healthy, and happier now I *have* to roam the fields and woods, no matter what the weather is doing. I now weigh 78.3 kg and I only have to reach 76 kg to get me back into a healthy BMI. I feel hardy, self-reliant, strong and very in tune with my world. I firmly shut out thoughts of ending this odyssey.

The weather forecast had warned of rain, but Gaïa is in a good mood today so it remains fine. I loop around a small section of the forest. I know it so well that I can walk it in my mind. I know every twist of the path, tree root trip hazard, ditch and bog. Most of all, I know the trees and their understorey companions, and my vision extends to beneath the ground as well. As I told Nick on the Toscaig pier while catching mackerel in August, it is like having X-ray vision in layers.

After a decade of foraging in this wood, I can 'see' the extent of the mycelium for every mushroom I've ever picked. Each one plucked created a waypoint, a dot on the map in my head. Over the years, as more and more markers have been added, the vision has become complete. Even when there are no mushrooms I can 'see' the mycelium as separate, fluffy neural networks, overlapping each other yet distinct, pulsing signals through the entire myconeural network. It's the same intimacy you find with a lover of many years whose thoughts you speak before they voice them. It is the spooky synchronicity of collective unconsciousness.

I greet each one in turn as we wind our way along the trail. Mostly in silence, in case I seem weird, but sometimes the joy of being in this place bubbles up and a spoken, 'Well, hello!' escapes me. They seem to have known I was coming and, happy to see me again, have put forth a cornucopia of treasures. I go deeper into the forest.

I return with firm penny buns, delicate tawny grisettes, flaming false saffron milkcaps, shaggy inkcaps, amethyst deceivers, bay boletes, hedgehog mushrooms, winter chanterelles and a handful of startling green aniseed funnels. Supper is sea beet from the large bag I picked that is keeping extremely well in the fridge. Winter chanterelles lightly fried in fallow deer fat – I rendered a large tub – and slices of venison with a herby rosehip purée crust complete a delicious meal.

## BEACH TALK

*South Queensferry, 10 October*

I walk along the South Queensferry foreshore with my cousin Felicity. I haven't seen her for ages. After a mile or so, we sit on a spectacular, throne-like, weathered volcanic rock. We talk of family, ageing, death. I am reminded of the birch wood with a single ancient beech in the middle. She thinks of heather still in flower, tiny dots of youthful purple among the dying bracken. I think of wounds that don't heal, and of forgiveness. I have realised that many of the wounds of my childhood have been healed by my connection with Gaïa, stronger now than ever. Someone somewhere said, 'Give a child a love of nature before they are ten and they will love her for life.' 'Someone' was right. Nature has been my salvation.

As we meander home we pick up plastic litter on the path. Then I find two huge shaggy parasol mushrooms. I carry them like babies cradled in my cardigan as I've used my emergency mushroom bag to collect the litter.

While I've been away, Matt has been out and found a huge basket of mushrooms. Kilos of penny buns, chanterelles, false saffron milkcaps, amethyst deceivers, charcoal burners, two types of red cracking bolete and some common puffballs. He weighs them all and adds the details to a spreadsheet of everything we've been foraging.

For supper, he cooks shaggy parasol schnitzels with a side of fried red cracking boletes. We have it with cold roast fallow deer shoulder, elderberry pontack sauce and sea beet. We'd collected a huge bag of sea beet. Its fleshy leaves keep well in the fridge, like the marsh samphire that lasted us a month in the summer.

## THE SCALES

*Daisylea, 12 October*

I weigh in at 76.7 kg. I have lost exactly 31 kilos since I started the wild food year. I've been using the infused lady's mantle oil to tighten my skin again, as I was getting a bit baggy. It's working a treat! This journey was never about weight-loss but I am delighted. I hadn't realised until now how unhappy I had been with my weight; not to the outside world, the trolls and the critics, but inside myself. We don't really grow up. In fact, I feel more childlike in many ways than I did forty years ago. But when your body no longer matches your spirit and you don't recognise your reflection in the mirror or a shop window, an ache creeps in.

## BLUE CHEESE

*Daisylea, 14 October*

I am reading a fascinating paper that found, on examining ancient faeces, that humans enjoyed drinking beer and eating blue cheese 2,700 years ago.[1] Salt miners in the Austrian Alps had a 'balanced diet', with an analysis of Bronze and Iron Age excrement finding the earliest evidence of cheese ripening in Europe.

I'm acutely aware of the cheeses in the fridge that I made earlier this year. They are almost black in the rind and I worry that they are possibly hardening too much inside. I've been resisting a taste until the year is over. It doesn't surprise me that people were fermenting and making blue cheese 2,700 years ago; it wasn't that long ago in the grand scheme of human history. We know our ancestors 300,000 years ago had the same cranial capacity and could easily have used a computer if they'd had access and tuition. If humans have always had this intelligence, why wouldn't they have wanted to experiment with food and cooking, or eat an interesting diet? The evolution of tools, from stick to whisk to blender; from clay oven to microwave to sous vide, has helped to provide more subtle techniques. It's allowed us to push the boundaries of what we can make, but our imagination has always fuelled our curiosity.

My energy levels are low today and it's dull and cold outside – a reminder that winter is, once again, around the corner. Should we be hibernating? It certainly feels like that. I'm not sure whether my low ebb is due to too few calories or a winter slowdown. The hens are moulting and have stopped laying. Brown feathers everywhere, but no bodies!

Norrie drops in on his way to work and has a cup of tea. We get onto the subject of badgers. There are, says Norrie, too many badgers in the area. He blames them for the lack of wildlife as they prey on hedgehogs and ground-nesting birds. The dry weather hasn't helped as there are fewer earthworms. Dozens get killed on the road every year. Between Slamannan and Limerigg, he says, he's seen fifteen carcasses this year, but even touching a dead badger is illegal in Scotland so there are no roadkill opportunities either. They dig out baby rabbits and wasp's nests – their natural prey. If it wasn't for intensive agriculture it wouldn't be a problem, but the population is too high and they have been spreading out. Ten years ago, the mosses had curlews, lapwings, skylarks – but all the wading birds have now gone. If the nests are raided every year then their populations eventually die out. I'm surprised as I rarely see badgers these days.

Last year, the telephone lines were weighted down with starlings but this year Norrie has not even seen starling nests, although the migrants are coming in now from Scandinavia, on their way south. I ask if he thinks the murmurations are still as plentiful as they were, in the areas where he used to see them. He says there are certainly far fewer – and in this last year they've just vanished.

Norrie blames the overuse of slug pellets and spraying for leather-jacket bugs. The pellets then come to the surface and are eaten by birds. The birds are poisoned. When he was young, he tells me, slug pellets weren't used indiscriminately but now they are every-where on many of the farms. The field behind him used to be full of starlings and jackdaws hunting for the leatherjackets; now there are none. 'There have been huge changes since my youth,' he says mournfully.

## THE END IN SIGHT

*Daisylea, 15 October*

I procrastinate over making breakfast. There is plenty of food. Well, plenty of mushrooms and meat, but I don't find the thought appetis-ing. I am keenly missing the abundance of green vegetables, especially now I know how long I'll be feeling like this – all winter – but the irony is that in six weeks this wild year ends and my pledge expires. Despite this, my mind is completely geared up for another year!

But . . . shouldn't I be overjoyed now that the end is so close in sight? Shouldn't the home stretch be easy? Strangely, I feel pangs of wistfulness at the thought of ending my wild year. My body has liked this diet – if you go by my weight, mood and overall energy. I don't miss the things that I thought I would, like coffee and chocolate. I would like to add a couple of ingredients in – especially during the winter – but that's it. I actually miss crunchy vegetables the most, such as courgettes, broccoli, olives, sweet peppers; fine ingredients for a chipotle chilli. I'm happy to forgo potatoes, bread and pasta for ever. I still have some sea beet in the fridge, but it won't last long. All around me the green of nature's palette is changing into hues of chestnut, gold and brown.

In my mind, I design a heavenly foraging paradise. It is full of vegetables. Big ones!

## MUSHROOM GENDER

*Stirling, 22 October*

I'm out foraging with Géza in the woods behind the Stirling University campus. There is never anything to eat in sycamore woods but from looking on Google Earth for a new spot to explore we didn't know there were *only* sycamores. However, it is beautiful. The woods are not only ablaze with the fiery russet, orange and ochre colours of autumn, but the earthy scent of soil, impregnated with fruiting fungi, permeates my nostrils unabashed. This is their mating smell.

We tend to think that only humans wear perfume but everyone is at it. Flowers luring their suitors with fragrance; mammals with musk; wrack antherozoids searching for odorous ova to fertilise in the summer seas. Why would fungi be any exception? Truffles are best known for their incredible scent and flavour. They live deep underground where it is difficult to find the perfect partner, the soil acting as an odour barrier. In Italy – where truffles are abundant – foragers use female pigs to find truffles, because this clever subterranean fungus mimics the scent of a wild boar's testicles when it is in rut. Sows love that smell so will go to great lengths to dig them up for us.

One thing that I didn't know until recently is that different genders of fungi – possibly all 36,000 - use different fragrance chemicals to advertise themselves, in the hunt for a perfect match. Mushrooms such as *Schizophyllum commune* and the inkcap, *Coprinus cinereus*, each have several thousand distinct mating types . . . Do they have as many distinct scents?

I read in an interesting essay that 'mycology is a science that, by its very nature, challenges paradigms and deconstructs norms. Mycology disrupts our mostly binary conception of plants versus animals, [and] two-sex mating systems, . . . [a] web-like network of fungal cells that extends . . . through substrate, performing sex, seeking nutrients, building multispecies and multi-kingdom symbioses.' [2] It's so true. Mushrooms are mind-blowing and regularly contradict all preconceived patterns of behaviour!

Exploring mushroom biology has challenged me to think more deeply about current discussions around gender and biological sex. LinkedIn and Instagram now allow pronouns but initially — despite no prejudices whatsoever — I just didn't see the point. However, as it is important to so many people, it became important for me to understand why it matters. On reflection I remembered that when I was growing up, everyone just assumed that if you referred to 'my doctor', 'my lawyer' or 'my bank manager', that you were talking about a 'he'. Early feminists fought to have 'chairman' become 'the chair' and 'policeman' become 'police officer' because these defaults excluded and alienated women. I was just married the year that Ms really took off. Before then you were often treated differently, both at work and socially, depending on whether you identified as Miss or Mrs. It was tiring to deal with assumptions.

I now understand that much of the gender pronoun debate is that neutral language helps us to avoid accidental prejudice by assuming nothing. Even if the pendulum has to swing far out to make the point, when it reaches the middle again, it will have been worth the effort to live in a more balanced, less judgemental society. Trying to understand another human may tax our brains, but it does not maim us like prejudice does. Compassion and empathy will lead us to the Symbiocene!

I shall now consciously state my pronouns as she/they.

Sleep is hard to find tonight with so many new thoughts to digest buzzing around my head. I wake at 3 a.m. and think that dawn is about to break. No. It is just light pollution hovering over the town in the distance. It is far worse than it was twelve years ago when we built this wooden house on the hill. The town is expanding rapidly, with new housing estates providing thousands of new homes. Now, instead of darkness punctured only by stars and the occasional intrusion of the moon, there is perpetual light in the east. I guess I will have to give in and make curtains.

I wonder about the effect that this has on our circadian rhythms. I find a survey by Anxiety UK, published in January, in which 1,200 of their members and supporters took part: '62.7% (770) reporting they are currently experiencing poor sleep while 34.4% (423) said they were not now but had in the past. Only 2.9% (36) said they had never experienced poor sleep.'[3]

# VISITING

*Treverlen, 23 October*

In the morning, I notice that one of the sheep is limping badly outside my window. I text Rab the farmer and he texts back to tell me that his son will be down to look at it, pronto. He arrives soon and gives it a shot of antibiotics.

I drive into town to see Christina and Maya. It's been too long. On my way down Briggis Hill I look out, as always, for the lone clump of Japanese knotweed. It must have died during the last winter; there hasn't been any sign of anyone spraying it but there were no shoots this spring. Perhaps it's not so tough after all when faced with over forty days of snow.

Invasive species are widely disliked but perhaps some of these come now in our time of need, bearing the gifts promised to our ancestors. Japanese knotweed, mouse-ear hawkweed, plantain, tumbleweed: they are all medicines for our time.

Darling Maya is teething; she is a veritable fountain of dribble. I wish I'd brought a piece of liquorice root for her to chew on. She's wearing a crocheted red hood with white spots, and a cardigan I embroidered with mushrooms and her name. I can't wait for her to grow up so that I can take her foraging. She is already fascinated by Christina's forest of houseplants, grasping their leaves tightly if she gets the chance. She will also gaze intently out of the window to watch the last of the roses swaying in the breeze as they ramble over the worn bricks. It is so natural for children to have this innate love of the wild world around them and tragic that so many no longer experience it. Writer and journalist Richard Louv, in his book about nature-deficit disorder, *Last Child in the Woods*, makes the point that, 'A kid today can likely tell you about the Amazon rainforest – but not about the last time he or she explored the woods in solitude, or lay in a field listening to the wind and watching the clouds move.'[4]

# BIRTHDAY

*Daisylea, 24 October*

It's my birthday! I was fifty-eight today at 00.14, just past midnight. Actually, because the clocks change at this time of year, I was also born yesterday at 23.14 Greenwich Mean Time. Since I discovered this, at the age of eighteen when one of my neighbours drew up my astrological chart, I have taken the opportunity of having a forty-eight-hour birthday ever since! Who wouldn't?

The only trouble with being over fifty is that you have to accept that you are also over halfway through life! Being realistic, I don't think I am going to make it to 116 years old even with great longevity genes. My grandmother was ninety-nine when she died, just five months short of her hundredth birthday, and it is very rare for anyone on my father's side to die under the age of ninety. As long as I can still get my leg over a barbed wire fence, I am planning to make it to 100. My great-grandmother Mabel lived to be almost 103. I can still see her face in my memory. Born in 1871, she was fond of muesli, cold showers and a run before breakfast. To balance her routine, she also enjoyed an after-dinner cigarette! After one visit, my father told me about all the changes she'd seen in her lifetime. I remember thinking that there would never be so much change in my time. Of course, there already has been. Our lives, before and after mobile phones and social media, are two distant worlds apart, as tangible a divide as Hadrian's Wall.

Longevity is something that we think has improved dramatically in this century although it is slowing down. The Office for National Statistics January report says, 'Latest life expectancy figures show the slowdown in improvements seen since 2011 has continued;

life expectancy at birth was 79.0 years for males and 82.9 years for females in the period 2018 to 2020.[5] People have a view that all Stone Age humans died by the time they hit their forties. In fact, this is not true; average lifespan is not as relevant as senescent mortality. In other words – if you take out causes of early death – how long do people live for when they die of relatively natural causes? The former include: infant mortality rate, volatile food supply, hunting accidents, violent injury or warfare. Those who survived these could often live to a ripe old age. A published research study of eight modern hunter-gatherer groups with little access to the modern world showed that some, like the Hazda, early death excluded, can live to an average age of seventy-eight.[6] Current life expectancy in Glasgow is still only 78.3 years![7] Worse still, National Records of Scotland statistics published in January reported that the *healthy* life expectancy at birth of Glaswegian men is just 54.6 years – followed by 23.7 years of poor health, we are left to assume.[8] Another study of contemporary female traditional foragers shows their life expectancy (at the age of twenty) is twenty to thirty years past the age of menopause[9] – so anywhere from sixty-five to eighty years old. Perhaps the menopause evolved just so we could be grandmothers? After all, no other land mammal shares this trait.

Overcrowding in early cities with no sanitation or clean water, and few green vegetables, led to disease on a major scale and a correspondingly poor average longevity. However, during the mid-Victorian era (1850–1880), when my great-grandmother was born, there was a short dietary golden age when urban people lived as long as we did today, but with 10 per cent *fewer* degenerative illnesses such as cancer, heart disease, stroke or respiratory diseases. According to a study of these thirty years, 'a generation grew up with probably the best standards of health ever enjoyed by a modern state'.[10] It is particularly astonishing as this period predates the National Health Service and the medical advances in surgery, infection control and drugs.

These Victorians consumed the British equivalent of a Mediterranean diet, with at least ten daily servings of fresh vegetables – brought into the cities by trains – with grass-fed beef and mutton, raw milk and dairy, fish, oats and bread that didn't have the 'improvements' of the Chorleywood bread process which is behind the modern sliced loaf. People also got a lot of physical exercise walking everywhere.

However, we're on shaky ground. Longevity is stalling and our children's generation will be the first that don't live longer than their parents due to the rise in obesity and its concomitant health problems. Without some major changes in diet and lifestyle, we seem to have reached as far as we can go. The big question is, do we just wait and hope that the drug companies will invent miracles, or are we going to take action ourselves? Sadly, our record of dealing with society's major problems is poor given our failure to tackle climate change, pollution, species extinction and migration. But dietary changes are ones that each of us can influence, up to a point.

Over the last couple of years, I have read extensively about the connection between longevity and diet in parts of the world as far apart as Georgia (Eurasia) and the Andes. Diets in these geographic pockets of longevity don't give up their secrets easily. Some of these old yins eat meat, some don't. Some eat fish, some don't. They all seemed to remain fairly physically active. Some smoked and drank, some didn't.

I would have put their advanced years down to genetic luck alone, but for one thing: each recollection, memoir or journal paper I read seemed to have one feature in common. One point so slight it was almost a postscript, a whisper. After going into some detail annotating and measuring 'diet', there would be an aside. *All these old people would also gather wild herbs to use in cooking or to make themselves medicinal teas.* I am struck by how obvious a link this seemed. We may have followed the '80:20 rule' for the bulk of our daily calories, but for flavour and health we added herbs.

Plants, especially the aromatic herbs, are crammed full of vitamins, flavonoids, polyphenols and antioxidants, along with immune-boosting, anti-inflammatory, cancer-fighting compounds. I later found out that drinking tea, especially green tea, is linked to a 10 per cent decrease in mortality risk amongst the very old in China and Japan.

I use herbs by the handful. A large bunch of chopped ground elder added to a soup. A springy bed of rosemary and yarrow under a roast. A handful of mixed herbs in a cafetière – not just a solitary teabag containing 1 gram of a herbal powder that lost its fragrance and volatile oils when it was finely ground, so it would run through a filling machine without clogging.

I am convinced that adding herbs to your food every day is the secret – if not to a long life, then most certainly to a healthy one!

# REFLECTIONS

*Daisylea, 28 October*

This morning, while looking for dryer trays, I found a tray of mouldy chestnuts that hadn't dried, half-hidden under a box. I have developed a terror of mould. Not personally, but for the destruction of our precious food supplies. Leaving them there was so stupid yet it's hard not to be careless when there's so much to do. There are few nut trees in this area and I have to drive to Falkirk to harvest what is left of them. I have an even greater respect for our ancestors; they didn't drive but walked everywhere and had to carry heavy loads or cache everything underground in souterrains, so it would last the long winter months. They must have covered some mileage. No wonder we have to have treadmills and rowing machines, or run to catch up.

Seventeen years ago, when I started teaching foraging, people asked me if I thought that this 'current interest' would last. Not only has it endured, but now it is joined by an interest in all things wild – wild swimming, wild singing! It feels that among the younger generations, there is a longing for self-reliance and reconnection. This can only be good for both people and the planet – as long as it is not co-opted and commercialised so that it loses its intrinsic wildness. The commodification of the wild, as entertainment activities, is like speed-dating to meet your soulmate. The strongest connections and deepest love take time.

In the afternoon, I walk up to the water meadow by the quarry and sit with marsh woundwort in the last cool rays of the autumn sun. Its leaves are curling, yellowing and slowly dying as its energy descends underground, focused on swelling into the long, crunchy, white tubers that will nourish me this winter. Raw or stir-fried, they taste like bean sprouts with a mild bitterness and keep their texture when lightly pickled or fermented. Marsh woundwort also calms allergy and gut flares. It reminds me to stop and be still. To cut back my daily activities and concentrate on nurturing myself.

'Be less reactive,' it whispers. 'Stop being so busy. Focus on what most nourishes you now.'

And it returns to storing subterranean starch for the winter ahead.

## BACK TO THE GARDEN

*Edinburgh, 31 October*

I'm thinking about the healing process today and not only how important the mind–body connection is, but also the human–nature connection. 'States of extreme distress are normal responses to abnormal stress,' to quote writer and herbalist Stephen Buhner,[11] who has taught me so much. 'We found that ultimately, for the most damaged people, bonding with wild landscapes was essential. There is an honesty there, a richness, that the neuro-atypical frequently must have for healing.'

In Fay Weldon's novel *Splitting* she defines the 'perforated personality'.[12] This is a state of feeling, arising from trauma, so fragmented that it is as though there are several different people inside us. However, unlike multiple personality disorder, there is not a completely defined split. Nowadays, I find that many people feel very fractured, due to the stress of modern life. Added to this is the burden of maintaining a separate social media persona, a work character and another – hopefully true self – for friends and family.

Nature has no desire for these fabricated selves. Wilderness calls to our authentic being, our own wild state within.

The twelfth-century philosopher and visionary Hildegard von Bingen believed that both humans and plants were nourished by 'viriditas'. (Viridian is a vivid green colour.) 'The soul is a breath of living spirit, that with excellent sensitivity, permeates the entire body to give it life,' she wrote.[13] 'Just so, the breath of the air makes the earth fruitful. Thus the air is the soul of the earth, moistening it, greening it.'

We all do something called *sensory gating*. It is the process by which we separate and filter out irrelevant environmental stimuli from meaningful messages. For example, can you name all the shops you pass on your walk to work? Or are there some gaps? The shops you forget because they have no interest to you? Or all the cars that passed you when waiting for a bus? Without this sensory self-censorship, we can suffer from sensory overload which, if we don't slow down, results in brain fog and confusion. The amygdala is a cluster of almond-shaped cells in the limbic system, near the base of the brain. It processes signals and stimuli from our environment, weighs up how important they are — whether they are a threat or a challenge — and then decides on the appropriate emotional response to generate.

After I had been teaching foraging for a few years, I noticed that something strange often happened, especially on mushroom iden-tification courses. At the beginning of a walk, I would point to the mushrooms and no one would see them. The winter chanterelles, out now, are particularly evasive. They have chosen to adopt the palette of the fallen autumn leaves that they love to fruit amongst — grey-brown caps and a dull yellow stem. Then after a spell staring at the ground, people suddenly began to spot them. First a few, then all of them. Nothing seemed to have changed except their perception.

However, I believe that looking for tiny plants and fungi on the ground suddenly forces our amygdala to pay attention. Suddenly we start to 'see' objects that before had eluded us. The amygdala pro-cesses not just sensory information but emotional response too. As my foraging students experience the 'opening' of their sensory gate, so their emotions change. Many are moved to tears – of joy.

'I haven't felt like this since I was a child.'

'I haven't thought about my email and texts for four hours.'

'Time just stopped.'

There is nothing we need to do, or engineer, to create the emotional freedom that accompanies a heightened sense of perception. All we need to do is to spend time in nature – just pottering about, looking.

Caitlin, my daughter, teaches forest bathing – the art of being mindful in nature, known as 'shinrin-yoku'. Feeling connected to nature and slowing right down relaxes people, lowers their blood pressure and increases feelings of well-being. However, she is careful not to claim she is offering a therapy. 'Nature is the therapist,' she explains. 'The guide just opens the door.'

There is a prevailing mood in society; it is one of both anger and profound sadness at the state of the planet, our inequitable economic systems, our busy stressful lives, the lack of meaning and our disconnect with nature. It's reflected in our physical and mental health as much as in the earth's physical and spiritual health. This mood undermines discourse. It lashes furiously through a thin veneer of civility.

We need to learn from the wisdom of viriditas. To let go of self-harming feelings, once the immediate danger has passed, but to learn from experience – and remain connected to the community that supports us through the web of life. The joy of nature connection nourishes the soul. Anger is needed; it has its rightful place, but it must arise from a joyful heart.

# PART SIX

# FINAL DAYS

# CHAPTER TWENTY-NINE

# TOWARDS COP26

*'There is almost a sensual longing for communion*
*with others who have a large vision. The immense*
*fulfilment of the friendship between those engaged*
*in furthering the evolution of consciousness*
*has a quality impossible to describe.'*

Pierre Teilhard de Chardin, *Hymn of the Universe*

## REWILDING

*Alladale, 1 November*

I track down my friend Paul Lister for a chat today. It's been a long time since we caught up. He owns an estate here in the Scottish Highlands called Alladale. At this time of year, Alladale is one of the most dramatically beautiful places to be.

The term 'orogeny' is used to describe the mountain range that is formed when two land masses collide. The Caledonian orogeny forced up the mountains of the Scottish highlands when the Iapetus Ocean closed, as the continents of Laurentia, Baltica and Avalonia crashed together. Standing at their feet, I am filled with an awe so deep it makes me shiver. Hewn from granite some 400 million years ago, these majestic peaks seem immortal.

There is a point at Alladale, halfway between the Alladale Lodge and Deanich Lodge, where the impact of Paul's vision hits you.

Looking south-west down An Gleann Mòr high above Abhainn a' Ghlinne Mhoir toward Beinn Dearg at 1,084 metres, Cona' Mheall (978 metres) and Meall nan Ceapraichean (977 metres), the mountains are giants.

Or, to put it another way: looking south-west down The Great Glen high above the River of the Big Valley toward the Red Mountain at 1,084 metres, the Adjoining Hill (978 metres) and the Hill of the Stubby Hillocks (977 metres), the mountains are giants. There are so many words in Gaelic, our beautiful aboriginal language, to describe our experience of place.

Heather and bracken carpet the lower slopes, as on most Scottish mountains, but at higher altitudes they give way to stone and scree. Dramatic waterfalls gouge silvery snaking lines through the bare granite. This is the Scotland that we are familiar with.

Yet, looking back towards Alladale Glen, it is totally different. As far as the eye can see, the hillside is a tumultuous riot of russet, green, ochre and scarlet as the Glencalvie Forest races uphill towards Carn Feur-Lochain. It is exultant and glorious. As if a choir of all the trees in the world has assembled in this vast landscape to belt out the 'Hallelujah Chorus' from Handel's *Messiah*.

Paul and his team have been planting trees. Not just a couple, as he does nothing by halves. At Alladale they have planted a million saplings over the last eighteen years. Paul is trying to restore the once Great Forest of Caledon – only 1 per cent remains today. This year they are planting more juniper, hawthorn, crabapple, rowan, aspen, Scots pine and hazel, to support more birds and red squirrels, and, above 450 metres, dwarf birch and dwarf willow.

Looking back down the Great Glen the naked mountains now seem like a desert. They are, but we can change this.

# GUILTY CONSCIENCE

*Daisylea, 3 November*

My optimism has plummeted. For supper I'm eating crow. A local man, who heard about my wild food year, sent a bag over via a neighbour. He shot the crows to keep them off a farmer's crops.

I feel so sad, desperately sad. I would never have chosen to kill a crow. I love the intelligence and character of the corvids, but I ate it so it didn't die in vain. Somehow, it seemed more respectful that way. I will never do this again. Yet all the corvids, except the vegetarian rooks, are thriving, their numbers booming. That should be a good thing, but it's not. When their numbers are too great, the small birds, their prey, decline. As with any over-population, too many is not always a good thing and has a knock-on 'domino effect' on many other species.

Professor of environmental and forest biology Robin Wall Kimmerer says, 'Sadly, since we cannot photosynthesize, we humans must take other lives in order to live. We have no choice but to consume, but we can choose to consume a plant or animal in a way that honours the life that is given and the life that flourishes as a consequence. Instead of avoiding ethical jeopardy by creating distance, we can embrace and reconcile that tension. We can acknowledge food plants and animals as fellow beings and through sophisticated practices of reciprocity demonstrate respect for the sacred exchange of life among relatives.'[1]

So many animals are killed to protect agricultural crops. We need to think, not just about domesticated animal welfare, but about the wild animals. What sort of nature do we want? What wildlife? And what are we prepared to do to manage that environment?

Supporting unfettered, intensive agriculture is not the answer to avoiding animal suffering. We need to stop looking at everything through the black-and-white lens of media polarisation and acknowledge that it is difficult to feed a planet of 7.8 billion people and find the right sustainable, humane and environmental solutions.

This last year, 99 per cent of my food has been sourced within 50 miles of my house and 90 per cent of the plants and fungi from within 6 miles. To do this, I had to eat meat, as in feral Scotland there is no choice. There is no wild rice, no wild beans, peas or other alternative proteins in our hedgerows. In a warmer climate, it would be possible to be vegetarian again and still keep a low carbon footprint, with local food miles. Imagine if there were no borders. We could all choose to live near the foods we want to eat. I would probably move to Portugal!

It is a tough debate.

I put the crow breasts into the smoker. This helps to remove them one stage from the living beings they once were – although polystyrene trays and plastic wrap disguise meat much better. It tastes like a gamey, strong-flavoured, smoked wild duck or pheasant. The texture is grainy and a bit tough. It's not unpleasant but my heart isn't in it. I procrastinate and leave most of it so long in the fridge that it goes mouldy – and then I feel guilty about the waste. And although we all die and go mouldy in the end I cannot reconcile myself to eating it.

## CHRISTMAS HUMBUG

*Bathgate, 5 November*

Many of the shops are dressed up in their Christmas finery. I've nothing against Christmas except that it's an environmental disaster. Hundreds of thousands of trees are grown in battery farms on depleted acid soil by monoculture, just so that they can make a two-week appearance in our living room covered in plastic baubles. And that's not counting the acres of wrapping paper and plastic discarded, or the strip mining of bauxite to make all that tinfoil to cover a million stuffed turkeys. I'm not a grinch but let's celebrate with a tree with roots that we can plant afterwards, or just a branch adorned with home-made ornaments and eco-conscious gifting. Christmas shouldn't have to cost the earth.

Foraging for wild food really focuses my mind. The longer I spend foraging, the more I detest the idea of shopping in a supermarket. The more time I spend outside looking for something to eat, the more time I really notice what is in season. As we tune in to nature, we change.

No tinsel sparkles like an iridescent icicle.

# COP26

*Glasgow, 6 November*

The house has been busy this week with friends passing through *en route* to Glasgow. After the quiet of lockdown socialising is a shock to the system, but I love these visits. Each of our guests brings stories, opinions, reactions and discussions that challenge and educate me – for which I am grateful. It reminds me of African hospitality: a bed, a hot bath and a fragrant meal for the traveller and all we asked in exchange was a story. When I was nine years old my family moved to Nairobi from Tigoni and my parents took in some sailors for Christmas. Their ship had docked and they were far from their families. I was entranced by Chris's golden eagle, tattooed in full flight, outstretched across his suntanned chest, and I perched on the arm of his chair for hours demanding tales of the sea. And 'the overlanders' – intrepid travellers, driving from Cairo to the Cape, who camped in the garden and relayed hair-raising adventures into the darkest hours of the night.

Lucy, from Wild Awake Ireland, has taken refuge with me from the tumult of Glasgow city. This morning, we set off over the Heights for Blackridge Station, to rendezvous with my friend Amy, who's brought seven-year-old Lola along. We're going to the COP26 protest march – all 100,000 of us. I'm excited but not sure what to expect. Glasgow is not as busy as I'd anticipated and we find Łukasz, who has joined us from Poland, easily enough on Sauchiehall Street. It's become pedestrianised with a double row of trees down the middle of the street for about a mile – hazelnut trees! Our little band, four foragers and a seven-year-old, make short work of collecting the nuts and soon I have both pockets full. I'm glad they have thick shells as I fish them off the pavement from between cigarette butts. Ironically, one of the COP26 issues is food security and here we are picking up free food from the concrete slabs.

Today, all roads lead to Kelvingrove Park and people converge from every direction. We find Łukasz's family and join the Extinction Rebellion bloc. There's a long wait, but the drummers engage us and people are smiling – especially at Lola, perched high on my shoulders. It is civil. People give each other plenty of space. Most are wearing fabric masks. There is no lurking aggression and we feel perfectly safe. Finally, after several false starts, we are off and, swaying to the drumbeat, out into the streets.

The procession is both a wake for Gaïa and also a celebration of 100,000 passionate people. After the Covid years of Zoom calls and seeing so few people in the flesh, I had forgotten that there is a tribe, a community, a fraternity. From one end of the street to another, all you can see is people. Walking alone along West George Street towards the square, I am nothing more than an ant, but as a 100,000-people-strong community we create a human ripple as far as the eye can see in both directions. Our action is visible and streamed, from the helicopters overhead, into living rooms across the globe. We started many conversations. If 100,000 people now change their daily actions to walk lightly and gently on the earth, leaving no footprints, *and* bear witness to it by speaking out, refusing to buy *anything* from the big polluters, campaigning and, above all, being visible, then maybe another 100,000 will follow, and another. I believe we can turn the tide.

It gives me hope. If we all vote with our wallets as well as the ballot, if we all speak out, surely there will be change.


# ECO-ACTIVISM

*Daisylea, 10 November*

Six o'clock is too early to start the day in winter. I go back to bed with a cup of hot linden, rose and birch twig tea, while the sun rises predictably over the horizon following its 4.6-billion-year-old daily routine. That's a hard habit to break!

Today, the leading and most respected climate analysis coalition, Climate Action Tracker (CAT), has predicted that we are heading for global warming of 2.4 degrees centigrade – not the 1.5 degrees that governments hoped for – based on the current political pledges to reduce emissions by 2030.[2] We are now at 1.2 degrees up and seeing the consequences. 2.4 degrees centigrade will be catastrophic.

We have been talking for far too long. Let's not forget, Rachel Carson wrote *Silent Spring* in 1962, an eco-conscious canary in the coal mine. Here is an excerpt from the Dalai Lama published in 1990:[3]

> *Clearly this is a pivotal generation. Global communication is possible, yet confrontations take place more often than meaningful dialogues for peace. Our marvels of science and technology are matched, if not outweighed, by many current tragedies, including human starvation in some parts of the world and extinction of other life forms. Exploration of outer space takes place at the same time the earth's own oceans, seas, and freshwater areas grow increasingly polluted, and their life forms are still largely unknown or misunderstood. Many of the earth's habitats, animals, plants, insects and even microorganisms that we know as rare may not be known at all by future generations. We have the capability and the responsibility. We must act before it is too late.*

I know that eco-grief is shared by many. There is an Irish Gaelic word that sums up this sadness perfectly – *díláthair* – described by Irish writer and traveller Manchán Magan as the feeling of loss or 'absence when something or somewhere has been depopulated or destroyed by other humans'.[4] *Mothaím pian na díláithreach* – I feel the grief of destruction.

This is an exquisitely beautiful planet, a truly marvellous expression of 'Life' now diseased. I am so in love with it; and, like watching your life partner die of cancer, my emotions bundle sadness, tenderness and devastation with hope for the miraculous. I cling to the faint possibility that there is a novel drug or new surgical technique that will keep my lover alive. However, even if there is a technological solution, there will be change. Like a cancer patient post treatment, this world may be a different place: scarred, exhausted, a shadow of its former self. Will the spirit be lost? Will we lose the exuberance and lust for living expressed through the myriad, awe-inspiring variety of the plant, fungi, insect and animal species, that we are decimating today?

I don't think so. The mistake in the publicity around climate change now is that we are waving placards that say 'Save the Planet', when really they should say 'Save the Human Race'. Nature is ancient, enduring, and has recovered countless times before. Nature and Life are the same being and the fractals of evolution will continue to churn out new life forms. *Homo sapiens* will survive. We are ingenious, flexible and enough of us care passionately. What we need to choose is a way of life on this planet that gives us quality of life.

Call me an idealist but I want to live in a world where 25 per cent of children are not depressed, where there is no hunger, and no conflict. The political approach to solving the inequality that creates these conditions is the same approach that will address climate change, protect the environment and respect non-human species.

It's too late to resolve global warming now, but it's not too late to ameliorate the effect. Television and the internet beam the consumption of the rich Western world into every refugee camp, every rickety hut, every slum. Chaos will come when the dispossessed, already needing water, food and opportunity, are pushed too far by climatic events. Chaos will come when the millions who live at sea level must move to higher ground as the oceans rise. While we are fighting, prepping, barricading our borders and protecting our wealth, nature will create new life forms adapted to a new climate to replace the koalas, giraffes, polar bears, birds and flowers. It is our children and their children who will miss them the most.

What we, the politically powerless, can do now is to embrace equality, consume less and live simpler lives, seeking out the spiritual over the material.

American writer and motivational speaker Leo Buscaglia once

said, 'Worry never prevents tomorrow's sorrows. It just robs today of its joy.' I know, from my own experience, that the deepest joy doesn't come from chasing money. It is in the development of soul, and in a union with the infinite, that we discover our truest selves. The reconnection with nature, outside and within, is the love affair we all crave.

I'm on a high from the connection with people who feel the same way that I do. Mobilising works! The power of individual people to influence change in the world is greater now than it ever has been. Companies are starting to act as consumers raise their voices, and even the board members of global corporations and investment banks have children who are learning at school that we need to protect our Earth. It's a slow process, though, balancing the need for change against the pressure for profits and the ideology of growth at any cost.

The same connectedness via the internet and social media that leaves us drained and depressed by the daily diet of bad news, also empowers us when we choose to speak out. Just four years ago, a fifteen-year-old schoolgirl started skipping school on a Friday to sit outside the Swedish Parliament holding a sign up that read '*Skolstrejk för klimatet*' (School strike for climate). Now, more people across the world recognise the name of Greta Thunberg and can tell you what she stands for, than could name most world leaders and their policies.

# CHAPTER THIRTY

# BRAVE NEW WORLD

*'Let's think the unthinkable, let's do the undoable.*
*Let us prepare to grapple with the ineffable itself,*
*and see if we may not eff it after all.'*

Douglas Adams,
*Dirk Gently's Holistic Detective Agency*

## THE UNIVERSE

*22 November*

To thrive on this planet there are some really difficult and unpopular decisions for society to make. I don't have solutions. I wish I did. All I know how to do is to ask questions . . . and then question the answers. That's why I got expelled from my physics class when I was fourteen years old – for questioning the fixed laws of the universe because I take nothing for granted. Perhaps I was right? Nobody then knew about the Higgs boson; or that recently observed unexpected behaviour by sub-atomic 'beauty quark' particles may reveal fissures in the principles of the decades-old Standard Model theory (the current operator manual for the universe).

In the third quadrant of my life, I am governed by *The Hitchhiker's*

*Guide to the Galaxy* author, Douglas Adams's, Rule No. 3: 'Anything invented after you're thirty-five is against the natural order of things.' I am also afflicted by a deep nostalgia for the planet that I adore. Yet, I have to stay open-minded. I have to remain open to new learning and new possibility. I have to have hope.

Humans are extremely good at coming up with solutions but not as good at thinking through their long-term effects: atom bombs, agrichemicals, plastics, capitalism. So I hope that the next generation will, like my fourteen-year-old self, ask questions – plenty of them – then question the answers, and question some more. After all, as the American politician Benjamin Franklin's maxim goes, 'failing to plan is planning to fail', and so failing to ask questions results in questioning why we failed. So before we throw the baby out with the bathwater, let's really think through the consequences as we introduce technology to change the weather, genetically modify crops and manufacture protein in the laboratory!

The Slow Food movement published a statement after COP26 which read:

> We need to tackle the causes of climate change at its source by ending the world's hunger for global commodity crops such as soya, palm oil at its source. Until we do this, global food will continue to drive climate change . . . There are many other things the world needs to do: from ending fossil fuel use, to overhauling transportation and our electricity supplies – but our food system has the potential to be a carbon sink, and is an opportunity lost.[2]

I, for one, shall continue to eat slowly and with nostalgia. Natural, wild, home-grown, organic and unmodified food produced or found locally, with exotics only an occasional treat. This way, for me, is the most sustainable.

## FOOD TOMORROW

*Daisylea, 23 November*

I sort through the crabapples, separating out those of an identical size, with stalks intact, to cover the bottom of a frying pan. In five days' time, I will simmer them in water, sugar and butter to make miniature toffee apples. This will be a celebratory treat after a year of eating only what nature has provided on my doorstep. I'm thinking of having a few luxuries: a wonderful wild-fusion curry that I've talked Vinod, the talented chef at Indie Roots, into making; a glass or two of exceptional red wine; and vegetables. I will munch once more on courgettes, broccoli, kale, carrots, cabbage, chillies and Brussels sprouts! I have missed vegetables so much.

Will I still eat wild food? Of course. It has changed me for the better, even though it was tough love at times. I still plan to avoid supermarkets – I didn't miss them – but I would like some more choice, especially in the dark Scottish winter. I also don't want to eat much meat nor can I expect Bob to give or barter it freely for ever! This coming year I will grow my own organic fruit and vegetables again, buying what I cannot grow from an organic wholesaler; keep the hens; get a sack or two of British cobnuts; bake the occasional homemade sourdough loaf with organic einkorn or bere barley; buy milk to make butter and cheese and just a little meat, now and then, from small, organic farmers at the weekly market. And of course I will forage!

## THE RIFT

*Dirleton, 24 November*

I've picked up Christina and Maya and we've headed for the coast. Standing on the vast sandy beach, ankle deep in the low tide, I face the endless ocean. The water breaks rhythmically, running a riff from left to right, sending rippling waves barely higher than my out-stretched hand to run over my feet. The sun is rapidly descending and the water's sparkle fades to a patchwork of greys, mauves and dusky grey-pinks. Above Berwick Law, the moon appears, showing only half her face. She looks huge which surprises me, as we are well past the perigee. The rhythm of the vast ocean echoes the pulse of Gaïa's beating heart, while a few tiny, silhouetted figures – adults, children and dogs – still dance across the flat sands. Maya sleeps peacefully in a sling, nestled close to the love of Christina's beating heart. In this tranquillity there is a sense of the infinite – an eternity.

As a child, I loved crossing the Rift Valley in Kenya on our visits north to our friends in Molo. Every time, before the descent, my father parked the Kombi and we got out to stand on the brink of the rift looking out into the vast, timeless landscape. The Kerio Valley, 1,000 metres below, stretched into the distance for 90 kilometres before rising sharply again in the west. The descending road ahead, a thin silver ribbon reflecting the sun, snaked tortuously down through hairpin bends so tight that when I think of it my stomach lurches even now, in anticipation. Here in the Rift, planet Earth has been splitting apart for millennia. The dramatic cliffs of the escarpments frame both glittering freshwater and soda lakes nestled on the valley floor. Mountain ranges peak in volcanic cones that break up the flat expanse. Down below, I saw waves of thousands of minuscule wildebeest – smaller than my childhood Airfix model animals – migrate across the plain in pulsing ripples not unlike the waves before me today. I could spot the distinctive shape of a Maasai manyatta – a circular group of perfectly ecological sustainable homes, and was filled with awe.

This is where our story began with Lucy, the hominid who lived here some 3 million years ago. Even Lucy was not the first. Another hominid ancestor *Nakalipithecus* goes back 10 million years, and it was from this Nakali ape parent that our cousins – the gorillas, chimpanzees, bonobos and other apes – all descended as well as us.

Like the miniature figures playing on the flat expanse of sandy beach today, we are tiny creatures. Our lives, over in a flash, settle quickly back into the dust with little trace unless we leave a legacy;

a poem that speaks to the soul, a piece of music that transports us, a book or a play that upturns our thoughts – or, darkly, casting the evil of a dictator's curse or a nuclear bomb. In this last century, though, we have left more than a trace. Collectively, we have left a poisonous slick of pollution. One study found that the collective weight of our anthropogenic mass of manmade plastics, metals, tarmac, 'from concrete bridges and glass buildings to computers and clothes', is about to exceed the weight of *all* living things on this planet.[3]

At this time of year, in open woodland, you will often find a fascinating creature called the dog's vomit slime mould: its Latin epithet *Fuligo septica* is not much better. The bearer of this unfortunate name is not actually a fungus, although you'd be forgiven for jumping to that conclusion when finding a bright lemon yellow blob-on-a-log or an orange globule clinging to a woodrush blade. From the kingdom Protista, a slime mould is actually a collection of single-celled organisms, each one entirely capable of living life on its own when food is abundant.

However, if there is a food shortage, these tiny individual organisms find each other and congregate. Massing together, they then start to act and move as a single body. As a larger entity, they change shape and each takes on a different function that serves the whole community. United, they are sensitive to airborne chemicals and can find sources of food. There is scope for diversity as they take on their different roles. Some even create stalks while others become the fruiting bodies on their tips and send out countless spores into the universe. Each spore a tiny message of DNA – a promise of life for future generations. A trillion times smaller than us, light enough to be carried on the wind, these smallest of creatures prevail through collective cooperation.

Now, dusk rapidly becomes darkness, as Christina and I step sure-footed on the narrow path back across the dunes. There is a chill in the air but we're wrapped up well in scarves and gloves. Despite the half-light we are still not yet done. I can see the familiar outlines of the plants and sense their identity. Almost back at the car park, three generations of women – myself, Christina and baby

Maya – stop to gather alexanders leaves for supper. As women have done for thousands of years.

## OPEN EYED

*Treverlen, 25 November*

Straddling the muddy path, wearing the wrong boots – the slippy sort – I'm taking the dog out for a walk so Christina and Maya can sleep in, cuddled up in their nest. The grass is wet with dew and the whole world still slumbers, just woman and wolf climbing the hill. I'm suddenly snared by a dog rose, its scarlet-jewel hip made vivid by the grey-brown landscape of a dying season. Straying from the path, I stop and pick a pocketful – mindful to top and tail them now to prevent hours of work later. The wolf runs off and returns occasionally to see if I've finished, then patiently hunkers down beside me. Eventually, my pockets are full and we head back to the path.

A crabapple tree is in my way. There's not a leaf or fruit on it, just dusky grey branches silhouetted against a grey sky. Then, at eye level, I notice a single yellow-green crabapple caught fast as it fell on a spike. I mourn that I have come too late to enjoy the harvest.

And then, I remember to look down!

Below the tree are hundreds of crabapples, in a range of sizes and coloured in all shades of yellow to green, clustered several layers thick in the grass and leaf fall. I fill a cloth bag in no time while the wolf, with a sigh, has a nap.

I think of my young friends, especially Christina and Maya; everyone should have friends across the generations. They are my reminder to look down as well as up. Not to get so fixed in my views that I miss discovering a different perspective and get stuck in a rut while the world around me evolves. I often catch myself out – it's the curse of nostalgia which, while it is always so comforting to look back and slip into the past, quickly renders the present an alien place. When I am a hundred, I pray I still have friends whose future stretches before them, just as my past trails behind me, to challenge me and lead me to fresh understanding. Gaïa, you are billions of years old but still delight in the new. Remind me always to look in every direction and never, doggedly, to follow only one path!

## BLACK FRIDAY

*Daisylea, 26 November*

It's Black Friday again. Outside in the garden, a climbing rose has come into flower – in late November?

With a cup of herb tea to warm me as it's only 3 degrees centigrade, and a belly full of fried mushrooms for fuel, I'm planting a new strip of woodland in the little valley that borders my land. It's a wildlife corridor, used by the deer travelling off the high Riggmoss Heath down to the woodland by the old mill. I'm planting 365 native trees. Hawthorn. Rowan. Birch. Cherry. Oak. One for each day that I was fed by Gaïa. I won't be alive to see the magnificence of these slender saplings as they mature, but Maya's generation will. My hope is that they grow up together and find new ways of sharing this Earth.

At midnight tonight, my 365 days of eating only wild food ends. It feels so sudden! I can't believe it is over and I feel quite sad that this chapter of my life is ending. The year has gone so fast.

The final weigh-in shows Matt is 70 kilos. He has lost 12 kilos overall and then gained back 4 of them. He's on the skinny side. I was very overweight and lost a staggering 31 kilos. I now weigh 76 kilos with a healthy BMI. At my Covid lockdown peak, I was a size 18/20. I am now the same size 12 that I was twenty-five years ago.

Matt and I sent off stool samples as each food season changed to track what was happening internally. We will do a final test today, then one in three months as a reference point, so it will be a while before I have all the results. The early signs from the first microbiome tests appear to show that our guts have become super-responders. Meaning that different bacteria species rise and fall, sometimes dramatically, according to the foods that we eat. Apparently this doesn't usually happen unless you're taking antibiotics or probiotics. When all the results come back it will take me some time to digest it all!

Overall we ate so well, far better than I'd expected, and never starved. Yes, there were periods of low blood sugar, winter monotony and February blues, but this was balanced by the joy of sudden bounty, birth, community and an exhilarating freedom of spirit – and this was all given to me for free! I learnt *so* much. Both by looking deeper into the science behind my everyday experience, and from simply sitting quietly outdoors: observant, open and receptive.

Now I feel like a new – or should I say – *renewed* person. Mentally and mood-wise, I feel brighter, younger and lighter. Full of energy, vitalised, alert, aware and far more ethereal – yet simultaneously more grounded. My approach to life seems kinder, gentler and more accepting – less critical and less cynical. Becoming intimately aware of Gaïa's immense power to remediate and rebalance, I feel humbled and hopeful. Ironically, I feel more trepidation returning to 'normal' than I did a year ago when I embraced the wild but, more than anything else, my abiding feeling is one of loving peace.

# CHAPTER THIRTY-ONE

# THANKSGIVING

*'Those who contemplate the beauty of the earth find reserves of strength that will endure as long as life lasts.'*

Rachel Carson, *The Silent Spring*

Without this strong connection I have to the land, I am lost. O Terra Madre, our relationship is the umbilical cord that binds me to you, the earth. You prevent me from getting lost among the stars and the endless emptiness of space.

Some people are rooted in their kin. They know their families, their tribes, their lineage and heritage. Many are rooted in the lands where they were born – with local dialects, menus and customs; it is a secure familiarity. Others have tenure – owning the land on which all our mothers gave birth. We – who grew up in exile, away from the land of our ancestors, split from families, fractured – belong nowhere. In adopted lands, our accent or customs or skin colour give us away. The native has a keen ear and a sharp eye for the outsider.

The nomad with no roots carries an incessant restlessness. At best we entertain with traveller's tales, at worst we leave a trail of destruction and broken hearts. Constantly in motion, trying on identities or places, in case one should suddenly fit like a glove or a crystal slipper. We dream of walking. Walking the entire surface of the earth, searching in vain, as the moment of our belonging to terroir – that deep sense of place - has passed.

I am a Londoner, Kikuyu, Kenyan, Vincentian, English, Malawian, Tongan Scot and yet none of them. Even my DNA denies me a home. I am a north-western European with English, Irish, Scottish, French, German and Scandinavian genes plus a splash of Neanderthal. No country or culture claims me. Yet Terra Madre has taken this orphan under her wing.

Now I need soil under my feet. The yielding earth, snapping twigs, crackling leaves, rustle of grasses, damp dew, or dry leg-scratching whipping burs. The concrete, tarmac and steel of the city underfoot make me crazy. Only in soil does my battered spirit take root. A spirit that knows no home but Earth.

I forage to live, in body and spirit. The algae, animals, plants and fungi are my kin. Here there is no judgement and all are welcome who step softly, with gratitude in their hearts.

I started this year expecting scarcity and hardship.

Instead, I found abundance.

# APPENDIX

## DIVING DEEPER

Thank you for reading this book. There was so much more I wanted to say that at times I feel like I've barely skimmed the surface. But I hope I have inspired you to be curious about the world that is your home. Explore and enjoy!

## STARTING FORAGING

Wild foods are your communion with nature. Do try foraging. You have this superpower and here are some suggestions to get you started.

There is a huge range of edible plants and fungi available to forage. Bewildered first-time foragers ask me, 'So many of them look the same. How will I ever tell all these apart from each other?' The answer to the question is simple . . . just begin! If you can tell the difference between a cabbage and a lettuce, then you have the mental power to be an excellent forager. Every small child quickly learns to tell apart the red ball-shaped fruit that could either be a small crimson apple or a large beefsteak tomato! Many two-year-olds could catalogue a standard grass lawn and, by six, many indigenous children will know the same number of species of foragable goodies as the average adult. They learn daily.

It is much easier to learn 'in the field' than from books. Find a teacher, for example from the Association of Foragers, and sign up for a course. This helps you to get a feel for texture, scent, ambience and a species' relationship to its habitat that are hard to comprehend from books.

A key to becoming proficient at foraging is to learn one new plant or fungus species every week. You probably already know a dozen or more, so at the end of two years, you'll be able to identify well over a hundred with confidence.

I suggest you start on a Monday. During the week, most people are more hectic, but a little reading can be squeezed in. Read about your chosen species in a field guide first to familiarise yourself with it. This way when you do venture online you can spot the mislabelled photographs! Then read as much as you can about it – its food use, medicines, crafting and folklore – from as wide a variety of reliable sources as you can manage. Try to find your chosen one in a walk after work: pick it; press it to make your own herbarium species; put it into a vase or pot and gaze at it; prop its picture next to your bed; smell it, inhaling deeply; touch and caress it; admire and compliment it; nibble and taste it (knowing it's 100 per cent correctly identified and edible).

Lao Tzu said, in the Tao Te Ching a long time ago, 'To gain knowledge add a little every day, but to gain wisdom subtract.'

Even if you stop learning at this point, you will have gathered enough knowledge about the plants to identify them and will be a competent forager, able to add many nutritious foods to your daily diet.

## EXPANDING AWARENESS

For those interested in a deeper intimacy with Gaïa, you need to go further than the facts, the science and the learning. This can feel uncomfortable for, as a culture, the British have a deep disconnect with nature – the second lowest in a survey of eighteen nations. We also have a disconnect with the intuitive side of our humanity. Add the West's reductionist thinking; scientific focus on the behaviour of isolated objects as opposed to interconnected systems; learning solely to pass exams; the media and society's focus on emotions; polarised opinion and intolerance – and we end up with an imbalanced lack of discernment on one hand, and an ignorance of intuition and soul on the other. The latter two qualities have to be actually experienced for the rational mind cannot imagine them and so is blind to their existence.

When knowledge has filtered deeply into our subconscious memory, it can then be expressed through the intuitive, to reach a depth of intimacy that reveals holistic truths we cannot otherwise reach. These are the eureka moments.

Once you have acquired your plant knowledge during the week, set aside some time at the weekend to meet them in their natural setting. Make sure you are warm enough and perhaps take a canvas square to your spot to sit on. Now spend an hour just sitting, gazing at your muse. Let your knowledge drift into the background and allow your entrained heart to well up and speak to you. Once it has spoken, faintly at first but stronger with practice, you will hear the voices of the wild ones. If you find this so awkward that you are struggling, consider a guide to help direct you past your sceptical, chattering-monkey mind. Try forest bathing, eco-yoga, plant spirit journeying, drumming circles and shamanic courses.

Some people skip the learning and try to establish knowledge only through intuition. In an age of instant gratification, they seek instant experience. 'The plants just spoke directly to our ancestors,' they argue. I agree that you will absorb some awareness of plants this way, however, our ancestors' deep knowledge of them was carved epi-genetically onto their DNA. Even the plants have these DNA Post-it notes of experiential memory. Without this type of ancestral lineage spanning the last few generations of your family, it is degraded and far less accessible – especially, for example, if you were brought up in a city with little interest in nature amongst your family and friends. Here, book learning is like restocking the epigenetic herbarium of your body. It doesn't discount or invalidate the intuitive experience; instead, it helps to avoid clouding wisdom and truth through a lack of discernment.

An easier way to explain this is to make a comparison with the expression, 'Cravings are your body telling you what it needs, so listen to them and eat what you desire.'

That's all very well if you have a healthy, intact microbiome. Then if your body craves seafood it may well be calling for iodine. If you suddenly fancy liver and onions, or vegan nettle cakes, you may well need iron. However, if you have microbial dysbiosis then there is more than one voice screaming to be fed. An overgrowth of *Candida albicans* – a gut fungus that causes thrush – will crave and demand sugar, for example. Listening to that voice just makes the situation worse as feeding *Candida* increases the size of the colony and further unbalances your gut microbiome. Excessive thirst – dehydration or diabetes? Craving for salt – mineral deficiency or Addison's disease? A guide-practitioner, prior experience or formal study, help to inform us as to the wisdom of having that sugary pudding that's calling to us!

## DEVELOPING DISCERNMENT

Jung described four cognitive functions: Thinking, Feeling, Sensing and Intuition. (You might have come across them at work as Red Hat Thinking, Myers-Briggs or other personality assessments and thinking exercises beloved by human resources professionals.) Initially I taught myself to take difficult decisions using these cognitive 'tools' to reach balanced outcomes. I since learnt that they also help me to understand the way that other living organisms in the natural world 'communicate' with us. I ask the four sentries of my mind:

What do you *think*?
What do you *sense*?
What do you *feel*?
What do you *intuit*?

*Thinking* is informed by rational thought, intellect, learning, education, critical analysis, logic, debate.

*Sensing* is informed by vision, hearing, touch, shape, size, texture, odour, taste, spatial awareness, kinaesthesia, proprioception. 'What does it smell like?' is an oft forgotten (occasionally critical) fungus identification tool. Aniseed? Curry? Iodine?

*Feeling* is informed by the heart, emotional context, repressed memory, mood, hormones, love, fear, anxiety, conviction, faith.

*Intuition* is channelled from the unconscious voices of the soul, ancestral memory, epigenetics, microbiomes, the 'gut feeling', bacteria, plants, fungi, animals, the collective unconscious, the numinous.

As both intuitions and feelings can have a sense of 'being given' or 'being self-evident', the inexperienced can sometimes find it hard to tell them apart from each other. This is the challenge. Is the message you're getting a pure communication? Or is it influenced or usurped by your feelings, mood or emotions?

Consciously asking the four questions as a 'balance check' helps to encourage your mind to reach its fullest potential – especially when you are encountering the numinous.

Good luck!

# SPECIES TABLE

The following tables cover all the plants, algae and fungi that I encountered during each season. Every species that I saw or mentioned is listed, not just those that I ate. If you look up a common name from the text, you can see the scientific name. This is important as while species may have several different common names, the scientific name is a universal constant. Look for the word by the main noun. For example, Japanese knotweed will be found under K – Knotweed, Japanese and bigflower vetch under V – Vetch, Bigflower unless both words are indivisible, such as ground elder which comes under G. The main use is also included. 'Edible' means some part of the species is eaten as a food. 'Herbal tea' means it is only used as a tea, flavouring or spice. This is a rough guide and you should investigate the correct use and preparation of each species before consuming them.

**\* and bold text identifies those species eaten during the course of my wild year.**

*TABLE 1: PLANTS*

| COMMON NAME | SCIENTIFIC NAME | EDIBILITY |
| --- | --- | --- |
| Agrimony | Agrimonia eupatoria | Herbal tea |
| **\*Alexanders** | **Smyrnium olusatrum** | Edible |

| COMMON NAME | SCIENTIFIC NAME | EDIBILITY |
|---|---|---|
| Alfalfa | Medicago sativa | Edible |
| *Almond, Wild | Prunus amygdalus | Edible |
| *Angelica, Wild | Angelica sylvestris | Edible |
| Anise | Pimpinella anisum | Edible |
| *Apple, Feral | Malus domestica | Edible |
| Arrowgrass, Marsh | Triglochin palustris | Edible |
| *Arrowgrass, Sea | Triglochin maritima | Edible |
| Artichoke, Jerusalem | Helianthus tuberosus | Edible |
| *Aster, Sea | Tripolium pannonicum | Edible |
| Ash | Fraxinus excelsior | Edible |
| Asparagus | Asparagus officinalis | Edible |
| Aspen | Populus tremula | Not eaten |
| Aubergine | Solanum melongena | Edible |
| Banana | Musa sp. | Edible |
| *Barberry, Common | Berberis vulgaris | Edible |
| *Barberry, Darwin's | Berberis darwinii | Edible |
| *Barley, Bere | Hordeum vulgare | Edible |
| Barley, Mediterranean | Hordeum hystrix | Edible |
| Barley, Sea | Hordeum marinum | Edible |
| Barley, Smooth | Hordeum glaucum | Edible |
| Barley, Wild | Hordeum spontaneum | Edible |
| *Bay | Laurus nobilis | Edible |
| Bean, Green | Phaseolus vulgaris | Edible |
| Bean, Mung | Vigna radiata | Edible |
| *Bedstraw, Heath | Galium saxatile | Edible |
| Bedstraw, Limestone | Galium sterneri | Edible |
| Bedstraw, Round-leaved | Galium rotundifolium | Edible |
| *Beech tree | Fagus sylvatica | Edible |
| *Beet, Sea | Beta vulgaris subsp. maritima | Edible |
| Beetroot | Beta vulgaris | Edible |
| Betony | Stachys betonica | Herbal tea |

| COMMON NAME | SCIENTIFIC NAME | EDIBILITY |
|---|---|---|
| **\*Bilberry** | **Vaccinium myrtillus** | Edible |
| Bindweed, Field | Convolvulus arvensis | Not eaten |
| **\*Birch, Downy** | **Betula pubescens** | Edible (sap) |
| Birch, Dwarf | Betula nana | Edible (sap) |
| **\*Birch, Silver** | **Betula pendula** | Edible (sap) |
| Bird's-foot Trefoil, Common | Lotus corniculata | Not eaten |
| **\*Bittercress, Hairy** | **Cardamine hirsuta** | Edible |
| **\*Bittercress, Wavy** | **Cardamine flexuosa** | Edible |
| **\*Blackthorn / Sloe** | **Prunus spinosa** | Edible |
| Blueberry | Vaccinium sect. Cyanococcus | Edible |
| Bracken | Pteridium aquilinum | Rarely eaten |
| **\*Bramble / Blackberry** | **Rubus fructicosus agg.** | Edible |
| Brazil nut | Bertholletia excelsa | Edible |
| Broccoli | Brassica oleracea var. italica | Edible |
| Brome, Archaeological | Bromus pseudobrachystachys | Not eaten |
| Brome, Meadow | Bromus commutatus | Not eaten |
| Brussels sprout | Brassica oleracea var. gemmifera | Edible |
| **\*Buckthorn, Sea** | **Hippophae rhamnoides** | Edible |
| **\*Burdock** | **Arctium lappa** | Edible |
| Burdock, Woolly | Arctium tomentosum | Edible |
| Burnet, Greater | Sanguisorba officinalis | Edible |
| **\*Cabbage, Wild** | **Brassica oleracea var. capitata** | Edible |
| Caltrop, Water / Water chestnut | Trapa natans | Edible |
| Cardamom | Elettaria cardamomum | Edible |
| **\*Cardoon** | **Cynara cardunculus** | Edible |
| Carrot, Domestic | Daucus carota, subsp. sativus | Edible |

| COMMON NAME | SCIENTIFIC NAME | EDIBILITY |
|---|---|---|
| **\*Carrot, Wild** | **Daucus carota** | Edible |
| Cashew nut | Anacardium occidentale | Edible |
| Celery | Apium graveolens | Edible |
| **\*Celandine, Lesser** | **Ficaria verna** | Edible |
| Chamomile | Matricaria chamomilla | Herbal tea |
| Chamomile, Dyer's | Anthemis tinctoria | Herbal tea |
| Cherry, Bird | Prunus cerastrum | Edible |
| **\*Cherry, European Bird** | **Prunus padus** | Edible |
| **\*Cherry, Plum** | **Prunus cerasifera** | Edible |
| **\*Cherry, Wild** | **Prunus avium** | Edible |
| Chervil, Bulbous | Chaerophyllum bulbosum | Edible |
| **\*Chestnut, Sweet** | **Castanea sativa** | Edible |
| Chestnut, Water | Eleocharis dulcis | Edible |
| **\*Chicory** | **Chicorum intybus** | Edible |
| **\*Chickweed** | **Stellaria media** | Edible |
| **\*Chickweed, Great** | **Stellaria neglecta** | Edible |
| Chilli | Capsicum annuum | Edible |
| Chives | Allium schoenoprasum | Edible |
| **\*Chokeberry, Black** | **Aronia melanocarpa** | Edible |
| Cinnamon | Cinnamomum verum | Edible |
| **\*Cleavers** | **Galium aparine** | Edible |
| **\*Clover, Red** | **Trifolium pratense** | Edible |
| **\*Clover, Suckling** | **Trifolium dubium** | Edible |
| **\*Clover, White** | **Trifolium repens** | Edible |
| **\*Coltsfoot** | **Tussilago farfara** | Edible |
| Cocoa | Theobroma cacao | Edible |
| Coconut | Cocos nucifera | Edible |
| Coffee | Coffea arabica | Edible |
| **\*Comfrey, Common** | **Symphytum officinale** | Edible |
| **\*Comfrey, Tuberosum** | **Symphytum tuberosum** | Edible |
| **\*Coriander** | **Coriandrum sativum** | Edible |

| COMMON NAME | SCIENTIFIC NAME | EDIBILITY |
|---|---|---|
| Corn/maize | Zea mays | Edible |
| Cottongrass, Common | Eriophorum angustifolium | Not eaten |
| Courgette | Cucurbita pepo | Edible |
| *Cow parsley | Anthriscus sylvestris | Edible |
| *Cowslip | Primula veris | Edible |
| *Crabapple | Malus sylvestris | Edible |
| *Cranberry, Wild | Vaccinium oxycoccos | Edible |
| Cranesbill | Geranium pratense | Herbal tea |
| Crosswort | Cruciata laevipes | Edible |
| *Cuckooflower / Lady's smock | Cardamine pratensis | Edible |
| Cucumber | Cucumis sativus | Edible |
| *Currant, Black | Ribes nigrum | Edible |
| *Currant, Flowering | Ribes sanguineum | Edible |
| *Currant, Red | Ribes rubrum | Edible |
| *Daisy | Bellis perennis | Edible |
| Daisy, Heart-leaf / Yellow Ox-eye | Telekia speciosa | Not eaten |
| *Daisy, Ox-eye | Leucanthemum vulgare | Edible |
| *Damson plum | Prunus insititia | Edible |
| *Dandelion | Taraxacum officinale agg. | Edible |
| *Dead-nettle, Red | Lamium purpureum | Edible |
| *Dead-nettle, White | Lamium album | Edible |
| *Dill | Anethum graveolens | Edible |
| *Dittany / Sea horseradish | Lepidium latifolium | Edible |
| *Dock, Broad-leaved | Rumex obtusifolius | Edible |
| Dodder, Greater | Cuscuta europaea | Not eaten |
| Dutchman's pipe | Monotropa hypopitys | Not eaten |
| *Einkorn / Wild wheat | Triticum monococcum | Edible |
| *Elder | Sambucus nigra | Edible |

| COMMON NAME | SCIENTIFIC NAME | EDIBILITY |
|---|---|---|
| *Elder, European | Sambucus racemosa | Edible |
| *Elecampane | Inula helenium | Edible |
| *Elm, Wych | Ulmus glabra | Edible |
| Emmer, Wild wheat | Triticum dicoccoides | Edible |
| *Eyebright | Euphrasia sp. | Edible |
| *Fat hen | Chenopodium album | Edible |
| *Fennel, Wild | Foeniculum vulgare | Edible |
| *Fern, Male | Dryopteris filix-mas | Rarely eaten |
| Fescue, Red | Festuca rubra | Edible |
| *Fir, Silver | Abies alba | Edible |
| Foxglove | Digitalis purpurea | Toxic |
| Foxtail | Alopecurus articulatus | Edible |
| Foxtail, Creeping meadow | Alopecurus arundinaceus | Edible |
| Foxtail, Green | Setaria viridis | Edible |
| *Fuchsia, Feral | Fuchsia magellanica | Edible |
| *Gallant soldiers | Galinsoga ciliata | Edible |
| Garlic | Allium sativum | Edible |
| Garlic, Crow | Allium vineale | Edible |
| *Garlic, Hedge / Garlic mustard | Alliaria petiolata | Edible |
| *Garlic, Rosy | Allium roseum | Edible |
| *Garlic, Victory | Allium victorialis | Edible |
| *Garlic, Wild / Bears | Allium ursinum | Edible |
| Gherkin | Cucumis sativus | Edible |
| Ginger | Zingiber officinale | Edible |
| Ginger, European Wild / Asarabacca | Asarum europaeum | Rarely eaten |
| Goat grass | Aegilops sp. | Edible |
| *Goat's-beard | Tragopogon pratensis | Edible |
| *Goji berry | Lycium chinense | Edible |
| Goldenrod, European | Solidago serotina | Edible |

| COMMON NAME | SCIENTIFIC NAME | EDIBILITY |
| --- | --- | --- |
| *Golden saxifrage | Chrysosplenium | Edible |
| *Goldenrod | Solidago virgaurea | Edible |
| *Good King Henry | Chenopodium bonus-henricus | Edible |
| *Gooseberry | Ribes uva-crispa | Edible |
| *Goosefoot, Many-seeded | Chenopodium polyspermum | Edible |
| *Gorse | Ulex europaeus | Edible |
| Grape | Vitis vinifera | Edible |
| Grass, Alkali | Puccinellia convoluta | Edible |
| Grass, Cock's-foot | Dactylis glomerata | Edible |
| Grass, Cockspur | Echinochloa crus-galli | Edible |
| Grass, Marram | Ammophila arenaria | Edible |
| *Ground elder | Aegopodium podagraria | Edible |
| *Ground ivy | Glechoma hederacea | Edible |
| *Guelder rose / Cramp bark | Viburnum opulus | Edible |
| Harebell | Campanula rotundifolia | Not eaten |
| Hawkbit, Rough | Leontodon hispidus | Not eaten |
| Hawkweed | Hieracium sp. | Not eaten |
| *Hawthorn | Crataegus monogyna | Edible |
| *Hazel | Corylus avellana | Edible |
| *Heartsease | Viola tricolor | Edible |
| Heather | Calluna vulgaris | Herbal tea |
| Hemlock, Poison | Conium maculatum | Toxic |
| Herb-paris | Paris quadrifolia | Toxic |
| *Himalayan balsam | Impatiens glandulifera | Edible |
| *Hogweed, Common | Heracleum sphondylium | Edible |
| Hogweed, Giant | Heracleum mantegazzianum | Dangerous |
| *Honeysuckle | Lonicera pericyclamen | Edible |
| *Hops | Humulus lupulus | Edible |
| *Horseradish | Armoracia rusticana | Edible |

| COMMON NAME | SCIENTIFIC NAME | EDIBILITY |
|---|---|---|
| Horsetail, Field | Equisetum arvense | Herbal tea |
| Horsetail, Great | Equisetum telmateia | Edible |
| *Jostaberry | **Ribes x nigridolaria** | Edible |
| *Juneberry / Saskatoon | **Amelanchier alnifolia** | Edible |
| *Juniper | **Juniperus communis** | Edible |
| Kale | Brassica oleracea var. sabellica | Edible |
| *Kale, Sea | **Crambe marítima** | Edible |
| Knapweed | Centaurea nigra | Not eaten |
| Knapweed, Greater | Centaurea scabiosa | Not eaten |
| Knotweed, Curly-topped | Polygonum lapathifolium | Edible |
| Knotweed, Japanese | Polygonum cuspidatum | Edible |
| Knotweed, Prostrate | Polygonum aviculare | Edible |
| Lady's bedstraw | Galium verum | Herbal tea |
| *Lady's mantle | **Alchemilla vulgaris** | Edible |
| *Larch, European | **Larix decidua** | Edible |
| Lavatera | Lavatera thuringiaca | Edible |
| Lavender | Lavendula angustifolia | Herbal tea |
| *Leek, Babington's | **Allium ampeloprasum** | Edible |
| *Leek, Few-flowered | **Allium paradoxum** | Edible |
| *Leek, Three-cornered | **Allium triquetrum** | Edible |
| *Lime, European | **Tilia x europaea** | Edible |
| Lemon | Citrus limon | Edible |
| Lentils, Wild | Lens culinaris subsp. orientalis | Edible |
| Lettuce | Lactuca sativa | Edible |
| *Lingonberry | **Vaccinium vitis-idaea** | Edible |
| Liquorice | Glycyrrhiza glabra | Edible |
| *Lovage | **Ligusticum officinale** | Edible |
| *Lovage, Scots | **Ligusticum scoticum** | Edible |
| *Mallow, Tree | **Malva arborea** | Edible |

| COMMON NAME | SCIENTIFIC NAME | EDIBILITY |
|---|---|---|
| Maple, Field | Acer campestre | Edible |
| *Marigold, Pot | Calendula officinalis | Edible |
| *Marjoram, Wild | Origanum vulgare | Edible |
| Marshmallow | Althaea officinalis | Edible |
| Mayweed, Scentless | Tripleurospermum inodorum | Not eaten |
| Meadow rue, Shining | Thalictrum lucidum | Edible |
| *Meadowsweet | Filipendula ulmaria | Edible |
| Medlar | Mespilus germanica | Edible |
| *Mint, Wild / Horse | Mentha longifolia | Edible |
| Monkshood | Aconitum napellus | Toxic |
| *Mugwort | Artemisia vulgaris | Edible |
| *Mulberry, Black | Morus nigra | Edible |
| *Mulberry, White | Morus alba | Edible |
| *Mullein, Common | Verbascum thapsus | Edible |
| Mullein, Dense-flowered | Verbascum densiflorum | Herbal tea |
| *Mullein, Dark | Verbascum nigrum | Herbal tea |
| *Mustard, Black | Brassica nigra | Edible |
| *Myrtle | Myrtus communis | Edible |
| *Myrtle, Bog | Myrica gale | Edible |
| *Navelwort | Umbilicus rupestris | Edible |
| *Nettle | Urtica dioica | Edible |
| *Oak, Evergreen | Quercus ilex | Edible |
| *Oak, Pedunculate | Quercus robur | Edible |
| *Oak, Sessile | Quercus petraea | Edible |
| *Oak, Turkey | Quercus cerris | Edible |
| Oat | Avena sativa | Edible |
| Oat, Slender wild | Avena barbata | Edible |
| Oat, Wild | Avena fatua | Edible |
| Okra | Abelmoschus esculentus | Edible |
| Onion | Allium cepa | Edible |
| *Onion, Everlasting | Allium cepa perutile | Edible |
| Onion, Spring | Allium fistulosum | Edible |

| COMMON NAME | SCIENTIFIC NAME | EDIBILITY |
| --- | --- | --- |
| *Orache, Common | Atriplex patula | Edible |
| *Orache, Frosted | Atriplex laciniata | Edible |
| *Orache, Grass-leaved | Atriplex littoralis | Edible |
| *Orache, Scot's | Atriplex glabriuscula | Edible |
| *Orache, Spear-leaved | Atriplex prostrata | Edible |
| Orange | Citrus x sinensis | Edible |
| Orange, Wild | Citrus sp. | Edible |
| Orchid, Common spotted | Dactylorhiza fuchsii | Rarely eaten |
| *Oregon grape | Mahonia x media | Edible |
| *Ox-tongue, Bristly | Helminthotheca echioides | Edible |
| Palm, African white | Elaeis guineensis | Edible |
| Parsley | Petroselinum crispum | Edible |
| Parsnip, Wild | Pastinaca sativa | Edible |
| Pea, Pigeon | Cajanus cajun | Edible |
| *Pea, Tuberous | Lathyrus tuberosus | Edible |
| *Pear | Pyrus communis | Edible |
| Pecan | Carya illinoinensis | Edible |
| *Pennycress, Field | Thlaspi arvense | Edible |
| *Peppermint | Mentha piperita | Edible |
| Pepper, Black | Piper nigrum | Edible |
| *Pignut | Conopodium majus | Edible |
| Pine, Pinyon | Pinus sect. Sembroides | Edible |
| *Pine, Scots | Pinus sylvestris | Edible |
| Pineapple | Ananas comosus | Edible |
| *Pineappleweed | Matricaria discoidea | Edible |
| *Plantain, Ribwort | Plantago lanceolata | Edible |
| *Plantain, Sea | Plantago maritima | Edible |
| *Plums, Feral (prunes) | Prunus domestica | Edible |
| Poppy, Field | Papaver rhoeas | Edible |
| Potato | Solanum tuberosum | Edible |

| COMMON NAME | SCIENTIFIC NAME | EDIBILITY |
|---|---|---|
| Potato, African | Hypoxis hemerocallidea | Edible |
| *Primrose, Common | Primula vulgaris | Edible |
| Primrose, Evening | Oenothera sp. | Edible |
| Pumpkin | Cucurbita pepo | Edible |
| *Purslane, Pink | Claytonia sibirica | Edible |
| *Purslane, Sea | Atriplex portulacoides | Edible |
| *Quince | Cydonia oblonga | Edible |
| Quinoa | Chenopodium quinoa | Edible |
| *Radish, Black | Raphanus sativus niger | Edible |
| *Radish, Sea | Raphanus maritimus | Edible |
| Ragwort, Common | Senecio jacobaea | Toxic |
| Rape, Oil Seed | Brassica napus | Edible |
| *Raspberry, Wild | Rubus idaeus | Edible |
| *Reed mace | Typha latifolia | Edible |
| Rhubarb | Rheum x hybridum | Edible |
| Rice | Oryza sativa | Edible |
| *Rocket, Sea | Cakile maritima | Edible |
| *Rocket, Sweet / Dame's violet | Hesperis matronalis | Edible |
| *Rocket, Wild | Diplotaxis tenuifolia | Edible |
| *Rose, Burnet | Rosa pimpernellifolia | Edible |
| Rose, Cabbage | Rosa centifolia | Edible |
| *Rose, Dog | Rosa canina | Edible |
| *Rose, Eglantine / Sweet briar | Rosa rubiginosa | Edible |
| Rose, Garden | Rosa chinensis | Edible |
| *Rose, Japanese | Rosa rugosa | Edible |
| Rosemary | Rosmarinus officinalis | Edible |
| *Rowan | Sorbus aucuparia | Edible |
| Rye brome | Bromus secalinus | Edible |
| *Sage | Salvia officinalis | Edible |
| Salsify | Tragopogon porrifolius | Edible |

| COMMON NAME | SCIENTIFIC NAME | EDIBILITY |
|---|---|---|
| Salsify, Meadow | Tragopogon pratensis | Edible |
| *Samphire, Golden | Inula crithmoides | Edible |
| *Samphire, Marsh | Salicornia europea | Edible |
| *Samphire, Rock | Crithmum maritimum | Edible |
| *Sandwort, Sea | Honckenya peploides | Edible |
| Scabious, Devil's-bit | Succisa pratensis | Edible |
| Scabious, Field | Knautia arvensis | Edible |
| *Scurvy grass, Common | Cochlearia officinalis | Edible |
| Scurvy grass, Danish | Cochlearia danica | Edible |
| *Scurvy grass, English | Cochlearia anglica | Edible |
| *Seablite, Annual | Suaeda maritima | Edible |
| *Sedge, Pendulous | Carex pendula | Edible |
| *Selfheal | Prunella vulgaris | Edible |
| Sensitive plant | Mimosa pudica | Not eaten |
| *Shepherd's purse | Capsella bursa-pastoris | Edible |
| Sickleweed | Falcaria vulgaris | Edible |
| *Silverweed | Potentilla anserina | Edible |
| *Sneezewort | Achillea ptarmica | Edible |
| Soapwort | Saponaria officinalis | Toxic |
| *Solomon's seal | Polygonatum multiflorum | Edible |
| Sorghum | Sorghum bicolor | Edible |
| *Sorrel, Common | Rumex acetosa | Edible |
| *Sorrel, Sheep's | Rumex acetosella | Edible |
| *Sorrel, Wood | Oxalis acetosella | Edible |
| Southernwood | Artemisia arbrotanum | Not eaten |
| Soybean | Glycine max | Edible |
| *Speedwell, Heath | Veronica officinalis | Herbal tea |
| Spelt | Triticum spelta | Edible |
| *Spring beauty / Miner's lettuce | Claytonia perfoliata | Edible |
| *Spruce, Norway | Picea abies | Herbal tea |

| COMMON NAME | SCIENTIFIC NAME | EDIBILITY |
|---|---|---|
| *Spruce, Sitka | **Picea sitchensis** | Herbal tea |
| *Spurrey, Sea | **Spergularia marina** | Edible |
| Strawberry | Fragaria x ananassa | Edible |
| *Strawberry, Wild | **Fragaria vesca** | Edible |
| Sunflower | Helianthus annuus | Edible |
| Sweet Annie | Artemisia annua | Herbal tea |
| *Sweet cicely | **Myrrhis odorata** | Edible |
| *Sweet vernal grass | **Anthoxanthum odoratum** | Edible |
| *Swinecress | **Lepidium didymum** | Edible |
| Swiss cheese plant | Monstera deliciosa | Edible |
| *Sycamore | **Acer pseudoplatanus** | Edible |
| **Tansy** | **Tanacetum vulgare** | Not eaten |
| *Tarragon | **Artemisia officinalis** | Edible |
| Tea | Camelia sinensis | Herbal tea |
| *Thistle, Brook | **Cirsium rivulare** | Edible |
| *Thistle, Common / Bull / Spear | **Cirsium vulgare** | Edible |
| *Thistle, Creeping | **Cirsium arvense** | Edible |
| *Thistle, Marsh | **Cirsium palustre** | Edible |
| *Thistle, Sow | **Sonchus oleraceus** | Edible |
| Thrift/Sea Pink | Armeria maritima | Not eaten |
| *Thyme, Wild | **Thymus polytrichus** | Edible |
| *Thyme, Broad-leaved | **Thymus pulegioides** | Edible |
| Tomato | Solanum lycopersicum | Edible |
| Tonka bean | Dipteryx odorata | Edible |
| Tormentil | Potentilla erecta | Herbal tea |
| Turnip | Brassica rapa | Edible |
| *Valerian | **Valeriana officinalis** | Edible |
| Valerian, Pyrenean | Valeriana pyrenaica | Herbal tea |
| Vanilla | Vanilla planifolia | Edible |
| *Vetch, Bigflower | **Vicia grandiflora** | Edible |
| *Vetch, Bush | **Vicia sepium** | Edible |

| COMMON NAME | SCIENTIFIC NAME | EDIBILITY |
|---|---|---|
| **\*Vetch, Common** | **Vicia sativa** | Edible |
| Vetch, Hairy | Vicia villosa | Edible |
| **\*Vetch, Lentil / Smooth tare** | **Vicia tetrasperma** | Edible |
| Vetch, Purple crown | Securigera varia | Edible |
| **\*Vetch, Tufted** | **Vicia cracca** | Edible |
| **\*Violet, Dog** | **Viola riviniana** | Edible |
| **\*Violet, Wood** | **Viola odorata** | Edible |
| Viper's bugloss | Echium vulgare | Not eaten |
| **\*Walnut** | **Juglans regia** | Edible |
| **\*Watercress** | **Nasturtium officinale** | Edible |
| Water lily, Giant | Victoria amazonica | Edible |
| **\*Watermint** | **Mentha aquatica** | Edible |
| **\*Water pepper / Arsesmart** | **Polygonum hydropiper** | Edible |
| Water-dropwort, Hemlock | Oenanthe crocata | Toxic |
| Wheat | Triticum aestivum | Edible |
| **\*Whitebeam, Swedish** | **Sorbus intermedia** | Edible |
| Willow, Dwarf | Salix herbacea | Herbal tea |
| Willow, Goat | Salix caprea | Herbal tea |
| Willow, White | Salix alba | Herbal tea |
| **\*Willowherb, Rosebay** | **Chamaenerion angustifolium** | Edible |
| **\*Wineberry, Japanese** | **Rubus phoenicolasius** | Edible |
| **\*Wintercress** | **Barbarea vulgaris** | Edible |
| **\*Woodruff, Sweet** | **Galium odoratum** | Edible |
| Woodrush, Greater | Luzula sylvestris | Edible |
| Wormwood | Artemisia absinthia | Herbal tea |
| **\*Wormwood, Sea** | **Artemisia maritima** | Edible |
| **\*Woundwort, Hedge** | **Stachys sylvestris** | Edible |
| **\*Woundwort, Marsh** | **Stachys palustris** | Edible |

| COMMON NAME | SCIENTIFIC NAME | EDIBILITY |
|---|---|---|
| *Yarrow | **Achillea millefolium** | Edible |
| *Yucca | **Yucca filamentosa** | Edible |

## TABLE 2: FUNGI

| COMMON NAME | SCIENTIFIC NAME | EDIBILITY |
|---|---|---|
| *Artist's bracket | **Ganoderma applanatum** | Medicinal |
| *Beefsteak fungus | **Fistulina hepatica** | Edible |
| Birch polypore | Piptoporus betulinus | Medicinal |
| *Blewit, Field | **Lepista saeva** | Edible |
| *Blewit, Sordid | **Lepista sordida** | Edible |
| *Blewit, Wood | **Lepista nuda** | Edible |
| *Blusher | **Amanita rubescens** | Edible |
| *Bolete, Bay | **Imleria badia** | Edible |
| *Bolete, Brown birch | **Leccinum scabrum** | Edible |
| *Bolete, Cow | **Suillus bovinus** | Edible |
| Bolete, Devil's | Rubroboletus satanas | Toxic |
| *Bolete, Ghost | **Leccinum holopus** | Edible |
| *Bolete, Larch | **Suillus grevillei** | Edible |
| *Bolete, Mottled | **Leccinum variicolor** | Edible |
| *Bolete, Orange birch | **Leccinum versipelle** | Edible |
| *Bolete, Peppery | **Boletus piperatus** | Edible |
| *Bolete, Pine | **Boletus pinopilus** | Edible |
| *Bolete, Red cracked | **Xerocomellus chrysenteron** | Edible |
| *Bolete, Red cracked | **Xerocomellus cisalpinus** | Edible |
| *Bolete, Scarletina | **Neoboletus luridiformis** | Edible |
| *Bolete, Slippery jack | **Suillus luteus** | Edible |
| *Bolete, Velvet | **Suillus variegatus** | Edible |
| *Brittlegill, Blackening | **Russula nigricans** | Edible |

| COMMON NAME | SCIENTIFIC NAME | EDIBILITY |
|---|---|---|
| *Brittlegill, Common yellow | Russula ochroleuca | Edible |
| *Brittlegill, Crowded | Russula densifolia | Edible |
| *Brittlegill, Greasy grey | Russula grisea | Edible |
| *Brittlegill, Green | Russula cutifracta | Edible |
| *Brittlegill, Oil slick | Russula ionochlora | Edible |
| *Brittlegill, The flirt | Russula vesca | Edible |
| *Brittlegill, Yellow swamp | Russula claroflava | Edible |
| Button mushroom | Agaricus bisporus | Edible |
| *Cauliflower fungus | Sparassis crispa | Edible |
| *Chaga | Inonotus obliquus | Medicinal |
| *Chanterelle | Cantharellus cibarius | Edible |
| Chanterelle, False | Hygrophoropsis aurantiaca | Not eaten |
| *Charcoal Burner | Russula cyanoxantha | Edible |
| *Chicken-of-the-woods | Laetiporus sulphureus | Edible |
| *Deceiver, Amethyst | Laccaria amethystina | Edible |
| *Deceiver, Scurfy | Laccaria proxima | Edible |
| *Deceiver, The | Laccaria laccata | Edible |
| *Dryad's saddle | Polyporus squamosus | Edible |
| Ergot | Claviceps purpurea | Toxic |
| *Fairy ring mushroom | Marasmius oreades | Edible |
| False morel | Gyromitra esculenta | Toxic |
| *Field mushroom | Agaricus campestris | Edible |
| Fly agaric | Amanita muscaria | Toxic |
| Funeral bell | Galerina marginata | Toxic |
| *Funnel, Aniseed | Clitocybe odora | Edible |
| *Funnel, Trooping | Clitocybe geotropa | Edible |
| *Giant polypore | Meripilus giganteus | Edible |
| *Grisette, Orange | Amanita crocea | Edible |
| *Grisette, Tawny | Amanita fulva | Edible |

| COMMON NAME | SCIENTIFIC NAME | EDIBILITY |
|---|---|---|
| *Grisette, The | Amanita vaginata | Edible |
| *Hedgehog fungus | Hydnum repandum | Edible |
| *Hedgehog, Terracotta | Hydnum rufescens | Edible |
| *Hen-of-the-woods | Grifola frondosa | Edible |
| *Honey fungus | Armillaria mellea | Edible |
| *Horn of plenty | Craterellus cornucopioides | Edible |
| *Horse mushroom | Agaricus arvensis | Edible |
| Inkcap, Grey | Coprinus cinereus | Edible |
| *Inkcap, Shaggy | Coprinus comatus | Edible |
| Liberty cap / Magic mushroom | Psilocybe semilanceata | Medicinal |
| Lion's mane | Hericium erinaceus | Edible |
| *Milkcap, Coconut-scented | Lactarius gloiciosmus | Edible |
| *Milkcap, Curry-scented | Lactarius camphoratus | Edible |
| *Milkcap, False saffron | Lactarius deterrimus | Edible |
| *Milkcap, Oak | Lactarius quietus | Edible |
| *Milkcap, Peppery | Lactifluus piperatus | Edible |
| *Milkcap, Saffron | Lactarius deliciosus | Edible |
| *Miller, The | Clitopilus prunulus | Edible |
| *Morel mushroom | Morchella esculenta | Edible |
| *Oyster mushroom | Pleurotus ostreatus | Edible |
| *Oyster, Branched | Pleurotus cornucopiae | Edible |
| *Oyster, Summer | Pleurotus pulmonarius | Edible |
| *Oysterling, Olive | Sarcomyxa serotina | Edible |
| *Parasol | Macrolepiota procera | Edible |
| *Parasol, Shaggy | Chlorophylum rhacodes | Edible |

| COMMON NAME | SCIENTIFIC NAME | EDIBILITY |
|---|---|---|
| *Penny bun / Ceps / Porcini | Boletus edulis | Edible |
| *Porcelain fungus | Oudemansiella mucida | Edible |
| *Puffball, Common | Lycoperdon perlatum | Edible |
| *Puffball, Giant | Langermannia gigantea | Edible |
| *Puffball, Meadow | Lycoperdon pratense | Edible |
| *Puffball, Mosaic | Calvatia exipuliformis | Edible |
| *Puffball, Stump | Lycoperdon pyriforme | Edible |
| Roundhead, Dung | Protostropharia semiglobata | Not eaten |
| *Saint George's mushroom | Calocybe gambosa | Edible |
| *Scarlet elf cups | Sarcoscypha coccinea | Edible |
| Slime mould / Dog's vomit | Fuligo septica | Not eaten |
| Split gill | Schizophyllum commune | Not eaten |
| Tinder hoof | Fomes fomentarius | Medicinal |
| Truffle, White | Tuber magnatum | Edible |
| *Turkey tail | Trametes versicolor | Medicinal |
| *Velvet shank | Flammulina velutipes | Edible |
| *Waxcap, Blackening | Hygrocybe conica | Edible |
| *Waxcap, Heath | Gliophorus laeta | Edible |
| *Waxcap, Meadow | Cuphophyllus pratensis | Edible |
| *Waxcap, Parrot | Gliophorus psittacina | Edible |
| *Waxcap, Scarlet hood | Hygrocybe coccinea | Edible |
| *Waxcap, Snowy | Cuphophyllus virgineus | Edible |
| *Winter chanterelle | Craterellus tubaeformis | Edible |
| *Wood ear / Jelly ear | Auricularia auricula-judae | Edible |
| *Wood mushroom, Blushing | Agaricus langei | Edible |
| *Woodtuft, Sheathed | Kuehneromyces mutabilis | Edible |

## TABLE 3: SEAWEEDS (algae)

| COMMON NAME | SCIENTIFIC NAME | EDIBILITY |
|---|---|---|
| *Bladderwrack | Fucus vesiculosus | Edible |
| *Carragheen | Chondrus crispus | Edible |
| *Dabberlocks | Alaria esculenta | Edible |
| *Double ribbon weed | Ulva linza | Edible |
| *Dulse | Palmeria palmata | Edible |
| *Dumont's tubular weed | Dumontia contorta | Edible |
| *Grape pip weed | Mastocarpus stellatus | Edible |
| *Gutweed | Ulva compressa | Edible |
| *Gutweed | Ulva intestinalis | Edible |
| *Laver / Nori | Porphyra spp. | Edible |
| Mermaid's tresses / Bootlace weed | Chorda filum | Edible |
| *Oarweed / Tangle | Laminaria digitata | Edible |
| *Pepper dulse | Osmundea pinnatifida | Edible |
| *Royal fernweed | Osmundea osmunda | Edible |
| *Sea lettuce | Ulva lactuca | Edible |
| *Sea spaghetti | Himanthalia elongata | Edible |
| *Sugar kelp | Laminaria saccharina | Edible |
| *Velvet horn | Codium tomentosum | Edible |
| *Wrack siphon weed | Polysiphonia lanosa | Edible |
| *Wrack, Channelled | Pelvetia canaliculata | Edible |
| Wrack, Estuary / Horned | Fucus ceranoides | Edible |
| *Wrack, Serrated | Fucus serrata | Edible |
| *Wrack, Spiralled | Fucus spiralis | Edible |

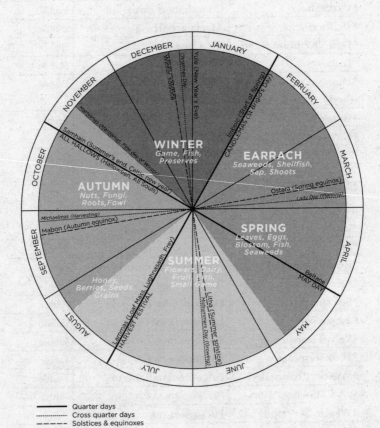

Quarter days
Cross quarter days
Solstices & equinoxes

**WINTER**
*Game, Fish,
Preserves*

**EARRACH**
*Seaweeds, Shellfish,
Sap, Shoots*

**AUTUMN**
*Nuts, Fungi,
Roots, Fowl*

**SPRING**
*Leaves, Eggs,
Blossom, Fish,
Seaweeds*

**SUMMER**
*Flowers, Dairy,
Fruit, Fish,
Small Game*

*Honey,
Berries, Seeds,
Grains*

JANUARY
FEBRUARY
MARCH
APRIL
MAY
JUNE
JULY
AUGUST
SEPTEMBER
OCTOBER
NOVEMBER
DECEMBER

Yule (New Year's Eve)
Christmas Day
Winter SOLSTICE
Imbolc (Start of Spring)
CANDLEMAS (St Brigid's Day)
Ostara (Spring equinox)
Lady Day (Planting)
Beltane
MAY DAY
Litha (Summer solstice)
Midsummer Day (Growing)
Lammas (Loaf Mass Lughnasadh Frey)
HARVEST FESTIVAL
Mabon (Autumn equinox)
Michaelmas (Harvesting)
Samhain (Summer's end Celtic new year)
ALL HALLOWS (Halloween, All Souls)
Martinmas (Martinmas, First day of Winter)

# CALENDAR

## THE CELTIC CALENDAR

| | |
|---|---|
| 31 October – 1 November: | Samhain (Celtic new year) |
| 21/22 December: | Yule (winter solstice) |
| 31 January – 1 February: | Imbolc (start of Earrach) |
| 21/22 March: | Ostara (spring equinox) |
| 30 April – 1 May: | Beltane (May Day) |
| 21/22 June: | Litha (summer solstice) |
| 31 July – 1 August: | Lùnastal (harvest festival) |
| 21/22 September: | Mabon (autumn equinox) |

## THE WILDERNESS CURE SEASONS

| | |
|---|---|
| Winter: | Samhain to Imbolc |
| Earrach: | Imbolc to Ostara |
| Spring: | Ostara to Beltane |
| Summer: | Beltane to Lùnastal |
| Autumn: | Lùnastal to Samhain |

# NOTES

## PART ONE: WINTER

### Chapter One: The Day Before

1 Schnorr, S. L., Candela, M., Rampelli, S., Centanni, M., Consolandi, C., Basaglia, G., Turroni, S., Biagi, E., Peano, C., Severgnini, M., Fiori, J., Gotti, R., de Bellis, G., Luiselli, D., Brigidi, P., Mabulla, A., Marlowe, F., Henry, A. G., and Crittenden, A. N. (2014). 'Gut microbiome of the Hadza hunter-gatherers.' *Nature Communications*, 5(1). https://doi.org/10.1038/ncomms4654.

2 Turner, P. G., and Lefevre, C. E. (2017). 'Instagram use is linked to increased symptoms of orthorexia nervosa.' *Eating and Weight Disorders — Studies on Anorexia, Bulimia and Obesity*, 22(2), 277–284.

3 Cornélio, A. M., de Bittencourt-Navarrete, R. E., de Bittencourt Brum, R., Queiroz, C. M., and Costa, M. R. (2016). 'Human brain expansion during evolution is independent of fire control and cooking.' *Frontiers in Neuroscience*, 10, 167.

4 Pierotti, R., and Fogg, B. R. (2017). *The First Domestication*. Yale University Press.

5 Stiner, M. C., Munro, N. D., Buitenhuis, H., Duru, G., and Özbaşaran, M. (2022). 'An endemic pathway to sheep and goat domestication at Aşıklı Höyük' (Central Anatolia, Turkey). *Proceedings of the National Academy of Sciences*, 119(4).

6 Mazoyer, M., and Roudart, L. (2006). *A History of World Agriculture: From the Neolithic age to the current crisis*. NYU Press.

7 Bollongino, R., Nehlich, O., Richards, M. P., Orschiedt, J., Thomas,

M. G., Sell, C., ... and Burger, J. (2013). '2000 years of parallel societies in Stone Age Central Europe.' *Science*, 342(6157), 479-481.

8    Clark, P. (ed.). (2013). *The Oxford Handbook of Cities in World History*. OUP Oxford.

9    Fairlie, S. (2009). 'A short history of enclosure in Britain.' *The Land*, 7, 16–31.

10   Wrigley, E. A. (2013). 'Energy and the English industrial revolution.' *Philosophical Transactions of the Royal Society A: Mathematical, Physical and Engineering Sciences*, 371(1986), 20110568.

11   Hughes, M. (2013). 'The Victorian London sanitation projects and the sanitation of projects.' *International Journal of Project Management*, 31(5), 682–691.

12   Cancer Research UK. https://www.cancerresearchuk.org/health-professional/cancer-statistics/risk accessed 29 Jan 2022.

13   Robin, Marie-Monique. (2014). *Our Daily Poison: From pesticides to packaging, how chemicals have contaminated the food chain and are making us sick*. New York and London: The New Press.

14   Draper., H. (1977). 'The aboriginal Eskimo diet in modern perspective.' *American Anthropologist*, 79, 2, 309–316. https://doi.org/10.1525/aa.1977.79.2.02a00070

15   Provenza, F. (2018). *Nourishment: What animals can teach us about rediscovering our nutritional wisdom*. Chelsea Green Publishing.

16   Logan, A. C., Katzman, M. A., and Balanzá-Martínez, V. (2015). 'Natural environments, ancestral diets, and microbial ecology: is there a modern "paleo-deficit disorder"?' Part II. *Journal of Physiological Anthropology*, 34(1), 1–21.

## Chapter Two: Early Days

1    Hartley, D. (1964). *Food in England* (1954). MacDonald & Co.

## Chapter Three: Foraging Habitat

1    Binford, L. R. (1980). 'Willow smoke and dogs' tails: hunter-gatherer settlement systems and archaeological site formation.' *American Antiquity*, 45(1), 4–20.

2    Burnham, A. (ed.). (2018). *The Old Stones: A field guide to the megalithic sites of Britain and Ireland*. Watkins.

3    Bassett, R., Young, P. J., Blair, G. S., Cai, X. M., & Chapman, L. (2020).

'Urbanisation's contribution to climate warming in Great Britain.' *Environmental Research Letters*, 15(11), 114014.

4   Ballin, T. B. (2018). *Reindeer Hunters at Howburn Farm, South Lanarkshire: A late Hamburgian settlement in southern Scotland — its lithic artefacts and natural environment.* Archaeopress Publishing Ltd.

5   Ma, K. W. (1992). 'The roots and development of Chinese acupuncture: from prehistory to early 20th century.' *Acupuncture in Medicine*, 10(1_suppl.), 92–99.

6   Dorfer, L., Moser, M., Bahr, F., Spindler, K., Egarter-Vigl, E., Giullén, S., ... & Kenner, T. (1999). 'A medical report from the stone age?' *The Lancet*, 354(9183), 1023–1025.

7   Deryabina, T., Kuchmel, S., Nagorskaya, L., Hinton, T., Beasley, J., Lerebours, A., & Smith, J. (2015). 'Long-term census data reveal abundant wildlife populations at Chernobyl.' *Current Biology*, 25(19), R824–R826. https://doi.org/10.1016/j.cub.2015.08.017

### Chapter Four: Digging Roots

1   Kelly, R. L. (2013). *The Lifeways of Hunter-gatherers: The foraging spectrum.* Cambridge University Press.

### Chapter Five: Broken Land

1   McKie, R. (2020, December 21). 'Early humans may have survived the harsh winters by hibernating.' *Guardian.* https://www.theguardian.com/science/2020/dec/20/early-humans-may-have-survived-the-harsh-winters-by-hibernating

2   Bartsiokas, A., & Arsuaga, J. L. (2020). 'Hibernation in hominins from Atapuerca, Spain half a million years ago.' *L'Anthropologie*, 124(5), 102797.

### Chapter Seven: Game

1   Butnariu, M., & Samfira, I. (2013). Vegetal metabolomics to seeds of Galium aparine. *Journal of Bioequivalence & Bioavailability*, 5, e45.

2   Duke, J. A. (2017). *Handbook of Edible Weeds: Herbal reference library.* Routledge.

3 Ferrero, D. M., Lemon, J. K., Fluegge, D., Pashkovski, S. L., Korzan, W. J., Datta, S. R., Spehr, M., Fendt, M., & Liberles, S. D. (2011). 'Detection and avoidance of a carnivore odor by prey.' *Proceedings of the National Academy of Sciences*, 108(27), 11235–11240. https://doi.org/10.1073/pnas.1103317108

# PART TWO: EARRACH

## Chapter Nine: Celebrating Imbolc

1 Foster, J., Sharpe, T., Poston, A., Morgan, C., & Musau, F. (2016). 'Scottish passive house: insights into environmental conditions in monitored passive houses.' *Sustainability*, 8(5), 412.

2 Mattingly, D. (2007). *An Imperial Possession: Britain in the Roman Empire, 54 BC–AD 409 (Vol. 1).* Penguin UK.

3 Carradice, P. (2013, June 27). *The death of the druids.* BBC Wales. https://www.bbc.co.uk/blogs/wales/entries/375ec5d4-a10c-3f1a-929c-12d9697f3f58

4 Bell, M. and Neumann, H. (1997). 'Prehistoric intertidal archaeology and environments in the Severn Estuary, Wales.' *World Archaeology*, 29(1), *Riverine Archaeology*, pp. 95–113 (on Bronze Age human footprints)

5 Miller, M. (2015, October 1). 'Bronze Age steam room may have been used by select Orkney settlers for rites.' Ancient Origins. https://www.ancient-origins.net/news-history-archaeology/bronze-age-steam-room-may-have-been-used-select-orkney-settlers-rites-020550

6 Loktionov, A. (2013). 'Something for everyone: a ritualistic interpretation of Bronze Age burnt mounds from an ethnographic perspective.' *The Post Hole*, 26, 137.

7 Bradley, J. (2018). The Irish Sweathouses, with special reference to Carrickmore's.' *Seanchas Ardmhacha: Journal of the Armagh Diocesan Historical Society*, 27(1), 130–144.

8 Wilson, P. L. (1999). *Ploughing the Clouds: The search for Irish soma.* City Lights Books.

## Chapter Ten: The Hungry Gap

1 Schulting, R. J., & Richards, M. P. (2002). 'The wet, the wild and the domesticated: The Mesolithic–Neolithic transition on the west coast of Scotland.' *European Journal of Archaeology*, 5(2), 147–189. https://doi. org/10.1179/eja.2002.5.2.147

2 Dolina, K., & Luczaj, L. (2014). 'Wild food plants used on the Dubrovnik coast (south-eastern Croatia).' *Acta Societatis Botanicorum Poloniae*, 83(3).

3 Kang, Y., Łuczaj, Ł., Kang, J., & Zhang, S. (2013). 'Wild food plants and wild edible fungi in two valleys of the Qinling Mountains (Shaanxi, central China).' *Journal of Ethnobiology and Ethnomedicine*, 9(1), 1–20.

4 Vanhanen, S., & Pesonen, P. (2016). 'Wild plant gathering in stone age Finland.' *Quaternary International*, 404, 43–55.

5 Melamed, Y., Kislev, M. E., Geffen, E., Lev-Yadun, S., & Goren-Inbar, N. (2016). 'The plant component of an Acheulian diet at Gesher Benot Ya 'aqov, Israel.' *Proceedings of the National Academy of Sciences*, 113(51), 14674–14679.

6 Colledge, S., & Conolly, J. (2014). 'Wild plant use in European Neolithic subsistence economies: a formal assessment of preservation bias in archaeobotanical assemblages and the implications for understanding changes in plant diet breadth.' *Quaternary Science Reviews*, 101, 193–206. https://doi.org/10.1016/j.quascirev.2014.07.013

7 Klok, M. D., Jakobsdottir, S., & Drent, M. L. (2007). 'The role of leptin and ghrelin in the regulation of food intake and body weight in humans: a review.' *Obesity Reviews: An Official Journal of the International Association for the Study of Obesity*, 8(1), 21–34. https://doi. org/10.1111/j.1467-789X.2006.00270.x

## Chapter Eleven: On Seaweed

1 Wrangham, R. (2010). *Catching Fire: How cooking made us human.* Profile Books.

## Chapter Twelve: Sap Rising

1 Svanberg, I., Sõukand, R., Łuczaj, Ł., Kalle, R., Zyryanova, O., Dénes, A., Papp, N., Nedelcheva, A., Šeškauskaitė, D., Kołodziejska-Degórska,

I., & Kolosova, V. (2012). 'Uses of tree saps in northern and eastern parts of Europe.' *Acta Societatis Botanicorum Poloniae*, 81(4), 343–357. https://doi.org/10.5586/asbp.2012.036

2  Simard, S. (2016). *Exploring How and Why Trees 'Talk' to Each Other*. Yale Environment, 360(1).

3  Simard, S. (2021). *Finding the Mother Tree: Uncovering the wisdom and intelligence of the forest*. Penguin UK.

4  Trewavas, A. (2003). 'Aspects of plant intelligence.' *Annals of Botany*, 92(1), 1–20.

5  Calvo, P., Gagliano, M., Souza, G. M., & Trewavas, A. (2020). 'Plants are intelligent, here's how.' *Annals of Botany*, 125(1), 11–28.

6  Gagliano, M., Renton, M., Depczynski, M., & Mancuso, S. (2014). 'Experience teaches plants to learn faster and forget slower in environments where it matters.' *Oecologia*, 175(1), 63–72.

7  Witzany, G. (2016). 'The biosemiotics of plant communication.' *The American Journal of Semiotics*, 24(1/3), 39–56.

8  Łuczaj, Ł., Wilde, M., & Townsend, L. (2021). 'The ethnobiology of contemporary British foragers: Foods they teach, their sources of inspiration and impact.' *Sustainability*, 13(6), 3478.

9  George, R. (2021, March 26). 'I've sailed the Suez canal on a cargo ship – it's no wonder the Ever Given got stuck.' *Guardian*. https://www.theguardian.com/commentisfree/2021/mar/25/suez-canal-cargo-ship-ever-given-stuck

10  George, R. (2013). *Ninety Percent of Everything: Inside shipping, the invisible industry that puts clothes on your back, gas in your car, and food on your plate*. Macmillan.

### Chapter Thirteen: The Sweetest Thing

1  Naito, Y., Uchiyama, K., & Takagi, T. (2018). 'A next-generation beneficial microbe: Akkermansia muciniphila.' *Journal of Clinical Biochemistry and Nutrition*, 63(1), 33–35. https://doi.org/10.3164/jcbn.18-57

### Chapter Sixteen: The Wonder of Trees

1  New Scientist Limited. (2019). 'What is the body made of?' *New Scientist*. Retrieved May 7, 2021, from https://www.newscientist.com/question/what-is-the-body-made-of/#ixzz7BkWE6Wj9

2   Mitchell, R.J. (1970). 'Woodstock' Recorded by Joni Mitchell. On
    *Ladies of the Canyon*. Reprise Records.

3   Waits, T.A. & Brennan, K.P. (2004). 'Green Grass'. Recorded by Tom
    Waits. On *Real Gone*. ANTI-.

4   McClatchie, M., Bogaard, A., Colledge, S., Whitehouse, N. J.,
    Schulting, R. J., Barratt, P., & McLaughlin, T. R. (2014). 'Neolithic
    farming in north-western Europe: Archaeobotanical evidence from
    Ireland.' *Journal of Archaeological Science*, 51, 206–215.

## Chapter Seventeen: The Fish Course

1   Meller, G. (2016). *Gather*. Quadrille, Hardie Grant Publishing.

## Chapter Eighteen: Transhumance

1   Costello, E. (2020). *Transhumance and the Making of Ireland's Uplands,
    1550–1900*. Boydell Press.

2   Juler, C. (2014). 'După coada oilor: long-distance transhumance and its
    survival in Romania.' *Pastoralism*, 4(1), 1–17.

## Chapter Twenty: Summer Solstice

1   Woolf, J. (2015). 'Dowsing at Torphichen and Cairnpapple.' The Hazel
    Tree website. https://www.thehazeltree.co.uk/2015/07/10/dowsing-a
    t-torphichen-and-cairnpapple/

2   Coppens, P. (2007). *Land of the Gods: How a Scottish landscape was sanctified
    to become Arthur's Camelot*. Frontier Publishing.

3   Van Wyk, B. E., & Gericke, N. (2000). *People's Plants: A guide to useful
    plants of Southern Africa*. Briza publications.

4   Curtis, R. & Elton, B. (writers) and Fletcher, M. (director). (1987,
    September 17). 'Dish and Dishonesty' (Series 3 Episode 1) In J. Lloyd
    (Executive Producer), *Blackadder the Third*. BBC.

5   Tarmac Dunbar Plant. (2021, February 18). 'How to "bee
    kind" this February: bee hotel giveaway.' Dunbar Quarry.
    Retrieved June 29, 2021, from https://dunbar.tarmac.com/news/
    how-to-bee-kind-this-february-bee-hotel-giveaway/

6  Tarmac. (2021). 'Environmental stewardship: Tarmac sustainability report 2020.' Tarmac Sustainability Report 2020 Website. Retrieved June 29, 2021, from https://sustainability-report.tarmac.com/planet/environmental-stewardship/

## Chapter Twenty-one: Flowers and Fruit

1  Goodare, J., Martin, L., Miller, J., & Yeoman, L. (2003, January). 'The survey of Scottish witchcraft: 1563–1736.' Scottish History, School of History and Classics, The University of Edinburgh. Retrieved July 2, 2021, from https://www.shca.ed.ac.uk/Research/witches/introduction.html

2  Scott, A. M., McAndrew, E., & Carroll, E. (2019, September 11). 'Survey of Scottish witchcraft database: Places of residence for accused witches.' University of Edinburgh | Witches. Retrieved July 2, 2021, from https://witches.is.ed.ac.uk/

3  Halperin, D. M. (2003). 'The normalization of queer theory.' Journal of Homosexuality, 45(2-4), 339–343.

4  'Bee Facts: Honey.' (2017, October 20). British Beekeepers Association. Retrieved July 3, 2021, from https://www.bbka.org.uk/faqs/honey-faqs

5  Powell, J. (2016). 'Learning from wild bees and tree beekeeping.' The Beekeepers Quarterly, 123. The Natural Beekeeping Trust. http://www.naturalbeekeepingtrust.org/learning-from-wild-bees-trees

6  Gerard, J. (1963). (1597). The Herball or Generall Historie of Plantes. Bonham & John Norton. Pp. [xviii], 1392, 72.

7  Save Our Magnificent Meadows partnership & Plantlife. (2018, June). Hay Festival? Action now for species-rich grasslands. Plantlife. https://www.plantlife.org.uk/uk/our-work/campaigning-change/meadows

## Chapter Twenty-three: Grasses and Grains

1  Marren, P. (2012). 'Our Vanishing Flora: How wild flowers are disappearing across Britain' (J. Bromley, T. Dines, N. Hutchinson, & D. Long, eds). Plantlife. https://www.plantlife.org.uk/uk/our-work/publications/our-vanishing-flora

2  Purvis, A., & de Palma, A. (2021, October). 'Biodiversity indicators: The biodiversity trends explorer.' The Natural History Museum | PREDICTS Project. https://www.nhm.ac.uk/our-science/data/biodiversity-indicators.html

3 White, M. P., Elliott, L. R., Grellier, J., Economou, T., Bell, S., Bratman, G. N., Cirach, M., Gascon, M., Lima, M. L., Lõhmus, M., Nieuwenhuijsen, M., Ojala, A., Roiko, A., Schultz, P. W., van den Bosch, M., & Fleming, L. E. (2021). 'Associations between green/blue spaces and mental health across 18 countries.' *Scientific Reports*, 11(1). https://doi.org/10.1038/s41598-021-87675-0

4 NHS website. (2021, November 25). 'Understanding calories.' https://www.nhs.uk/live-well/healthy-weight/managing-your-weight/understanding-calories/

5 Mercader, J. (2009). 'Mozambican grass seed consumption during the Middle Stone Age.' *Science*, 326(5960), 1680–1683. https://doi.org/10.1126/science.1173966

6 Lippi, M. M., Foggi, B., Aranguren, B., Ronchitelli, A., & Revedin, A. (2015). 'Multistep food plant processing at Grotta Paglicci (Southern Italy) around 32,600 cal BP.' *Proceedings of the National Academy of Sciences*, 112(39), 12075–12080.

7 Barton, H., Mutri, G., Hill, E., Farr, L., & Barker, G. (2018). 'Use of grass seed resources c. 31 ka by modern humans at the Haua Fteah cave, northeast Libya.' *Journal of Archaeological Science*, 99, 99–111.

8 Weiss, E., Wetterstrom, W., Nadel, D., & Bar-Yosef, O. (2004). 'The broad spectrum revisited: evidence from plant remains.' *Proceedings of the National Academy of Sciences*, 101(26), 9551–9555. https://doi.org/10.1073/pnas.0402362101

9 Özkan, H., Willcox, G., Graner, A., Salamini, F., & Kilian, B. (2011). 'Geographic distribution and domestication of wild emmer wheat (Triticum dicoccoides).' *Genetic Resources and Crop Evolution*, 58(1), 11–53.

10 Lorenz, K., & Hoseney, R. C. (1979). 'Ergot on cereal grains.' *Critical Reviews in Food Science & Nutrition*, 11(4), 311–354.

## Chapter Twenty-four: Lùnastal

1 IPCC Working Group 1. (2021, August 6). 'Sixth Assessment Report, Climate Change 2021: The physical science basis.' The Intergovernmental Panel on Climate Change (IPCC). Retrieved August 11, 2021, from https://www.ipcc.ch/report/sixth-assessment-report-working-group-i/

2 Carson, R. (2002). *Silent Spring*. Houghton Mifflin Harcourt.

3 Waddell, E. (2021, July 27). 'Three in five Brits want to shop seasonally to become more sustainable.' Public Sector Catering. Retrieved August

10, 2021, from https://www.publicsectorcatering.co.uk/news/three-fiv
e-brits-want-shop-seasonally-become-more-sustainable

4   The Miles Better Initiative. (2020, July). 'The Mushroom Miles
    Report.' Mushroom Miles. Retrieved August 10, 2021, from
    https://mushroommiles.com/wp-content/uploads/2020/07/
    Mushrooms-report-FINAL-FINAL.pdf

5   Lyons, J., & Sarkis, S. (2021, August 3). 'Larger-than-average
    Gulf of Mexico "dead zone" measured.' National Oceanic and
    Atmospheric Administration. Retrieved August 11, 2021, from
    https://www.noaa.gov/news-release/larger-than-average-gulf-o
    f-mexico-dead-zone-measured

6   Stein, T. (2021, July 21). 'Low-oxygen waters off Washington, Oregon
    coasts risk becoming large "dead zones."' NOAA Research News. Retrieved
    August 21, 2011, from https://research.noaa.gov/article/ArtMID/587/
    ArticleID/2779/Low-oxygen-waters-off-Washington-Oregon-coasts-
    risk-becoming-large-%E2%80%9Cdead-zones%E2%80%9D

7   Ordnance Survey. (2020, February 6). 'The Gaelic origins of place
    names in Britain.' Ordnance Survey, GetOutside. https://getout-
    side.ordnancesurvey.co.uk/guides/the-scots-origins-of-place-name
    s-in-britain/

8   Leopold, A. (1989). A Sand County Almanac, and Sketches Here and There.
    Oxford University Press, USA.

9   Albrecht, G. (2019). Earth Emotions: New words for a new world. Cornell
    University Press.

10  Jade, K. (2015, June 22). 'Nettle tea benefits.' Mother Earth News.
    Retrieved August 27, 2021, from https://www.motherearthnews.com/
    natural-health/nettle-tea-benefits-zbcz1506

11  Owyoung, S. D. (2013, June 2). 'Tianluoshan: Tea in the Neolithic era.'
    Tsiosophy. https://www.tsiosophy.com/2013/06/tianluoshan-tea-in-th
    e-neolithic-era-3/

Chapter Twenty-five: Nuts, Seeds and Honey

1   Levinson, S. C. (1997). 'Language and cognition: The cognitive conse-
    quences of spatial description in Guugu Yimithirr.' Journal of Linguistic
    Anthropology, 7(1), 98–131.

2   Pager, H. (1976). 'Cave paintings suggest honey hunting activities in Ice
    Age times.' Bee World, 57(1), 9–14.

3   Wood, B. M., Pontzer, H., Raichlen, D. A., & Marlowe, F. W. (2014).

'Mutualism and manipulation in Hadza–honeyguide interactions.' *Evolution and Human Behavior*, 35(6), 540–546.

4  Buhner, S. H. (2004). *The Secret Teachings of Plants: The intelligence of the heart in the direct perception of nature.* Inner Traditions/Bear & Co.

## Chapter Twenty-six: Mushrooms

1  Miller, K. (2020, May 9). 'How mushrooms can save the world.' *Discover Magazine*. Retrieved February 9, 2022, from https://www.discovermagazine.com/environment/how-mushrooms-can-save-the-world

2  Albrecht, G. A. (2021, October 8). 'Symbiosis is life, dysbiosis is death.' *Psychoterratica*. https://glennaalbrecht.wordpress.com/2021/10/08/symbiosis-is-life-dysbiosis-is-death/

3  Damialis, A., Bayr, D., Leier-Wirtz, V., Kolek, F., Plaza, M., Kaschuba, S., Gilles, S., Oteros, J., Buters, J., Menzel, A., Straub, A., Seubert, S., Traidl-Hoffmann, C., Gerstlauer, M., Beck, C., & Philipp, A. (2020). 'Thunderstorm Asthma: In search for relationships with airborne pollen and fungal spores from 23 sites in Bavaria, Germany. A rare incident or a common threat?' *Journal of Allergy and Clinical Immunology*, 145(2), AB336. https://doi.org/10.1016/j.jaci.2019.12.061

4  Thomas, S., Becker, P., Pinza, M. R., & Word, J. Q. (1998). 'Mycoremediation of aged petroleum hydrocarbon contaminants in soil' (No. WA-RD 464.1).

5  Schwarze, F. W. M. R., Baum, S., & Fink, S. (2000). 'Dual modes of degradation by Fistulina hepatica in xylem cell walls of Quercus robur.' *Mycological Research*, 104(7), 846–852.

6  Jianyang, J. Z. L. X. T., Jingui, C. H. L. Y. L., Peiyu, L. S. Y., & Boqi, H. Y. W. (2001). 'The nutritional assessment of Fistulina hepatica protein.' *Acta Edulis Fungi*, 8(04), 19.

7  Myers, J. P., Antoniou, M. N., Blumberg, B., Carroll, L., Colborn, T., Everett, L. G., Hansen, M., Landrigan, P. J., Lanphear, B. P., Mesnage, R., Vandenberg, L. N., Vom Saal, F. S., Welshons, W. V., & Benbrook, C. M. (2016). 'Concerns over use of glyphosate-based herbicides and risks associated with exposures: a consensus statement.' *Environmental Health: A Global Access Science Source*, 15(1), 1–13. https://doi.org/10.1186/s12940-016-0117-0

8  Boedeker, W., Watts, M., Clausing, P., & Marquez, E. (2020). 'The global distribution of acute unintentional pesticide poisoning: estimations based on a systematic review.' *BMC Public Health*, 20(1), 1–19.

9  Straw, E. A., Carpentier, E. N., & Brown, M. J. F. (2021). 'Roundup causes high levels of mortality following contact exposure in bumble bees.' *Journal of Applied Ecology*, 58(6), 1167–1176. https://doi.org/10.1111/1365-2664.13867

## Chapter Twenty-eight: October

1  Maixner, F., Sarhan, M. S., Huang, K. D., Tett, A., Schoenafinger, A., Zingale, S., ... & Kowarik, K. (2021). 'Hallstatt miners consumed blue cheese and beer during the Iron Age and retained a non-Westernized gut microbiome until the Baroque period.' *Current Biology*, 31(23), 5149–5162.

2  Kaishian, P., & Djoulakian, H. (2020). 'The science underground.' *Catalyst: Feminism, Theory, Technoscience*, 6(2).

3  Anxiety UK. (2021, January 3). 'Sleep survey reveals state of nation's poor rest patterns.' https://www.anxietyuk.org.uk/blog/sleep-survey-reveals-state-of-nations-poor-rest-patterns/

4  Louv, R. (2008). *Last Child in the Woods: Saving our children from nature-deficit disorder*. Algonquin Books.

5  'National life tables: life expectancy in the UK.' (2021, September 23). Office for National Statistics. https://www.ons.gov.uk/peoplepopulationandcommunity/birthsdeathsandmarriages/lifeexpectancies/bulletins/nationallifetablesunitedkingdom/2018to2020

6  Gurven, M., & Kaplan, H. (2007). 'Longevity among hunter-gatherers: a cross-cultural examination.' *Population and Development Review*, 33(2), 321–365 (p.335).

7  'Life expectancy in Scotland, 2018–2020.' (2021, September 23) National Records of Scotland. https://www.nrscotland.gov.uk/statistics-and-data/statistics/statistics-by-theme/life-expectancy/life-expectancy-in-scotland/2018-2020

8  'Healthy life expectancy in Scotland, 2017–2019.' (2021, January 28). National Records of Scotland. https://www.nrscotland.gov.uk/statistics-and-data/statistics/statistics-by-theme/life-expectancy/healthy-life-expectancy-in-scotland/2017-2019

9  Marlowe, F. (2000). 'The patriarch hypothesis.' *Human Nature*, 11(1), 27–42.

10 Clayton, P., & Rowbotham, J. (2009). 'How the Mid-Victorians worked, ate and died.' *International Journal of Environmental Research and Public Health*, 6(3), 1235–1253. https://doi.org/10.3390/ijerph6031235

11  Stevenson, M., & Buhner, S. (2017, January 7). 'Understanding Extreme States: An interview with Stephen Harrod Buhner.' Mad In America. Retrieved October 31, 2021, from https://www.madinamerica.com/2017/01/understanding-extreme-states-interview-stephen-harrod-buhner/

12  Weldon, F. (1996). *Splitting*. Atlantic Monthly Press.

13  Hildegard, S. (1903). *Hildegardis causae et curae* (P. Kaiser, ed.). In aedibus B.G. Teubneri.

## Chapter Twenty-nine: Towards COP26

1  Wall Kimmerer, R. (2020, July 29). 'Speaking of nature.' *Orion Magazine*. Retrieved November 3, 2021, from https://orionmagazine.org/article/speaking-of-nature/

2  Climate Action Tracker. (2021, November 9). 'Glasgow's one degree 2030 credibility gap: net zero's lip service to climate action.' Retrieved November 10, 2021, from https://climateactiontracker.org/publications/glasgows-2030-credibility-gap-net-zeros-lip-service-to-climate-action/

3  Rinpoche, Gyalwa (the 14th Dalai Lama). (1990). *My Tibet* (pp.79–80). Thames and Hudson Ltd.

4  Magan, M. (2020). *Thirty-Two Words for Field: Lost words of the Irish landscape*. Gill Books.

## Chapter Thirty: Brave New World

1  Adams, D. (2002). *The Salmon of Doubt: Hitchhiking the universe one last time* (Vol. 3). Harmony.

2  Holland, S. (2021, November). 'Further thoughts on COP26 and the changes our food system most desperately needs.' *Slow Food International*. https://www.slowfood.com/further-thoughts-on-cop26/

3  Stone, M. (2021). 'Human-made materials now equal weight of all life on Earth.' *National Geographic*. Retrieved December 31, 2021, from https://www.nationalgeographic.com/environment/article/human-made-materials-now-equal-weight-of-all-life-on-earth

# ACKNOWLEDGEMENTS

My deepest thanks to 'Mushroom Matt' Rooney, Géza Turi and Robert 'Bob' Smith for putting up with me, keeping me alive, on track, and sharing the journey. Your belief in me has been immeasurable.

To my literary agent, Claire Paterson Conrad, at Janklow & Nesbit, a huge thanks – without your enthusiasm and encouragement this book would have remained an unstructured collection of ideas and notes. Also to Holly Harris at Simon & Schuster, for going out on a limb for a new writer with a mad idea, and so ably assisted by Arzu Tahsin, Mary Chamberlain, Kat Ailes, illustrator Sian Wilson and many others.

A special thanks to Christina, Andy and precious Maya for welcoming me into your new family and allowing me to share your story. A blessing to Robert and Jean Paton whose farmland I roam and my neighbours Allan and Irene Leckie. My gratitude to Professor Łukasz Łuczaj for hosting me in Poland, challenging my many assumptions and often lazy thinking, and correcting botanical names.

For all gifts of food, both large and small, from an incredible band of fellow foodies, foragers, cooks and brewers: Abi Francis, Alex Baring, Ally Graham, Amy 'Hipsters and Hobos' Rankine, Andrea Ladas, Ben 'Wild Human' McNutt, Clare Holohan, Craig 'Edible Leeds' Worrall, Debs 'Wild Human' Nickolls, Ella 'Honey' Stone, 'Fergus the Forager' Drennan, Fred Gillam, Gitta Cooper, Graham and Christine Whitehouse, Jessie 'Oak and Smoke' Watson Brown, Jim 'Forage Box' Parums, Jos Fletcher, Kaeli Pettigrew, Lisa 'Edulis' Cutcliffe, Maisie Geelan, Mark 'Galloway Wildfood' Williams, Martin Theoboldt, Mary Cosnett, Millie Baring, Miles 'Forager' Irving, Natascha Kenyon, 'Nicki by the Sea' Slater, Nicola Hornsby of Achray Farm, Norrie 'Noz' Smith, Patrycja Kosiarska, Richard Mawby, Robert Irvine, the exceedingly generous Rupert 'the Bruce' Waites, Sarah Cameron, Szymon 'Foragerium' Szyszczakiewicz, Thomas and Lesley Kilbride, Ursula Humphrey, Yuliya Surnina, Zippy and all the members of the Association of Foragers. I just hope I've remembered you all. If not, please blame it on early dementia and not ingratitude!

Thank you also to John Wright for your encouragement, and to Dr Wojciech Maksymilian Szymański and Ivona Ziółkowska for information on harvesting bulbous-rooted chervil and showing me an extraordinary global collection of nettles!

Last but not least, to my long-suffering children who got saddled with a crazy mum and yes, I did hide seaweed in everything that you ate . . . Quite simply: I love you.

# INDEX

Species have been listed by their common names. For scientific names please use the Species Table on pages 305–323.